CAMBRIDGE AIR SURVEYS

ROMAN BRITAIN FROM THE AIR

THIS BOOK IS DEDICATED TO

IAN RICHMOND (1902–1965)
WHOSE GENIUS STILL ILLUMINATES
THE STUDY OF ROMAN BRITAIN

CAMBRIDGE AIR SURVEYS

Edited by DAVID R. WILSON

CURATOR IN AERIAL PHOTOGRAPHY, UNIVERSITY OF CAMBRIDGE

D. KNOWLES and J.K.S. ST JOSEPH

Monastic Sites from the Air
(out of print)

M.W. BERESFORD and J.K.S. ST JOSEPH

Medieval England
An Aerial Survey

E.R. NORMAN and J.K.S. ST JOSEPH

The Early Development of Irish Society
The Evidence of Aerial Photography

ROMAN BRITAIN FROM THE AIR

S.S. FRERE
PROFESSOR OF THE ARCHAEOLOGY OF THE ROMAN EMPIRE
IN THE UNIVERSITY OF OXFORD

J.K.S. ST JOSEPH
EMERITUS PROFESSOR OF AERIAL PHOTOGRAPHIC STUDIES
IN THE UNIVERSITY OF CAMBRIDGE

CAMBRIDGE UNIVERSITY PRESS

CAMBRIDGE
LONDON   NEW YORK   NEW ROCHELLE
MELBOURNE   SYDNEY

Published by the Press Syndicate of the University of Cambridge
The Pitt Building, Trumpington Street, Cambridge CB2 1RP
32 East 57th Street, New York, NY 10022, USA
296 Beaconsfield Parade, Middle Park, Melbourne 3206, Australia

First published 1983

Printed in Great Britain

Library of Congress catalogue card number: 82-9746

British Library Cataloguing in Publication Data
Frere, S.S.
Roman Britain from the air.—(Cambridge air
surveys; 4)
1. Aerial photography in archaeology
2. Great Britain—Antiquities, Roman
I. Title II. St Joseph, J.K.S.
936.1'04   DA145

ISBN 0 521 25088 9

CONTENTS

AERIAL PHOTOGRAPHS DESCRIBED IN THE TEXT

Each photograph has a caption which includes, besides the place name, county and direction of view, the national grid reference, the negative number and the date of photography

FIGURES IN THE TEXT

PREFACE

The contribution of aerial reconnaissance to the study of Roman Britain is extensive and well known, but there has never been a book devoted wholly to this subject. Aerial photographs of individual sites have been published in general works and in reports of discoveries and excavations. Since 1951, nine illustrated accounts of aerial reconnaissance relating to Roman Britain have been published in volumes of the *Journal of Roman Studies*. These papers have included results of research mainly on the relationship of military sites to recorded history, and the sites have been classified on a systematic basis. However, each report dealt only with results of reconnaissance during the previous few years: the series gives a cumulative but not an overall picture of discovery. Another series describing individual discoveries of all periods of British archaeology has appeared regularly since 1964 in *Antiquity*.

The reception accorded to the previous volume of the *Cambridge Air Surveys*, the second edition of *Medieval England* (1979), suggested that the present book be prepared on somewhat similar lines. Differences in the nature of the evidence and in the character of the sites themselves account for changes in overall treatment. As Roman sites usually feature *in* the present landscape rather than as organic parts of it, more emphasis has been placed on the detailed commentaries to the photographs.

The great value of aerial photography lies in its power of revealing unrecognised or buried sites, of many different categories, in their topographical contexts, often with much unexpected detail. Some fields of study have been profoundly changed during the last thirty years by the very volume of discoveries. This is particularly so with military remains, and here aerial reconnaissance has literally changed the map. Discoveries in large numbers can overturn accepted opinions based upon the distribution of sites, and may even have a bearing on such a fundamental topic as the size of the population in Roman times. By contrast, aerial photography can make only a limited contribution to the study of some other aspects of Roman Britain, such as industry, trade and religion.

To provide an account of the history and archaeology of Roman Britain has not been considered necessary, as general works on the subject are plentiful. The reader is referred to P. Salway, *Roman Britain* (Oxford, 1981); S.S. Frere, *Britannia, A History of Roman Britain* (London, rev. ed. 1978); M. Todd, *Roman Britain* (London, 1981); R.G. Collingwood and I.A. Richmond, *The Archaeology of Roman Britain* (London, 1969). Nor has any special discussion of the techniques of aerial photography been included, as these are for the most part well understood: attention is drawn in individual commentaries to noteworthy features. An introductory section to each chapter relates the sites chosen for illustration to their historical and archaeological contexts.

The present series of aerial surveys, begun in 1945, has since 1949 been conducted for the Cambridge Committee for Aerial Photography. The photographs in this book are all drawn from the University Collection of Aerial Photographs which now includes over half a million items. Amongst archaeological subjects there is coverage of almost every major Roman site in Britain, so that in range and variety the Collection will not easily be superseded: indeed, a number of the sites have been destroyed, or at least obscured from aerial view since they were photographed.

With so much material there has been no need for further surveys specially for this book: indeed, the difficulty has lain in selection. The photographs finally chosen comprise a sample illustrating the essential features of a wide range of sites differing in character and date. To choose a single view of a given site, from amongst a few hundred photographs taken over years under varying conditions and at different seasons, has not been easy. The text has had to be woven round the illustrations, and the evidence they provided has been supplemented from unpublished photographs. At a complicated site the amount of information conveyed by a single photograph and that revealed by repeated cover is well demonstrated by comparing the illustrations of Dalswinton and Glenlochar (74 and 76) with their respective plans (Figs. 14 and 3), which take account of all the evidence obtained over many years' reconnaissance. Repeated reconnaissance is not always necessary, but will seldom fail to add points of interest, and sometimes points of extreme value at complicated sites.

To carry out a wide-ranging series of surveys in the variable British climate has meant a continual struggle against time and weather. Sometimes conditions for photography were far from perfect: traces of buried features might be so faint that the image recorded on film could not be reproduced on a printed plate. Yet such photographs often yield important information to an interpreter. From 1945 to 1961 most of the reconnaissance took place in aircraft of the Royal Air Force engaged on training flights. In 1962 Mr A.G. Douglass was appointed as pilot to the University Committee for Aerial Photography and since then the flying has been undertaken in the University's aircraft, at first an Auster, and from 1965 a Cessna Skymaster. A glance through the Collection shows the importance of securing the best position for photography in the prevailing conditions of weather and lighting, and it will be apparent how much is due to the pilot's skill and patience, without which such widely ranging results could not have been obtained. The continuation of the surveys and the care of the Collection are now under the direction of Mr D.R. Wilson, who joined the Committee's staff in 1965.

That Roman Britain should be the subject of a volume in the *Cambridge Air Surveys* has long been intended, and the project was discussed many years ago by the three original editors. They hoped that Professor Sir Ian Richmond might be able to contribute the text, and he readily agreed when invited to do so. However, other work prevented him from undertaking this: the task was postponed, and he had not been able to make a start by the time of his death in 1965. The present book, which ensures that the intention of so long ago is fulfilled, is dedicated to him.

The authors have worked closely together in the preparation of this book. Drafts of the various sections were written by S.S.F. as commentaries on photographs chosen by J.K. StJ. Every site has been visited by one or other of the authors, and many by both together. The value of such visits to compare aerial photographs with actual remains on the ground needs no emphasis. Points of interpretation have been carefully considered, and the text has been discussed and revised in the light of evidence provided by such other photographs as were available. For the result the authors are jointly responsible.

S.S. Frere
J.K.S. StJoseph

ACKNOWLEDGEMENTS

All the photographs are from the Cambridge University Collection. Those reproduced as illustrations 3, 15, 23, 26–7, 33, 39, 41, 43–4, 48–9, 55–6, 69, 73–6, 82, 86, 88–92, 94, 96–7, 100, 107, 109–12, 114, 119, 123, 125, 130–3, 136–9, 142 are Crown Copyright, and are published by permission of the Ministry of Defence and the Controller of Her Majesty's Stationery Office. The remainder, which are the copyright of the University of Cambridge, are published by permission of the Committee for Aerial Photography.

Of the line drawings, Figs. 3, 6, 8–9, 11–14, and 16 are from surveys by J.K. St Joseph. Fig. 3 was drawn by Miss F.M. Browne; Figs. 6, 8–9, 12–13 by B.M. Thomason and Figs. 11, 14 and 16 by D.R. Wilson. Figs. 1–2, 4–5, 7, 10 and 17–18 were prepared by Mrs A. Wilkins specially for this book.

The authors wish to acknowledge the work of Mrs Lynda Smithson in the production of the finished typescript from many preliminary drafts.

ABBREVIATIONS USED IN THE REFERENCES AND FOOTNOTES

Antiq. Journ.	*The Antiquaries Journal*, Society of Antiquaries of London.
Arch. Aeliana	*Archaeologia Aeliana* (4th series, 5th series), Society of Antiquaries of Newcastle upon Tyne.
Arch. Camb.	*Archaeologia Cambrensis,* the Cambrian Archaeological Association, Cardiff.
Arch. Journ.	*The Archaeological Journal*, Royal Archaeological Institute, London.
B.A.R.	*British Archaeological Reports*, Oxford.
Berks. Arch. Journ.	*Berkshire Archaeological Journal*, Reading.
Bull. Board of Celtic Studies	*Bulletin of the Board of Celtic Studies*, Cardiff.
Cymmrodorion Soc. Trans.	*Transactions of the Honourable Society of Cymmrodorion*, London.
Glasgow Arch. Journ.	*Glasgow Archaeological Journal.*
I.L.S.	H. Dessau, *Inscriptiones Latinae Selectae.*
J. Brit. Arch. Assoc.	*Journal of the British Archaeological Association,* London.
J.R.S.	*Journal of Roman Studies*, Society for the Promotion of Roman Studies, London.
Proc. Cambridge Antiq. Soc.	*Proceedings of the Cambridge Antiquarian Society.*
Proc. Devon Arch. Soc.	*Proceedings of the Devon Archaeological Society,* Exeter.
Proc. Leeds Philosophical Soc.	*Proceedings of the Leeds Philosophical Society.*
Proc. Prehist. Soc.	*Proceedings of the Prehistoric Society,* Cambridge.
Proc. Soc. Ant. Scotland	*Proceedings of the Society of Antiquaries of Scotland*, Edinburgh.
Proc. Suffolk Inst. of Arch.	*Proceedings of the Suffolk Institute of Archaeology*, Ipswich.
R.C.A.H.M.	Royal Commission on Ancient and Historical Monuments (Wales, Scotland), Inventory.
R.C.H.M.	Royal Commission on Historical Monuments (England), Inventory.
R.I.B.	*The Roman Inscriptions of Britain*, Oxford, 1965.
Roy, W., *Military Antiquities*	William Roy, *Military Antiquities of the Romans in Britain*, London, 1793.
Trans. Birmingham Arch. Soc.	*Transactions of the Birmingham Archaeological Society.*
Trans. Cumb. and Westm. Antiq. and Arch. Soc.	*Transactions of the Cumberland and Westmorland Antiquarian and Archaeological Society*, Carlisle.
Trans. Dumfriesshire and Galloway N.H. and Antiq. Soc.	*Transactions of the Dumfriesshire and Galloway Natural History and Antiquarian Society*, Edinburgh
Trans. Perthshire Soc. of Nat. Science	*Transactions of the Perthshire Society of Natural Science*, Perth.

Trans. Shropshire Arch. Soc.	*Transactions of the Shropshire Archaeological Society*, Shrewsbury.
Trans. Thoroton Soc.	*Transactions of the Thoroton Society of Nottinghamshire*, Nottingham.
V.C.H.	The Victoria County History.
Wilts. Arch. Mag.	*The Wiltshire Archaeological Magazine*, Devizes.
Yorks. Arch. Journ.	*The Yorkshire Archaeological Journal*, Leeds.

KEY TO LOCATION MAP

1 Allington Hill
2 Arbury Banks
3 Ardoch
4 Ashwell
5 Badbury Rings
6 Bainbridge
7 Balmuildy
8 Bartlow Hills
9 Baylham House
10 Beckfoot
  Bennachie, *see* Durno
11 Biglands
12 Birdoswald
13 Birrens
14 Brancaster
15 Buckton
  Bullock's Haste, *see* Willow
    Farm
16 Burnswark
17 Caerhun
18 Caerleon
19 Caerwent
20 Caistor by Norwich
21 Camelon
22 Cappuck
  Car Dyke, *see* Willow Farm
23 Carpow
24 Castor
25 Catterick Bridge
26 Cawthorn
27 Chedworth
28 Chesterholm
29 Chesterton (Water Newton)
30 Chew Green
31 Chichester
32 Chignall St James
33 Chisenbury Warren
34 Church Stretton gap
35 Cirencester
36 Corbridge
37 Crawford
38 Cromwell
39 Croy Hill
40 Dalginross
41 Dalswinton
42 Dorchester

43 Durisdeer
44 Durno
45 Ewe Close
46 Forden Gaer
  Fyfield Down, *see*
    Totterdown
47 Gelligaer Common
48 Glenlochar
49 Gosbeck's Farm
50 Grassington
51 Greensforge
52 Haltwhistle Burn
53 Hardknott
54 The Herefordshire Beacon
55 Hod Hill
56 Holbeach
57 Housesteads
58 Inchtuthil
59 Irchester
60 Islip
61 Ixworth
62 Kelmscott
63 Kenchester
64 Kirmington
65 Landbeach
66 Leeming Lane
67 Lidgate
68 Limlow Hill
69 Little Milton
70 Llanfor
71 Lockington
72 Longthorpe
73 Lune Gorge
74 Maiden Castle
75 Malham
76 March
  Maumbury Rings, *see*
    Dorchester
77 Menai Strait
78 Mildenhall
79 Newstead
80 Newton Kyme
  Normangate Field, *see*
    Castor
81 Old Burrow
82 Old Carlisle

83 Pennymuir
84 Pen-y-Crogbren
85 Piercebridge
86 Portchester
87 Rey Cross
88 Rhyn
89 Richborough
90 Risingham
  Rookery Farm, *see* Spalding
    Common
91 Rossington
92 Rough Castle
93 Scarborough
94 Silchester
95 Smacam Down
96 Spalding Common
97 Stanway
98 Stoke Hill
99 Strageath
100 Thistleton Dyer
101 Thorpe
102 Tomen-y-Mur
103 Totterdown
104 Trawscoed
105 Troutbeck
106 Weycock Hill
107 Whitley Castle
108 Wilderness Plantation
109 Willow Farm
110 Woden Law
111 Wroxeter
112 Wycomb
113 York
114 Y Pygwn

PART ONE

GENERAL

1

GEOGRAPHICAL FEATURES AND IRON AGE HILL FORTS

The importance of aerial reconnaissance in archaeology lies in its power as an instrument of discovery. It can reveal sites hitherto unknown, where there may often be no features whatever to be seen on the ground; even at familiar sites the comprehensive view only attainable at a distance can bring new understanding of features that were vague or obscure. The technique can also, however, be very successful in complementing the map by vivid illustration of a site in its geographical context. Thus, panoramic views strikingly bring home the skill of Roman road engineers in hilly country (6, 10) or the tactical setting of a fort or fortress (20, 66).

Views of certain geographical features help the mind to picture the reality of past events, and two are included in this collection. The view of the Menai Strait (1) should be examined against the background of the evocative account by Tacitus of Suetonius Paullinus's crossing in A.D. 61. The island of Anglesey had given sanctuary to many intransigent refugees; conquest was an important objective because, in addition, the island's agricultural resources sustained the resistance of the Ordovices, just as its Druidical shrines were a powerful factor in maintaining their morale. The governor had prepared boats for the transport of his infantry; of the cavalry some relied on fords but others had been trained to swim with their horses. The Anglesey shore was lined with a dense throng of warriors among whom darted black-clad women with hair dishevelled like Furies, brandishing flaming torches; close by stood ranks of Druids with upraised arms, calling down curses. The sight momentarily brought the Roman forces to a standstill with a chill of superstitious fear, until with renewed shouts of encouragement they forced their landing and set about ending the resistance. The same fords were used seventeen years later by Agricola for his final subjection of the island.

The Firth of Tay at Carpow was the scene of another crossing used on more than one occasion by a Roman army, and may have been provided with a bridge of boats in the early third century. The controls exercised by the geography of the area (2) are well brought out.

Few Iron Age hill forts have been illustrated here, for important Roman associations can seldom be demonstrated. Maiden Castle (3) is included because of evidence of Roman capture and of much later use as a cult site. Its defences and those of the Herefordshire Beacon (4) or of Badbury (5) illustrate the character of the native strongholds which faced the Roman conquerors of Britain. The Beacon is only one of many powerful hill forts along the Welsh Marches, which must have played a significant role in delaying Roman efforts to conquer Wales. Hod Hill (49) illustrates another phenomenon, now recognised not to be unique – the occupation of a hill fort by a Roman garrison. Cadbury Castle in Somerset has been known for several years to have been held by a small Roman garrison, and in 1981 similar military reuse, probably on a more extensive scale, was proved at Brandon Camp near Leintwardine (Fig. 12) and at Hembury in Devon. It may well turn out that use of ready-made fortified sites, at least as *aestiva* (summer campaign camps), was more common than the evidence at present suggests, for little research has been done on this aspect of campaigning.

References

Tacitus, *Annales* XIV, 29–30; *Agricola* 18. Brandon Camp: *Britannia* XIII (1982), 'Roman Britain' report. Hembury: *ibid.* (forthcoming).

MENAI STRAIT, North Wales (1).

The Menai Strait divides the island of Anglesey (*Mona*, lying to left of the photograph) from the mainland of North Wales, and on two occasions, in 61 and 78, was the scene of contested crossings by the Roman army. On the first occasion the conquest of Anglesey had to be aborted because of the rebellion of Boudicca; on the second, Agricola completed the occupation. In both crossings mounted auxiliaries used the fords and others swam with their horses.

In the middle distance on the right, at the mouth of the Afon Seiont, lies Caernarvon with its Roman fort on the plateau above and its Edwardian castle by the foreshore. Here the Strait

1 **Menai Strait, North Wales**; looking NE from about the point SH 432597. AUN 68: June 1968.

is 1.6 km wide, though partly blocked by sand-banks. Towards the far end of the Strait, beyond a bend, lie the two bridges leading to Anglesey from Bangor; beyond them, again, the mouth broadens over a wide area of sandbanks. Today the Strait can be forded only near Caernarvon, and then only at certain conditions of low water; there is no ford at Bangor (where the width is a mere 200 m), or beyond. These facts may provide a clue to the site of the Roman crossings – both were undertaken at the same spot, for we are told that in 78 known fords were employed. Paullinus, indeed, had also prepared a fleet of flat-bottomed barges, but Agricola's campaign had been too suddenly undertaken for boats to be amassed in advance.

Reference

R.M. Ogilvie and I.A. Richmond, *De vita Agricolae* (Oxford, 1967), note to 18.4.

CARPOW, Tayside (2)

Carpow lies on the south shore of the Firth of Tay, 1.3 km east of its confluence with the Earn. At this point the Ochil range (background), which flanks the south side of Strathearn, approaches close to the Firth leaving little level ground between. Behind, the summits of the Lomond hills appear on the skyline. The 9.7 ha vexillation fortress of Carpow occupies the small plateau partly covered by trees above the south (further) shore; the dark line marking the two closely spaced eastern ditches can be seen running obliquely across a white field towards a short line of trees. The fortress has been proved by excavation to be of Severan date.

The site had first been occupied by a large marching-camp apparently Agricolan, and it is probable that Agricola's army crossed the river hereabouts in 83. However, his line of march north of the Tay is uncertain since no camps of

2 The Tay crossing at Carpow, Tayside (Perthshire); looking S. NO 207179. ATN 62: July 1967.

the expected size or date have been found along the coastal route beyond the Firth. Later, the same position at Carpow again served as the camping-ground for a Roman army. A level area of about 26 ha was enclosed between a large ditch laid out in three straight lengths on the landward (south) side and the edge of the plateau where the ground slopes down to the Firth. This enclosure also antedates the fortress. A series of 25.5 ha marching-camps, almost certainly marking the early third-century campaigns, extends from Craigarnhall, on the north side of the Forth, to Forteviot, 17 km WSW of Carpow, and again from Longforgan, 16 km north-east of Carpow on the north side of the Firth of Tay, to Oathlaw in the basin of the North Esk, a distance overall of some 120 km. This line of camps implies a crossing of the Tay at Carpow, where the 26 ha polygonal enclosure, corresponding in area to one of the camps, would serve as a base and springboard. The width of

exposed open water between the reed-beds on either shore is now some 550 m, and the depth at low water hardly more than 2 m, apart from occasional hollows; such conditions would present no great obstacle to the anchoring of pontoons. This is thought to be the point where a bridge of boats such as that depicted on a small bronze medallion of Caracalla, minted in 209, was thrown across the Firth. At the left-hand corner of the field in the foreground of the photograph, just right of the corner of a wood, a narrow dark line marks two sides and a rounded corner of a small camp lying above the low bank that rises from the landward edge of the reed-beds. Other photographs show a gate with *titulum* on the west side of this camp, which may well have been sited in relation to the north end of the bridge.

The fortress itself was constructed soon after the campaigns associated with these earthworks, and was held for a few years by detachments of

5

3 Maiden Castle, Winterbourne St Martin, Dorset; Iron Age hill fort and Romano-Celtic temple, looking NW. SY 670884. UM 78: April 1957.

Legions VI Victrix and II Augusta, whose stamped tiles have been found there. Although the buildings of the central range were in stone, the greater part of the fortress was of half-timbered construction.

References

J.K. St Joseph, *J.R.S.* LIX (1969), 110 (map); *J.R.S.* LXIII (1973), 222 (plan) with Pl. XVI, 2 (this view). A.S. Robertson in W.S. Hanson and L.J.F. Keppie (eds.), *Roman Frontier Studies 1979* (B.A.R. Int. Series 71 (1), Oxford, 1980) 131–9 (bridge of boats).

MAIDEN CASTLE, Dorset (3)

The great hill fort of Maiden Castle, 3 km south-west of Dorchester, is an earthwork of many periods. Sir Mortimer Wheeler's excavations of 1934–7 showed that there had been a Neolithic settlement on the eastern (nearer) summit, but that all the visible defences belong to the Iron Age. The eastern summit was surrounded by a rampart and ditch enclosing *c.* 6.5 ha, and although the hill fort was later expanded to embrace the western knoll, thus increasing the defended area to 19 ha, the denuded remains of the west side of the original hill fort can still be distinguished, running between decided kinks in the line of the later ramparts. At the climax of the structural sequence, towards the end of the Iron Age, the defences covered a band over 100 m wide and had a vertical measurement from rampart-top to ditch-bottom of up to 15 m. Of particular interest is the elaborate development of the entrance defences at each end of the site. Even at the less complicated eastern entrance, in the foreground, an attack would have had to penetrate 73 m of tortuous approach overlooked by platforms

6

4 The Herefordshire Beacon, Colwall, Hereford and Worcester; Iron Age hill fort looking S. SO 759398. AJC 30: June 1964.

manned by slingers. Such elaborate outworks were necessary because the great timber gates were always the weakest elements in a hill fort's defences. The point is reinforced by the fact that, although it has been established that Maiden Castle fell to Legion II Augusta during the Roman Conquest of southern Britain, the site shows no sign of siege-works or of causeways thrown across the ditches by storming parties.

The more complex western entrance has not been excavated, and so has produced no evidence; but an attack there may not have been necessary, the Roman onslaught being perhaps concentrated on the simpler eastern entrance. Here a cemetery containing the bodies of the British casualties, some of them showing evidence of terrible wounds, was created in the area between the twin portals and the covering hornwork, and the gates themselves were dismantled. The answer to the slings of the defenders had been to outrange them and drive them from the ramparts by means of fire from field *ballistae*.

Although the population was not evacuated immediately, the hill fort was deserted within a generation; presumably its inhabitants migrated to the growing Roman city of *Durnovaria* at Dorchester. About the middle of the fourth century a metalled roadway was laid through the northern portal of the eastern entrance and across the interior, and may have served undiscovered buildings in the western sector of the hill fort. Not long afterwards a Romano-Celtic temple and accompanying two-roomed house, presumably for a priest, together with a simple oval shrine nearby, were built within the original eastern hill fort, and a screen-wall and gate were provided at the old entrance. In the make-up for the temple were pieces of mosaic from an earlier building.

The temple (which measures 13.25 by 12.34 m) and the priest's house have been laid out in restored form at ground level and can be seen near the right-hand side of the original enclosure. They illustrate the well-attested revival of paganism in mid-fourth-century Britain.

References

R.E.M. Wheeler, *Maiden Castle, Dorset* (Oxford, 1943). R.C.H.M. *Dorset* II Pt 3 (London, 1970), 493–501.

THE HEREFORDSHIRE BEACON, Hereford and Worcester (4)

The Beacon is the more northerly of two hill forts at the southern end of the Malvern Hills, comprising a narrow outcrop of Pre-Cambrian rocks forming a ridge of steep-sided hills that dominate the plain of the Severn north of Gloucester. It is one of a large number of sizeable and well-defended Iron Age strongholds along the borders of Wales, and illustrates the difficulties facing Roman forces attempting the conquest of the region.

The hill fort makes skilful use of the terrain. The initial circuit has been doubled in size by the addition of wing-like extensions that enclose the ridge crest to north and south. The line of the defences has been carefully laid out on a change of slope, so that the effective height of the rampart has been considerably increased. Within the defences numerous scooped platforms can be seen; these presumably were occupied by houses or other buildings. The summit was reused as the site of an earthwork castle in the Norman period.

The complexity of the defences, of the gates and of the internal features of the hill forts in the Welsh Marches has been revealed by excavations at the neighbouring site on Midsummer Hill, 2 km away.

References

R.C.H.M. *Herefordshire* II (London, 1932), 55–7 with plan. J.K. StJoseph in W.F. Grimes (ed.), *Aspects of Archaeology in Britain and Beyond* (London, 1951), Pl. XV (oblique view looking west); *Antiquity* XXXIX (1965), 223–5 with Pl. XLI (this view).

2

ROADS

The Romans have left many traces of their presence on the face of Britain, not least in their choice of sites for towns and fortresses; but it is their roads which most frequently attract attention, whether on maps or in the direct experience of the modern traveller exploring the countryside by car, on a bicycle, or on foot. For many Roman roads are still followed by modern successors or can be traced by the remains of an *agger*, by alignments of footpaths and hedges, or by the documentary record of use as a boundary in medieval times.

Most of the principal Roman roads in Britain were military in origin, having been built in the conquest years to serve the communications and supply of Roman troops in their various fortresses or forts, and – especially in Wales and the North – to cordon areas of conquered territory and so facilitate patrolling, observation and the control of large-scale movement. Careful observation can sometimes discern how the road pattern reflects the history of the conquest, as where Ermin Street, approaching Gloucester from the south, aims at the early military site at Kingsholm, only later having been diverted to Gloucester itself; or where Watling Street, running from London to Chester, evidently had as its original objective some site not yet discovered near the junction with the Foss Way and was later extended on a changed alignment to Wroxeter, the connection with Chester being constructed only in a third phase later still.

In point of geology, south-eastern Britain is broadly composed of strata dipping successively to the south-east, forming ridges with an east–west or north-east–south-west orientation, so that a traveller setting out north-west from London crosses a succession of hills and vales. In prehistoric times long-distance trackways tended to keep to the ridges, avoiding the woodlands and undrained low-lying areas between them. It is no coincidence that the best-known trackways, such as the Icknield Way or the Jurassic route, run from south-west to north-east. Built roads were a novelty introduced by Rome; the construction of the Roman road network gave the island a new unity by breaking through hitherto almost impervious belts of coun-

try and by providing for the first time a system of purposeful communication, valuable alike to soldier and to merchant. These roads remained of vital importance for centuries after the end of Roman Britain: King Harold's forced march in 1066 to Yorkshire and back to Hastings usefully illustrates the point, for without the Roman roads it could not have been achieved with the necessary speed.

Close examination of the course of Roman roads, especially perhaps in mountainous country, must arouse admiration for the grasp of topography and for the skilful detailed surveys which were evidently their preliminary. Aerial photographs can often illustrate these characteristics within the limits of a bird's-eye view. 6 and 10 point to a masterly treatment of hilly terrain, and 8 shows the unswerving pursuit of a visible objective. For a wider view, recourse must be had to maps. It is well known that the first 19 km of Stane Street on its course from London Bridge to Chichester is aligned directly on the eastern gate of that city, 96 km away, and that the road running from Leicester south-eastwards to cover the 160 km to Colchester follows a course directly aimed at the *colonia*. Although long-distance alignments could have been laid down by a laborious system of trial and error, by moving intermediate markers, it is evidently more likely that accurate bearings had been worked out using astronomical data; and this in turn implies possession of accurate maps.

The network of principal roads will have been laid out by legionary surveyors and constructed either by soldiers or more probably by prisoners of war, or by labour exacted from the native tribes. These roads were solidly built, normally with a foundation of large stones capped by gravel and served by side-ditches; often the road itself is raised on an embankment (*agger*) for even better drainage. Their direct courses disclose a ruthlessness of purpose and disregard for private property consistent with the new order of a conquering power; aerial photographs sometimes record a Roman road striking across the boundary ditches of native farms.

To judge by milestones set up in the Emperor's

9

name, as well as by evidence from other parts of the Empire, these main roads remained a concern of the provincial government, which saw to their periodic repair. But as time went on the officials of the *civitates* took over increased responsibility in this field, at least as agents. Construction and maintenance of minor roads would always have been a local concern. The Roman names of individual roads in Britain are unknown; names such as Ermine, Stane or Watling Street are later attributions

Many of the major roads were used as regular routes by the imperial posting system (*cursus publicus*); along them, at the expense of the *civitas* concerned, rest-houses and posting houses were provided for the use of travelling officials and governmental couriers. Road-books and road-maps existed. The British section of the Antonine Itinerary lists numerous places along various routes together with the intervening distances, while the small surviving fragment of the British part of the so-called 'Peutinger Table' displays similar information in cartographic form.

Straightness was a characteristic of Roman main roads, but they were not undeviating. Once the basic direction had been determined, they were laid out from point to point (changing direction as necessary, normally on hill-tops from which the next section could be sighted) in order to maintain the most practicable route. Being designed for animal-drawn transport, they often took a much steeper course uphill than would be contemplated today; but on the steepest slopes short zig-zags were introduced, the road returning to the main alignment at the top (7). In mountainous country the course of Roman roads is naturally often much more sinuous; they prefer to climb to high, more open, ground and to strike directly along a ridge (83) or across a high plateau rather than to follow a narrow valley which, although more level, may offer a longer more wandering route through possibly dangerous defiles. When a Roman road does follow a valley, a middle course is preferred (6), that avoids the proximity of steep overlooking hills. But occasionally this could not be avoided (6, 9).

Examination of the Ordnance Survey *Map of Roman Britain* strongly suggests that we know only a small proportion of the minor roads which must once have existed; in general only through-roads and those with well constructed metalling have left detectable traces, or have survived long enough to become incorporated in later landscapes. Many others must have existed to serve local needs but have now disappeared. In addition, aerial photographs reveal, for instance in the Fenland (128) or on the chalk Downs (123) and

river gravels (125), a network of unmetalled drove-ways wandering through the fields from farm to farm or connecting villages in a manner very similar to the country lanes of today.

References

I.D. Margary, *Roman Roads in Britain* I and II (London, 1955). R.G. Collingwood and I.A. Richmond, *The Archaeology of Roman Britain* (2nd ed., London, 1969), Ch. 1. For the Antonine Itinerary and the Peutinger Map: A.L.F. Rivet and C. Smith, *The Place-Names of Roman Britain* (London, 1979).

BADBURY RINGS, Dorset (5)

Badbury Rings is a prominent hill fort of the Iron Age occupying a low summit 3 km north of the slow-flowing river Stour. The main Roman road to the South-West (Ackling Dyke), in the length from Old Sarum (*Sorviodunum*) to Dorchester (*Durnovaria*), passes close to the north (near) side of the hill fort, crossing the photograph obliquely from the bottom left to the top right-hand corner. Ackling Dyke is a noteworthy example of road engineering; where well-preserved, its *agger* is up to 19 m wide and 1.5 m high. A second road, that runs from Hamworthy (on Poole Harbour) in the direction of Bath, skirts the north-east side of the defences and then traverses the same arable field. At the intersection, the side-ditches of Ackling Dyke appear to cut across the other road, and this may suggest that the Hamworthy–Bath road had gone out of use when these ditches were dug. However, appearances may be deceptive: the ditches may not be original features, or alternatively they may have been continued as culverts beneath the north-bound road, and it is perhaps the traces of the collapsed culverts that show on the photograph.

The Romano-British settlement which grew up near the crossroads took the name *Vindocladia* ('White Ditches') for topographical reasons. The core of this settlement lies between the road and the hill fort in the top right-hand part of the photograph. The Iron Age defences have not been excavated, but the extensive ditch system shows that at least in their latest phases they belong to the first century B.C. The two inner ramparts are considered to represent an earlier phase of fortification.

However, the settlement did not determine the line of Ackling Dyke; the situation in regard to both roads is more complicated and more interesting than might appear at first sight. The last alignment of Ackling Dyke as it approaches the left foreground from the north-east aims at the east (left) side of the hill fort, but some 425 m from the hill fort the Dyke changes direction

5 Badbury Rings, Dorset; Iron Age hill fort and Roman roads, looking S. ST 965004. AT 42: June 1948.

through 40° to the west in order to pass the north flank of the defences. The point of change lies at the very bottom left corner of the photograph, which plainly shows a further continuation of the old alignment of the road to join the Hamworthy road where some trees now stand in a hedge. There is evidence for the existence at Hamworthy of a military supply base of the period of the conquest, while a military establishment as large as a vexillation fortress is known to have existed at Lake Farm on the same road some 9 km north of Poole Harbour, so that there is every probability that Ackling Dyke was originally designed to make for Hamworthy. Only later, though perhaps not much later, was the new length of main road constructed from Badbury on to Dorchester and ultimately to Exeter. Both these places were certainly in existence within 10–12 years of A.D. 43 (and Exeter was a legionary fortress), so the new road is not likely to be much later than this.

The Hamworthy–Bath road could hardly have become redundant in so short a time. The suggested fort at Shapwick (ST 949024), 1.5 km south-west of the hill fort towards the Stour, is crossed by the new road and, if indeed a military work, may belong to the intervening years.

References

J.K. St Joseph, *J.R.S.* XLIII (1953), 93 with Pl. XIV, 2 (similar view). I.D. Margary, *Roman Roads in Britain* I (London, 1955), 98–101. R.C.H.M. *Dorset* II Pt 3 (London, 1970), 528–9 with plan; *Dorset* V (London, 1975), pp. XXXII-IV. Shapwick: N. Field, *Britannia* VII (1976), 280–3.

WATLING STREET WEST, Shropshire (6)

The road, which even today is the most prominent man-made feature of the landscape, is marked by the continuous line of hedges of its modern

6 Watling Street West, Roman road, Wroxeter to Kenchester, entering the Church Stretton gap, Shropshire; looking S. SJ 5000. Y 84: July 1947.

successor. The route keeps to the centre of the level valley floor between hills (The Lawley and Caer Caradoc) on the left and the marshy valley of the Cound Brook on the right, beyond which rises the Long Mynd plateau. In the distance the road curves to enter the narrow Church Stretton gap, beyond which it continues past the forts at Stretford Bridge and Leintwardine on its way to the upper Wye Valley at Kenchester; there it forks to Gloucester and Usk. The course of this road demonstrates notable ability on the part of the military surveyors to choose a direct but well planned route through this tangled hill country, evidence that they had good maps on which to base their work. This road may well have been laid

down by the Roman army at an early stage of their attempt to conquer Wales, perhaps even briefly forming the backbone of a frontier system linking the legionary bases at Wroxeter and at Kingsholm near Gloucester.

Reference

I.D. Margary, *Roman Roads in Britain* II (London, 1957), 50–2 (Road 6b).

LEEMING LANE, North Yorkshire (7)

This view under snow shows the course of Leeming Lane about 9 km south-west of Darlington as it runs north from Scotch Corner (3 km behind the

12

7 Leeming Lane, Roman road near Scotch Corner, North Yorkshire; looking N. NZ 2109. CIF 92: January 1979.

camera) towards Piercebridge, 7 km away. Further south the Roman road is masked by the dual carriageway of the modern A 1 road; but here it is represented by a narrow lane, the B 6275, which gives an excellent impression of the directness of the Roman survey over comparatively level ground. In the foreground another characteristic of the Roman surveyor's work is illustrated, where the road has to descend a short steep bluff towards the farm of Low Hangbank (in the shadow) and deflects to take an easier gradient, only to resume the main alignment once it has done so. On the bluff itself are seen earthworks of unknown date. The important pre-Roman site of Stanwick lies on the left of the photograph in the middle distance.

Reference

I.D. Margary, *Roman Roads in Britain* II (London, 1957), 160–1 (Road 8c).

DERE STREET, Borders (8)

Dere Street, the Roman road from Corbridge northwards to Newstead and beyond, marks the line of the more easterly of the two main Roman routes into Scotland. The view is taken from near the small fort of Cappuck. In the distance, 19 km away, are the triple peaks of the Eildon Hills, to the right of which lay the large fort of Newstead; the fort derives its name *Trimontium* from the peaks. Eildon Hill North, the right-hand summit (404 m), was occupied by the largest native hill

13

8 Dere Street, Roman road, Borders (Roxburghshire); looking NW. NT 6922. CNA 2: August 1980.

fort in Scotland, with its many scooped hut-emplacements still visible, evidently one of the chief *oppida* of the Selgovae. In Roman times a signal station, comprising a timber tower surrounded by a circular ditch, was erected within the hill fort near the summit. The line of the road crosses the river Teviot in the middle distance and then inclines to the east to pass by the Eildons to the site of Newstead at their foot, beside the Tweed. The photograph strikingly illustrates the long-distance alignments often used by Roman road builders.

References

I.D. Margary, *Roman Roads in Britain* II (London, 1957), 213 (Road 8f). R.C.A.H.M. (Scotland), *Roxburghshire* I (Edinburgh, 1956), 24; II (1956), 467–9.

THE LUNE GORGE, Cumbria (9)

The photograph, taken in the winter after a fall of snow, looks north up the Lune Valley from the broken low ground west of Sedbergh to the gorge cut through the hills between the Lake District and the Pennines (Langdale Fell on right). The gorge thus marks one of the few routes northwards through this difficult country to avoid an ascent to a high watershed. Beyond the gorge lies Tebay, and in the distance on the left the height of Shap. Today the route is used both by the London–Carlisle railway and by the M6 motorway: in Roman times it was utilised by Agricola's road from Manchester to Carlisle and western Scotland. The line of the Roman road can be seen as an almost continuous hedgerow running northward on the right-hand side of the valley from the lower

9 The Lune Gorge, Cumbria (Yorkshire–Lancashire); Roman road, looking N. SD 6395. BLY 58: February 1973.

end of a prominent rectangular plantation. The site of the Roman fort of Low Borrow Bridge lies where the gorge widens half-way along. This fort does not appear to be an Agricolan foundation; the first fort on this sector of the road may have lain in the more open foreground, near Sedbergh.

Reference

I.D. Margary, *Roman Roads in Britain* II (London, 1957), 123 (Road 7c).

ROMAN ROAD NEAR CRAWFORD, Strathclyde (10)

In mountainous terrain Roman road surveyors were often compelled to choose routes less direct than in flat country, but even so often preferred to strike boldly up steep gradients or to keep to high plateaux, thus avoiding the long detours necessary for modern traffic. In this photograph the fort of Crawford lies in the left central background commanding the light-coloured flat basin where the Camps Water and Midlock Water join the river Clyde, beyond the first range of hills and just behind a small dark wood. The sites of

two marching-camps are known nearby. The Roman road, coming north from Carlisle, runs close to the line now followed by the modern A 74 dual-carriageway road, which can be seen passing from right to left, centre. The marching-camp of Little Clyde and the watch-tower at Beattock Summit lie beyond the right margin. The road skirts closely round the base of Bodsberry Hill (centre), on whose summit (401 m) there is a small Iron Age hill fort; the proximity of the marshy ground at the confluence of the Clydes Burn (right) with the river Clyde forces the Roman road into this unusual position at the base of a steep slope. It then keeps to the right bank of the Clyde as far as Crawford fort. But whereas the A 74 then curves left, keeping to the left bank of the Clyde to make a long detour round the high ground of Castle Hill (483 m), the Roman road regains the Clyde valley by striking boldly over the shoulder of Raggengill Hill and descending the steep side-valley of the Raggengill Burn which divides these hills from the main range of mountains to the right. The road then takes a NNE course behind the shadow-covered range in the right-hand middle distance towards the fortlets of

10 Roman road, Carlisle to Inveresk, near Crawford, Strathclyde (Lanarkshire); looking NE. NS 9617. BVL 26: July 1975.

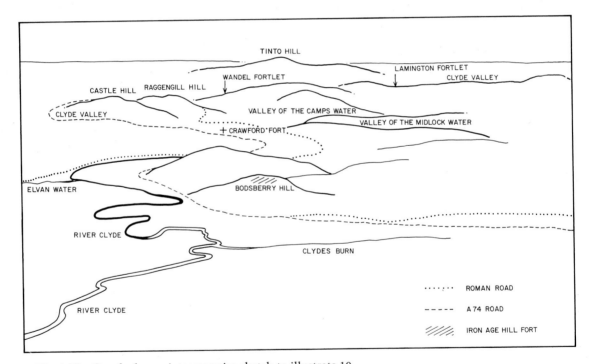

Fig. 1 The Crawford area: interpretative sketch to illustrate 10.

Wandel and Lamington, which lie out of sight in the Clyde valley this side of Tinto Hill. A second Roman road coming in from Nithsdale along the Elvan Water joins the first near the left centre of the photograph.

References

J.K. StJoseph in S.N. Miller (ed.), *The Roman Occupation of South-western Scotland* (Glasgow, 1952), 27–34 with Pls. X, XII (maps). I.D. Margary, *Roman Roads in Britain* II (London, 1957), 190, 195–6. R.C.A.H.M. (Scotland), *Lanarkshire* (Edinburgh, 1978), 128–33, 143–4.

PART TWO

MILITARY SITES

3

MARCHING-CAMPS

Roman troops on campaign, at least down to the third century, built at their halting-places each night defended camps in which their tented lines were set up. Vegetius (*Epitoma rei militaris* I, 21) writes that it was as if the Roman army carried everywhere with it a walled town. The site was chosen by an advance party, and when the army arrived a ditch (*fossa*) was dug and a rampart (*vallum*) built; this was sometimes made at least partly of turves, but sometimes of the earth or clay from the ditch, and was then crowned with a palisade. The shape of the camp was normally square or oblong except where the nature of the ground dictated otherwise, but the sides were almost invariably straight and the angles rounded. There were normally at least four gates, one on each side; larger, longer camps had six, but there are examples, normally of early date, with even more gates (13, Rey Cross).

The gates did not, of course, have timber towers or doors like those of forts, but were guarded by special details, who formed a wall of men across the gap in time of need, as descriptions in Livy, Caesar and Tacitus tell us.[1] The gates were normally protected in addition by an outlying length of bank and ditch (*titulum*, 16), intended to break up a direct charge, or else by the device known as a *clavicula* (11, 14). This consisted of an extension of the rampart in the form of a quarter-circle curving either inwards or outwards, or sometimes in both directions; the *clavicula* was so planned as to compel attackers to veer to the left, thus presenting their unshielded side to the missiles of the defenders on the rampart. Internal *claviculae* were accordingly attached to the right of the entrance viewed from outside, and external ones to the left. The *clavicula* was in use for only a comparatively short period; the earliest examples can be assigned to about A.D. 70 and no examples later than the reign of Hadrian (117–38) are known. *Titula* on the other hand can be of any date. These devices were only very rarely used at the gates of forts (48, Hod Hill). In Scotland there is a group of camps of first-century date possessing

gates that are protected by an interesting elaboration of the *clavicula*, known as the 'Stracathro type' from the camp at the site of that name. This type of *clavicula* is illustrated and discussed with the camp at Dalginross (78).

Camps normally possess only a single ditch, often of no great size, and this fact together with the area enclosed helps to distinguish them from forts or fortresses. The defences of marching-camps are particularly vulnerable to the plough, being neither so substantial nor so solidly constructed as the defences of forts. Many camps have been flattened by agriculture in later centuries, but even so the buried ditches can be detected by excavation, or distinguished on aerial photographs taken when suitable conditions of weather have favoured differential growth of crops. Frequently the crop-marks show no sign of gate-defence; this is doubtless because the original *claviculae* or *titula* were unaccompanied by ditches. It may be observed, for instance, that whereas external *claviculae* usually have the outward-curving rampart accompanied by a ditch, internal *claviculae* often comprise an inward curve of the rampart only. Thus, at the gates of camps where all earthworks have been levelled, the ditch alone being visible as a crop-mark, there may now be no remaining trace of an internal *clavicula*. That *titula* frequently lacked ditches is less certain; the examples at Rey Cross (13) might have been thought exceptional, the result of the presence of rock close to the surface, were it not for the fact that the gates at another camp in the same series, at Crackenthorpe, are also provided with ditchless *titula*. It remains true, however, that no camp still surviving in relief lacks gate-defences of one or the other kind. At the south camp at Chew Green (84, 85), where surface traces of *claviculae* have disappeared, excavation revealed remains of internal *claviculae*.

Of nearly four hundred temporary camps known in Britain, almost three-quarters have been discovered by aerial reconnaissance in the last thirty-five years. The country is particularly rich in camps still surviving in relief; on the continent of Europe almost all the camps which must once have marked the numerous great campaigns attested in history have entirely disappeared. Scarcely

---

1. Livy IV, 27; XXXIV, 46; XL, 25. Caesar, *B.G.* VI, 38. Tacitus, *Agricola* 26.

five or six are still upstanding, and the number known even from crop-marks is depressingly exiguous. The valuable and historic heritage of camps in Britain is under constant threat from forestry, from agriculture and from all kinds of 'development', so that the preservation of these comparatively slight earthworks calls for unceasing vigilance.

Marching-camps naturally varied in size with the composition of the forces which built them. Old camps conveniently situated were doubtless reused on occasion, and there are several examples of a small camp being placed within one of the corners of a larger one so as to save labour on the construction of two of its sides (16). The largest camps known anywhere in the Roman Empire belong to a series in south-east Scotland which cover 66.8 ha (165 acres). As there is reason to think that a single legion required only 7.3–8.1 ha (18–20 acres) for its camp (see 13, Rey Cross), it is clear that, even allowing ample space for baggage-trains and stores, these huge camps were built for a very large army indeed, which almost certainly was that with which the Emperor Septimius Severus invaded Scotland in 208. Another Scottish series is 25.5 ha (63 acres) in area, but camps of 7–12 ha occur much more frequently, suggesting that the need for assembling really large armies was rarely felt. Examples of camps as small as 0.5 ha are not infrequent, and these may represent single auxiliary units on the move. The great majority of camps seem thus to denote the passage of troops on the march or on campaign; but some can be classified as construction camps in which troops were housed while building e.g. a fort or fortress (21) or a frontier line such as the Antonine Wall, and others may be regarded as siege camps (p. 32). At some sites there are clusters of extremely small camps which are classified as practice camps since they are often really too small for occupation but seem to be exercises in constructing properly rounded angles in turf or in laying out *claviculae* or *titula*. Such camps may have only sufficient normal rampart in between to form a coherent earthwork (Fig. 16, p. 136).

As aerial photography gradually increases our total of camps and our knowledge of their areas, it should be possible to trace the actual course of individual campaigns. Much progress has been made towards this end in Scotland and the objective has been at least in part achieved; in Wales, which also was the scene of fierce and repeated cam-paigning in the first century, insufficient camps of similar size have yet been found to throw clear light on lines of advance, but at several places in the Marches there exist either very large camps

(e.g. Brampton Bryan (Fig. 12) near Leintwardine, 25.9 ha, 64 acres) or groups of camps, e.g. at Brompton (Shropshire) and Greensforge (Stafford-shire), which suggest the starting-points of invasion routes. A line of camps, each of about 16 ha (40 acres), extends from Wall in Staffordshire to Corwen in North Wales and may represent the campaigns in this area of either Ostorius Scapula or Suetonius Paullinus in the middle of the first century.

The internal arrangements of a camp are known from descriptions in Polybius and Hyginus to have varied greatly from those found in a fort or fortress, but very rarely does aerial photography or archaeology throw any additional light on this aspect. At Masada, in Israel, low dry-stone walls have preserved the outline of the accommodation used in the camps during the siege of that citadel; in Britain the rows of pits in the construction camps at Inchtuthil (21, 22) also give a clue to the arrangement of the tented lines. The tents them-selves were of leather; 'under skins' (*sub pellibus*) was the Latin equivalent for our 'under canvas'. Representations of tents are frequent on Trajan's Column and pieces of the leather sheets from which they were assembled are not uncommonly found at sites where conditions have been damp enough to preserve them.

References

I.A. Richmond, 'The Romans in Redesdale', *Northumber-land County History* XV (1940). R.G. Collingwood and I.A. Richmond, *The Archaeology of Roman Britain* (2nd ed., London, 1969), Ch. 2. V.E. Nash-Williams, *The Roman Frontier in Wales* (2nd ed. by M.G. Jarrett, Cardiff, 1969), 123–6. D.R. Wilson, 'Roman Camps in Britain', *Actes du IXe Congrès international d'Études sur les Frontières romaines* (Bucharest/Köln, 1974), 343–50. Groupings of camps in Scotland: J.K. St Joseph, *J.R.S.* LIX (1969), 113–29; *J.R.S.* LXIII (1973), 228–33; *Britannia* IX (1978), 277–81. Practice camps: see bibliography on p. 138. Masada: C.F.C. Hawkes, *Antiquity* III (1929), 195–213 (with aerial photographs). I.A. Richmond, *J.R.S.* LII (1962), 142–55 (aerial photographs and plans).

Y PYGWN, Dyfed (11)

The rounded summit of Trecastle Mountain (413 m), 7 km south-east of Llandovery, carries the earthworks of two successive marching-camps. The outer and larger can be seen to be the earlier, and it encloses *c.* 15.2 ha (37.5 acres); but even the inner camp, at 10.3 ha (25.5 acres), is still of legionary size. Both camps have gates defended by internal *claviculae*, that on the right of the inner camp (its *porta principalis dextra*) being among the best preserved anywhere in the Roman Empire. In Britain the use of *claviculae* seems virtually confined to the Flavian period.

11 Y Pygwn, Dyfed; Roman marching-camps, looking SW. SN 827313. AQE 47: October 1966.

The south-east (left) sides of both camps have been much damaged by subsequent tile-stone quarries. The later Roman road from Brecon to Llandovery passes obliquely from left to right behind the site and probably overrides the south corner of the larger camp. The original road bears slightly left, but has been replaced by a deeply cut series of medieval trackways bearing right, seeking an easier way down the escarpment. A Roman fortlet guarding the road at the top of the ascent lies just beyond the edge of the photograph; this fortlet was itself later occupied by a small medieval tomen or motte.

Although the forts of the permanent occupation tend to lie in valleys, the known marching-camps in South Wales, which housed large bodies of troops on campaign, are found for the most part on high open plateaux by way of which initial penetration was easier and where there was room for manoeuvre with less chance of being surprised. These two camps may represent successive campaigns by Legion II Augusta with varying numbers of accompanying auxiliary troops.

References

F. Haverfield, *Cymmrodorion Soc. Trans.* (1910), 62–3 with

12 Malham, North Yorkshire; Roman marching-camp, looking S. SD 913655. AQM 69: January 1967.

sketch plan. R.E.M. Wheeler, *Prehistoric and Roman Wales* (Oxford, 1925), 219 with (inaccurate) plan. J.K. St Joseph, *J.R.S.* XLIII (1953), 86. G.D.B. Jones, *Bull. Board of Celtic Studies* XXIII (1968), 100–3 with map and Pl. I (vertical) and II (ground view). V.E. Nash-Williams, *The Roman Frontier in Wales* (Cardiff, 1954), 4–6; *idem*, 2nd ed. (ed. by M.G. Jarrett, Cardiff, 1969), 123–4 with plan and Pl. XIB (vertical).

MALHAM, North Yorkshire (12)

This well-preserved marching-camp lies in the Pennines 2.2 km ESE of Malham Tarn, at an altitude of 380 m. With an area of 8.2 ha (20.25 acres) the camp is of legionary size, and is defended by a rampart of earth and stones and by a small ditch apparently lacking round parts of the circuit, where solid limestone rock comes close to the surface. There are four gates, each defended by an internal *clavicula*; two of these are clearly visible at the centres of the north and south sides. The *claviculae* point to a Flavian date, so that the camp may belong to the campaigns either of Cerialis or of Agricola which effected the conquest of this part of northern England. Like many of the marching-camps in Wales that at Malham lies on a plateau, terrain more suited to the passage or manoeuvring of sizeable forces than are the

13 Rey Cross, Cumbria; Roman marching-camp, looking S. NY 901124. BFW 83: July 1971.

narrow, steep-sided and often wooded valleys which cut through the hills. No further camps are known within a very large distance of Malham; the earthwork at Cross Green (SD 962474), about 19 km to the south, which has recently been claimed as a camp, is of very dubious Roman origin. Other camps in the same series as Malham must surely have existed at intervals of a day's march apart of *c*. 20 km or (in this hilly terrain) perhaps rather less. The camp at Malham is bisected by an old road, Mastiles Lane, which provides an easy east–west route between the valley of the Ribble, north of Settle, and that of the Wharfe near Grassington. In one or the other direction, this was possibly the line taken by the troops who encamped at Malham: a convenient north–south route hereabouts is far less easy to find, on account of deeply incised valleys and steep scarps.

References

J.K. St Joseph, *J.R.S.* XLVIII (1968), 97. Cross Green: *Britannia* XIII (1982), Roman Britain report.

REY CROSS, Cumbria (13)

This camp of 8.15 ha (20.14 acres) lies at an altitude of 451 m on the bleak and wind-swept summit of the Stainmore Pass, the route taken by the Roman road (and modern A 66) between Scotch Corner and Carlisle. The Roman road crosses the camp, making use of two of the gates, and changes direction through a slight angle at the east gate. These facts suggest that the camp was already in existence when the road was built, doubtless (at the latest) during Agricola's governorship. This deduction is supported by the square metation of the camp, a feature which was going out of use in Agricola's time, and is seldom found later. The camp is unusual in having as many as eleven gates. These features in combination give the camp an old-fashioned look, and support an attribution to the campaigns of Cerialis; this was the first occasion, as far as is known, when Roman troops campaigned so far north. Two other camps which appear to belong to the same series are known at day's-march intervals farther towards the north-west at Crackenthorpe and Plumpton Head, but hitherto none has been discovered in the other direction; they may represent a thrust by Legion IX from York towards the Eden valley and Carlisle, which must certainly have been one of the objectives during Cerialis's conquest of the Brigantes.

The south rampart, beyond the main road, lies above the steep side of a deep valley (somewhat flattened by perspective in the photograph) formed by the headwaters of the river Greta. In this rampart there are two gates; the others have three each, and all are defended by substantial *titula*. As the photograph shows, at those gates that remain sufficiently well preserved, a slight inward turn of the rampart occurs on either side of the gateway passage. There are traces here and there of a small ditch on the north and east sides, but the nearness of limestone rock to the surface has caused greater reliance than usual to be placed on the rampart, which at 6.4 m wide is much more substantial than normal and is probably built of turf and stones scraped up from the surface. In the south-west corner of the camp a large area has been disturbed by nineteenth-century quarrying.

The existence of eleven gates permits a reconstruction of the internal street system of the camp, as Richmond showed, with far greater probability than the normal quota of four or six gates would allow. In the diagram (Fig. 2), the *intervallum* street has been assigned a width of 10.6 m (35 ft) and the others a width of 7.6 m (25 ft); the double plot on the south side has been provisionally subdivided into Plots 13 and 14.

The fifteen plots thus outlined vary in size because of a basic distortion of the camp's layout; but even the two smallest, No. 1 (at 2230 sq. m) and No. 15 (at 2210 sq. m), are sufficient for a quingenary cohort, for they approximate closely to Hyginus's figure of 150 by 150 ft (2090 sq. m) for such a cohort's camping needs (*De munitione castrorum*, 2). This arrangement of the camp suggests that it accommodated the ten cohorts of a legion (whether or not at this time the first cohort of the legion was of double strength) and an additional complement of auxiliaries, partly no doubt cavalry. If this reasoning is correct, it allows the deduction that a legion on the march would require a camp of 7–8 ha (18–20 acres) and gives us a yardstick for a rough assessment of the forces represented by other camps.

References

W. Roy, *Military Antiquities* (London, 1793), Pl. XVII (plan). I.A. Richmond and J. McIntyre, *Trans. Cumb. and Westm. Antiq. and Arch. Soc.* (2nd series) XXXIV (1934), 50–61 (plan and discussion). R.G. Collingwood and I.A. Richmond, *The Archaeology of Roman Britain* (2nd ed., London, 1969), Fig. 2 (plan).

TROUTBECK, Cumbria (14)

This marching-camp of 4.03 ha (9.96 acres) forms one of a remarkable group of Roman military earthworks sited on an exposed moorland at *c.* 275 m in altitude, near Troutbeck Station, 13 km WSW of Penrith. A second and much larger camp of 16.66 ha (41 acres), with gates defended by both internal and external *claviculae*, lies beyond the left side of the photograph on higher ground. There are also two permanent but no doubt successive works, namely a fortlet of 0.72 ha (1.79 acres), just outside the photograph, to the left, and a fort of 1.42 ha (3.5 acres). The fortlet has a broad rampart and only two gates, which are, most unusually, like those of the camp, defended by double *claviculae*. This plan of gate is more typical of a temporary camp, and it is hard to see how a timber gateway could have been combined with the *claviculae*, or why these were provided if a timber gateway was envisaged. Nevertheless, the rampart seems too substantial for a temporary camp and the position of one of the gates is unusual. The first gate faces the road in a normal position in the centre of the south side, but the other lies close to the south-west corner. This suggests that the garrison had a close concern with traffic on the road. If, however, future excavation fails to reveal internal buildings such as would be expected in a road-post, an alternative interpretation might suggest that the earthwork

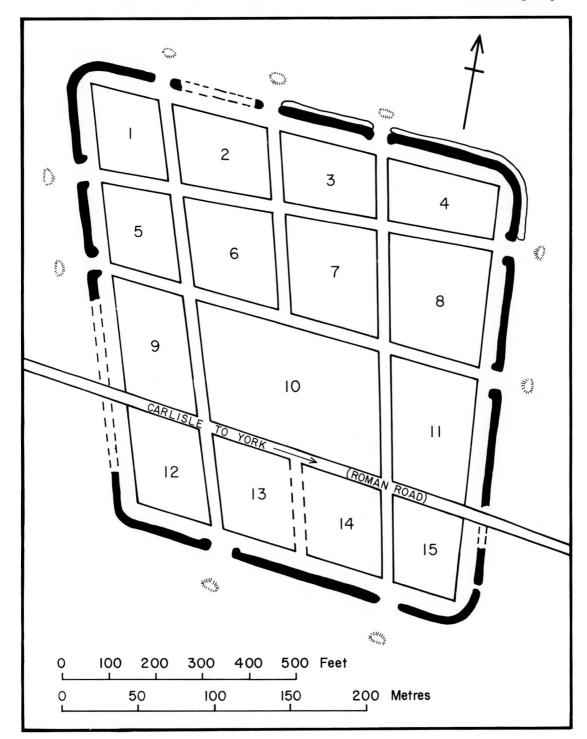

Fig. 2 The camp at Rey Cross (after I.A. Richmond), with street system restored.

is the construction camp for the fort, which lies on the opposite side of the road.

The fort, although plainly visible on the surface, remained undetected until 1973 when it was observed by Mr R.A.H. Farrar during a ground survey. The west rampart of the fort can be seen running at right angles to the modern A 594 road across the light-toned slope of a low knoll near the top left-hand corner of the photograph. The course of the eastern defences follows a parallel

25

14 Troutbeck, Cumbria; Roman marching-camp, looking SE. NY 379273. BPB 40: November 1973.

line in the meadow to the left of the hedge. The fort extends below the modern road to the hedgerow on the near side.

The marching-camp in the centre of the picture is remarkably preserved; the rampart of clay is 3.8 m wide and still stands 0.6 m high. The gates are defended by internal *claviculae*, two of which are clearly distinguishable. The possession of *claviculae* suggests that both camps are of the first century or at the latest of the early second. They probably represent the passage of successive forces from the neighbourhood of the fort at Brougham

south-east of Penrith, along the northern east–west route through the Lake District by way of Keswick. This area was probably not finally brought under military control until the reign of Trajan. The large camp could have accommodated two legions or their equivalent; the smaller camp held a force of the size of only half a legion.

References

J.K. StJoseph, *J.R.S.* XLV (1955), 83–4 with Pl. XVI, 1 (oblique view of fortlet from the SE), XVI, 2 (oblique

15 Glenlochar, Dumfries and Galloway; Roman marching-camp No. 1, looking ENE. NX 739642. DT 65: July 1949.

view of the small camp from the NW); *J.R.S.* LXIII (1973), 115. R. Bellhouse, *Trans. Cumb. and Westm. Antiq. and Arch. Soc.* LVI (1956), 28–36. *Britannia* V (1974), 412–13.

GLENLOCHAR, Dumfries and Galloway (15)

Glenlochar on the river Dee in south-west Scotland, some 3.5 km north-west of Castle Douglas, was an important strategic centre for the Roman army. The fort there is described elsewhere (p. 127). Aerial photography has also revealed an impressive group of marching-camps (numbers 1–7 on Fig. 3) extending over 1.25 km along the level valley floor east of the fort; one of them is seen here. Its ramparts have been ploughed away, but the ditch still survives below ground to yield crop-marks. The camp is large, enclosing 12.7 ha (31.5 acres), and is of a size to house a legion and a large force of attendant auxiliaries. It faces west towards the river; the positions of two lateral gateways defining the *via principalis* can just be made out in the fields on the near side of the transverse modern lane. The front and back gates are concealed from view but would have occupied the centres of their respective sides. Indications of either *titulum* or *clavicula* are lacking; a *titulum* would hardly have been built without its ditch, but a *clavicula* could have been made of turf alone and been ploughed away without trace. Alternatively, perhaps, no gate-protection was provided at all.

To the east half of the north side has been added an annexe measuring *c.* 230 by 75 m, itself divided by a cross-ditch and possessing at least two external gateways. Annexes attached to camps are unusual, and must be supposed to have housed either prisoners or bulky stores which it would be inconvenient to accommodate within the main camp. The only series of camps at which attached annexes regularly occur is the 25 ha (63 acre) series in eastern Scotland, which has been ascribed to the Severan campaigns.

The camp reveals another remarkable feature; lines of pits can be seen, some perhaps cooking pits or latrine pits along the rear of the rampart,

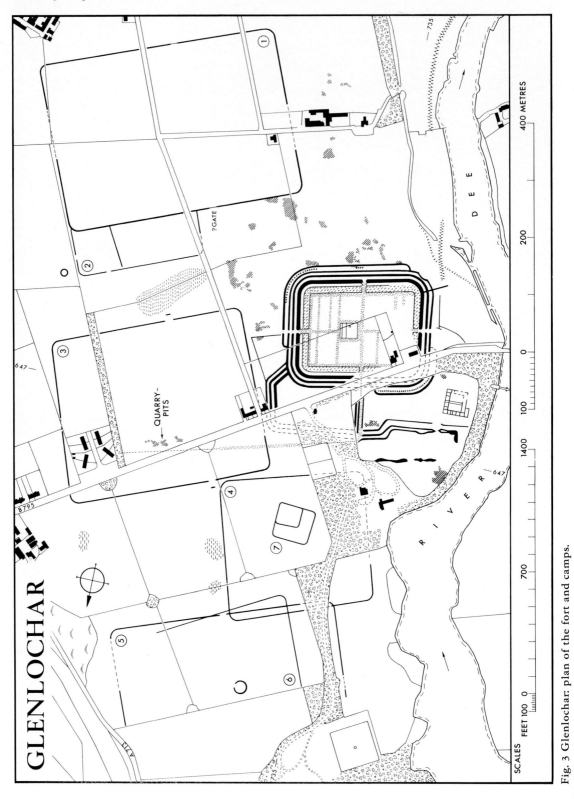

Fig. 3 Glenlochar: plan of the fort and camps.

16 Pennymuir, Oxnam, Borders (Roxburghshire); Roman marching-camps, looking S. NT 755139. Y 34: July 1947.

others orientated on either axis. These recall the pits in the construction camp at Inchtuthil (21) and suggest part of the arrangement of the tented lines. It would seem likely that the camp had been occupied for a longer period than normal – perhaps at the beginning of a campaigning season – so that digging rubbish pits in front of the tents became necessary. Too few of the pits are visible for useful analysis, but a total stripping of the camp by excavation might one day reveal remarkable information.

Reference

J.K. StJoseph, *J.R.S.* XLI (1951), 60 with Pl. VI, 2 (this view)

PENNYMUIR, Borders (16)

Beside the line of Dere Street (p. 36) lie two Roman camps, the larger enclosing 17 ha (42 acres), space sufficient to accommodate a force of two legions or their equivalent. The smaller, of 3.66 ha (9.04 acres), makes use of parts of the east and south sides of the larger camp, and its later

date is confirmed by the observation that its ditch cuts through the rampart of the latter. Each camp had six gateways defended by *titula*, two on the longer (east and west) sides and one on each of the shorter. A small embanked enclosure of no great age lies between the camps and the Roman road. A short distance north-east, off the picture on the other side of Dere Street, lies a third camp, in shape a parallelogram of 6.06 ha (14.99 acres), and south of it has been noticed the corner of a fourth camp, probably of much smaller size. It is clear that this site, close beside the Kale Water, was found to be a convenient halting-place for troops on the march after they had descended the steep north-west slope of the Cheviots, or before beginning the ascent. The camps also lie within 1.5 km of the practice siege-works of Woden Law (19) on the hill above to the south-east, and it has been reasonably considered that the large camp, and perhaps some of the others, were the base for these operations despite the fact that the camp itself seems to face north. The fact that the camp's ramparts are unusually massive, as if

29

17 Durno–Bennachie, Grampian Region (Aberdeenshire); suggested battle-field of Mons Graupius, looking SSW. NJ 699272. BVE 11: July 1975.

designed for a longer than normal occupation, reinforces this view.

At the date of photography these camps formed the best-preserved group in Scotland. Unfortunately they were badly and irresponsibly damaged in 1969 during forestry operations; but they have since been restored as far as possible to their original condition.

References

W. Roy, *Military Antiquities* (London, 1793), Pl. XXII. J.K. St Joseph, *Proc. Soc. Ant. of Newcastle upon Tyne* (4th series) VII (1935–6) 107–12. R.C.A.H.M. (Scotland), *Roxburghshire* II (Edinburgh, 1956) 375–7 with maps and plans. S.S. Frere, *Britannia, a history of Roman Britain* (London, 1967), Pl. 16 (this view).

DURNO–BENNACHIE, Grampian Region (17)

In the background lies Bennachie (528 m), a conspicuous granite mountain visible from afar and easily recognisable by its distinctive profile. In 1975 a very large Roman marching-camp was discovered in the fields in the foreground, ex-

tending over *c.* 58 ha (144 acres). Its north-east side enters the picture at Easterton, the steading in front of a wood on the left, runs to the pylon by the wood in the centre and turns two-thirds of the way across the large oval field on the right (where its line can just be distinguished), to continue west just to the right of a small clump of trees. It turns south in the field beyond the farm (Westerton) and crosses the belt of trees behind the farm to take up a line which is obscured by the slope of the ground. The line continues across the light-coloured, L-shaped field, and the south-west angle is in the part of that field which is surrounded by woods on three sides.

The claim that the ground between the Urie Water, flowing just beyond the camp, and the northern slopes of Bennachie was the site of Agricola's famous battle has been argued in *Britannia* IX, and need not be repeated in detail here. The evidence, which is largely circumstantial, is as follows: this unique camp, the largest north of the Antonine Wall, implies, in the context of Roman military affairs, a concentration at Durno,

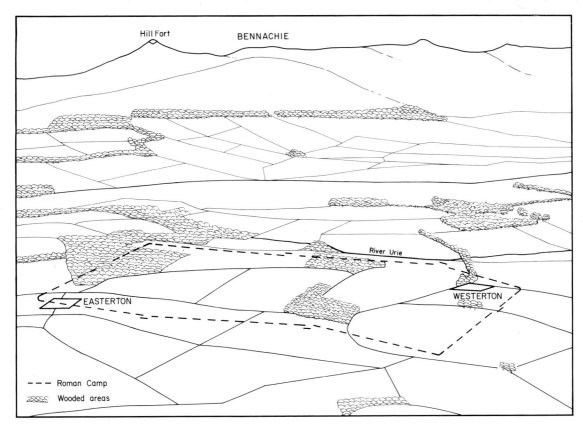

Fig. 4 Durno: interpretative sketch to illustrate 17.

for whatever purpose, of a force of overwhelming strength. The area of the camp is almost exactly equal to the sum of the areas of the only two series of camps known anywhere in the neighbourhood (within 55 km). One of the series (comprising two examples) is certainly Agricolan in date, so there are strong grounds for supposing that Durno is Agricolan too. The topography well matches the somewhat scanty hints provided by Tacitus (*Agricola* 35–8) about the battle and its terrain, while Bennachie itself is an unmistakable landmark, an eminently suitable rendezvous for Caledonian war-bands, offering ample gathering-ground for the large forces involved.

Reference

J.K. StJoseph, *Britannia* IX (1978), 271–87 with map and plan and Pls. XVIIIB (oblique of SW side of camp), and XIX (this view).

4

SIEGE-WORKS

Two sites illustrate Roman techniques of siege warfare. Strongly defended places could often withstand long sieges by the Roman army, when it was normally necessary to construct a wall of circumvallation to cut off the defenders' supplies and communications. Archaeological traces of such sieges are well known at such sites as Numantia, Hatra, Masada or Alesia; Masada in particular illustrates the enormous power and engineering skills which the Romans could exert when necessary, and the remains there are vividly complemented by Josephus's account of the almost contemporary siege of Jerusalem.

The defences normally encountered by the Roman army in Celtic Europe rarely called for similar exertions. As Caesar's account of his war in Gaul makes clear, such places could usually be captured by a *coup de main*; strong though the earthworks might appear, the gateways through them were vulnerable to fire or to the ram. Even at Maiden Castle (3), Dorset, whose breath-taking defences are known to have fallen to the Second Legion, there are no traces whatever of prolonged siege. At Hod Hill (49) the hill fort appears to have surrendered after a short bombardment by catapults. Occasionally the presence of a marching-camp in its vicinity may suggest that a hill fort was attacked, but other indications are rare.

At Burnswark and Woden Law Roman siege-works are identifiable, but in the past reasons have been suggested for thinking that neither indicates an actual act of warfare; instead, both have been taken to illustrate something much more rare in the archaeological record, training-grounds where troops could be taught the appropriate techniques. This conclusion, as will be seen, is by no means well-grounded for Burnswark, which may well have seen the abrupt suppression of a last stand by native rebels. Here a circumvallation is lacking, but two camps of unusual form clasp the hill; both are provided with emplacements from which the hill could be bombarded with catapult shot, and the North Camp was so placed that it could deny access to the only spring.

At Woden Law a circumvallation was begun but not completed, and it too seems to have had provision for catapult fire. But no attempt has been made to complete the lines of circumvallation along or below the steep north-western slopes down which the defenders of a real siege could have escaped, and the works themselves though logically of successive stages are none of them completed; all seem to show concern for the proper construction of small lengths rather than for the overall progress of the whole. Further, the hill fort itself is too slight to have called for such efforts. If there really was an actual siege it ended before the works were completed; but there are signs of more than one period in the siege-works, and it seems certain that they must have been undertaken for training. The absence anywhere in Britain, except possibly at Burnswark, of indications that the techniques learnt had been put to practical use should not lead us to suppose that the work involved was pointless: Roman legions could be, and were, transferred to other theatres of warfare, and experience learnt in one province could be valuable elsewhere.

References

Alesia: Caesar, *B.G.* VII, 68–90; J. Harmand, *Une campagne Césarienne: Alesia* (Paris, 1967).

Hatra: Dio LXXV 10, 1; 11, 1–12, 5; A. Birley, *Septimius Severus, the African Emperor* (London, 1971), 203–5; J. Bradford, *Ancient Landscapes* (London, 1957), 71–5 with Pl. 24, vertical view showing siege-works.

Masada: see references on p. 20.

Numantia: A. Schulten, *Numantia, der Ergebnisse der Ausgrabungen 1905–12* III–IV (München, 1927–9); M. Cary and H.H. Scullard, *A History of Rome* (ed. 3, London, 1975), 144–6 with plans.

BURNSWARK, Dumfries and Galloway (18)

The level skyline of Burnswark (less correctly Birrenswark) rises to an altitude of 286 m and is a well-known landmark of south-west Scotland, visible from afar. The hill is crowned by the denuded earthworks of a native hill fort, which excavation has suggested to have been obsolete and abandoned long before the Roman period. Nevertheless, a large siege camp of 5.3 ha (13 acres) is visible on the photograph, and another similar but rather smaller camp of 3.2 ha (8 acres) is out of sight behind the hill; it lies in front of the

18 Burnswark, Dumfries and Galloway; Roman siege camp, looking NW. NY 185787. CLX 25: May 1950.

more distant fir wood (Fig.5). The exceptional character of the Roman work is suggested by consideration of its gates. Those in the centre of the south side (foreground) and in the centres of the east and west sides are defended by normal *titula*: these are short lengths of detached rampart and ditch designed to break up a direct charge. Along the north side, however, which is pushed far up the slope towards the hill fort, three gateways are visible and each is defended by an exceptional *titulum*, higher than the others and circular in shape. These appear to have served also as the emplacement of catapults (*ballistae*) for the bombardment of the native defences. Lead *glandes* (catapult shot) have been found scattered on the hillside and over the defences, and the *titula* themselves were reinforced with stones. Thus the hill fort was certainly under fire; but the fact that its rampart was no longer serviceable has

led to the suggestion that we should recognise an army siege training school rather than an operation of real warfare. The 'lines of circumvallation' round the hill which were planned by General Roy are now thought to be later field boundaries, but the character and date of two small earthworks on the circuit have not been established.

The field-exercise theory is based on the premise that since even strongly defended hill forts in Britain did not call for siege-works, then *a fortiori* there would be no need for them here; and it has gained additional support from the claim of the 1898 excavators to have found buildings in the centre of the south camp, for buildings imply some permanency. Nevertheless, there are good reasons to doubt the idea. In the first place, excavations by George Jobey in the late 1960s failed to find any buildings although they confirmed the presence of a large area of paving or hardstanding just east of the small stream which bisects the south camp. In the second place, it is hard to see why a siege school would need the north camp as well as the larger south camp when there is no intervisibility between the two. The presence of two camps makes better sense in real warfare.

The recent excavations did find second-century pottery within the area of the hill fort, pointing to some occupation at that time. The absence of any sign of refortification may, however, merely indicate the suddenness of the emergency. Occupation of the hill-top by a large force of native warriors intent upon a last stand would certainly call for careful investment, for although the hill is not impregnable, its slopes are steep and its reduction by direct assault might be costly in the absence of preliminary bombardment. The so-called siege-works are preparations for exactly that. The siege itself need not have been long. If its aim was to reduce or dislodge a large war-band which had taken refuge on the top, the absence of circum-vallation was no doubt intentional; if the enemy could be induced to retire, they could more easily be dealt with on lower ground.

In the north-east corner of the camp lies a second small rectangular earthwork with a gateway in its south side. Despite the distance (nearly 500 m) from the Roman road, which runs beyond the photograph to the left, this is recognisable as a fortlet, one of a series which were built to protect the road in the Antonine period, in an attempt to economise manpower by placing full-sized forts at greater intervals. The date is confirmed by the discovery within it of second-century pottery. The reason for the fortlet's distance from the road is obscure. Although visible relationship of the fortlet to the earthworks of the camp suggests that it overlies them, this is an illusion; excavation has shown that the northern ditch of the fortlet lies buried beneath the rampart of the camp. Thus the siege camp is likely to date from the middle or second half of the second century, and the most probable context is either the rebellion which is thought to have occurred at the end of the first Antonine period in Scotland or else some later campaign, for instance that of Ulpius Marcellus.

The extension in the early sixties of a plantation over the south-west corner of the camp is a regrettable defacement of a monument of European importance.

References
W. Roy, *Military Antiquities* (London, 1793), pl. XVI. D. Christison and J. Barbour, *Proc. Soc. Ant. Scotland* XXXIII (1899), 198–249 (excavation report). R.G. Collingwood, *Trans. Dumfriesshire and Galloway N.H. and Antiq. Soc.* (3rd series) XIII (1927), 46–58 (excavation report). *Antiq. Journ.* VI (1926), 83. O.G.S. Crawford, *Antiquity* XIII (1939) with Pls. VIA and B (oblique views of N and S camps by G. Alington). E. Birley, *Arch. Journ.* XCVI (1940), 315–17 with plan. J.K. St Joseph in S.N. Miller (ed.), *The Roman Occupation of S.W. Scotland* (Glasgow, 1952), 6, 97–8, with Pls. XXXVI (S camp, oblique), XXXVII (N camp, oblique: photographs by G. Alington). G. Jobey, *Trans. Dumfriesshire and Galloway N.H. and Antiq. Soc.* (3rd series) LIII (1977–8), 57–104, excavation report with fig. 1 (plan), Pl. IV (oblique view from SE). *J.R.S.* LVIII (1968), 178. R.G. Collingwood and I.A. Richmond, *The Archaeology of Roman Britain* (2nd ed., London, 1969), Pl. IIIB (oblique view of fortlet and S camp from the E). S.S. Frere, *Britannia, A History of Roman Britain* (London, 1967), Pl. 13B (similar view).

WODEN LAW, Borders (19)

The summit of Woden Law (423 m), a westward spur of the Cheviots, is occupied by a small multivallate hill fort only 0.4 ha in size but of several periods, the latest being probably post-Roman; in this last phase the rampart consisted of a rough stone wall placed within the earlier banks and ditches. Running round the south and east sides of the hill fort is a second earthwork consisting of two prominent banks and three ditches; excavation in 1950 showed this to have the characteristics of Roman work, since turf was employed both as a base and as a revetment for the outer bank and as a revetment of the inner one. Between the turf cheeks the material of the outer bank had been laid in the reverse order of its excavation, with the rocky material at the bottom; and the bank itself had been widened and flattened in some sectors, particularly towards the north, perhaps for the placing of catapults. If this is so, the inner bank and ditch were intended to protect the artillery. While there were no signs that this earthwork had been dug in haste, it had evidently not been completed, and signs of unfinished work were even more obvious in two outer lines (right) and in the one at right angles (foreground). Near a gap in the latter is a circular *titulum* resembling the three at Burnswark (18) and perhaps, like them, intended as a *ballista* platform. The various investing lines do not appear to be all contemporary, and at one place had certainly been recut. Two further observations are relevant. The first is that though the series is successive, none of the stages is complete; the second, that many components had evidently been constructed by gangs without concern for the co-ordination of their work with that of their neighbours. All this points to the conclusion that Woden Law did not witness an actual siege, but rather was a training-ground in siege-craft, used on more than one occasion. The conclusion is reinforced both by the weak character

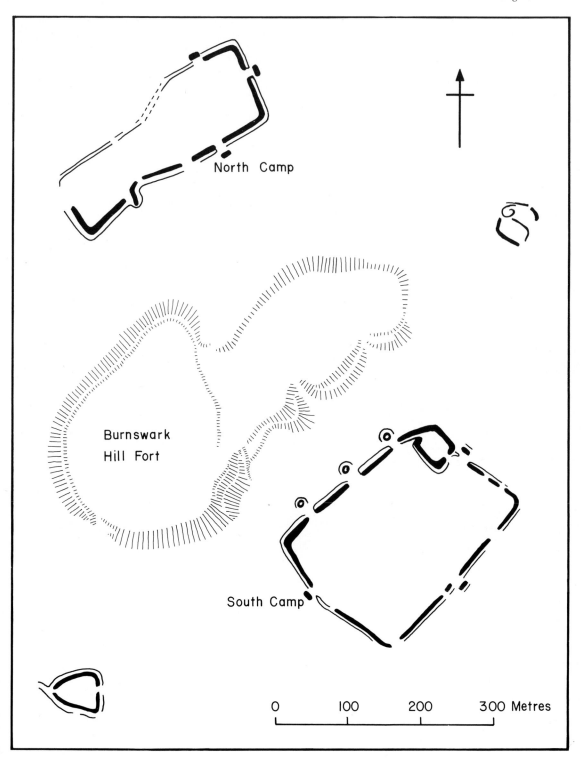

North Camp

Burnswark
Hill Fort

South Camp

0   100   200   300 Metres

Fig. 5 Burnswark: general plan.

19 Woden Law, Borders (Roxburghshire); native hill fort and Roman siege-works, looking NE. NT 768125. F 84: July 1945.

of the hill fort's defences, which hardly call for serious siege, and by the probability that the inhabitants had already been compelled to evacuate. The course of Dere Street can be seen running from right to left across the picture before it descends the steep declivity beyond the hill fort. Such a vital line of communication would not be allowed to remain under constant threat. There are no siege camps on the hill, as there are at Burnswark; but on the low ground at Pennymuir (16) 1.5 km to the north-west, close by where Dere Street crosses the Kale Water, lies a group of marching-camps, the largest of which occupies 17 ha (42 acres). The troops undergoing training were perhaps quartered here at a sheltered site with an adequate water supply.

References

R.C.A.H.M. (Scotland), *Roxburghshire* I (Edinburgh, 1956), 169–72, Woden Law with plan and similar oblique view; II, 375–77, Pennymuir with map and plans. S.S. Frere, *Britannia, A History of Roman Britain* (London, 1967), Pl. 16 (oblique view of Pennymuir camps). I.A. Richmond and J.K. St Joseph, *Proc. Soc. Ant. Scotland* CXI, forthcoming.

5

LEGIONARY AND VEXILLATION FORTRESSES

Roman military power was founded on the legion. There were rarely more than 30–33 of them in existence at any one time and Britain had four, a number reduced to three in the late first century. A legion consisted of something over 5000 heavily armed infantry, all being Roman citizens and all highly trained, not only in the art of combat but also in simple constructional engineering and in a variety of administrative duties. It was organised in ten cohorts, each consisting of six centuries (in the late first century the legion's first cohort was larger than the others, with ten centuries); although individual cohorts or groups of cohorts could be detached in vexillations for special duties, the whole legion normally occupied a single fortress.

The location of fortresses was naturally a matter of careful strategic decision, for the legions represented concentrations of military and of potentially political power, and they had a responsibility for internal security as well as for supporting the frontier troops or menacing the enemy. The legions formed the *ultima ratio regis* of the Roman world. The sites chosen for fortresses were often on navigable rivers, the cheapness and ease of water transport being of great importance for bulk supplies in both peace and war; they were naturally also well placed in relation to land routes.

In the early years of Roman Britain there was constant movement of legions as new military objectives appeared; but for a time, after the initial battles had been won and while the opposition was in disarray, the use of vexillations rather than of whole legions gave greater freedom of action. In the field, legionary troops always operated in close association with auxiliary cavalry and infantry, and the new strategic situation was served by establishing what are known as vexillation fortresses, in which two or three legionary cohorts were brigaded with auxiliary units, to effect control of a region. In recent years some 10–12 early vexillation fortresses have been identified, mainly by aerial photography; but except at Longthorpe (26) little light has been thrown on them by excavation. The majority of these vexillation fortresses belong to the first century, but as late as the reign of Severus one was established

at Carpow (2). Occasionally, as at Newstead (72) in the second century and perhaps at Hod Hill (48, 49) in the first, smaller legionary vexillations were outposted in forts of much smaller size. Particularly interesting is the evidence at Corbridge (30) that in the third century there was a permanent legionary outstation near Hadrian's Wall, manned by vexillations engaged in the manufacture of weapons and no doubt other military necessities. This was a period when the legions themselves rarely changed their bases, even in time of war, but when increasing use was made of vexillations; such detachments were sometimes away for very long periods on service overseas or in distant parts of the province. The point is illustrated also by the vexillation fortress at Carpow, which was held, on what was intended to be a permanent basis, by legionaries from York and Caerleon.

When the attempt to conquer Wales became prolonged, it was realised that greater force must be applied; legions were once more reunited for the purpose. By the mid-50s of the first century the positions occupied by the legions become better known, but some obscurity still surrounds their movements before this; the positions of their fortresses or those of their vexillations have still very largely to be discovered. At this time the distinction between *aestiva* and *hiberna* was still operative. During the winter legions returned to their *hiberna*, but during the campaigning months they might move to summer quarters situated near the scene of fighting and substantially established. Two such *aestiva* may perhaps be recognised at Rhyn (29) and at Brandon Camp (pp. 98–100).

Until 49, Legion XX Valeria continued to hold its fortress at Colchester, but this did not of course preclude employment of the legion elsewhere during the campaigning season. Legion IX Hispana had established a fortress at Lincoln by 61–2, and we may therefore assume that the two vexillation fortresses in the same area, at Longthorpe and Newton on Trent, represent its earlier positions with at least one other still to be identified (which may have occupied a different site at Lincoln itself). Longthorpe has yielded evidence of occupation from perhaps 47 to 61; where the legion was before 47 is unknown.

Legion XIV Gemina reached Wroxeter perhaps a little before 60; its earlier positions (some of them no doubt successive) are therefore probably to be identified at Mancetter, Wall, Kinvaston and Leighton, where vexillation fortresses are known. But even these sites seem unlikely to have been established before 47; still earlier positions are to be sought, possibly at Leicester and in the Northampton region.

Legion II Augusta is known to have been engaged in the south, and was certainly established at Exeter from some date in the mid-50s. An earlier fortress of unknown size has been found at Lake near Wimborne, Dorset and, earlier still, vexillations may have been in station at Fishbourne and at Chichester.

In 49 Legion XX left Colchester for the south Welsh front, and by the mid-50s seems to have been united in a single fortress at Usk. Before that time it may have been divided among vexillations; fortresses suitable for these are known at Clifford and Clyro in the Wye valley and perhaps at Kingsholm near Gloucester; another possibility recently suggested is Weston under Penyard, west of Kingsholm, though here the absence of a water supply would have caused difficulties.

By 61–2, therefore, Legion IX was at Lincoln, Legion XIV at Wroxeter, Legion XX at Usk and Legion II at Exeter; however, the unusually small size of the fortresses at Lincoln (17 ha, 42 acres) and Exeter (15.4 ha, 38 acres) suggests that cohorts were still outposted on a permanent basis. Part of Legion IX may have occupied the vexillation fortress at Rossington (28) at this time.

The next changes were a consequence of the removal from Britain in 67 of Legion XIV Gemina for Nero's war in the East. The position of Wroxeter was too important to be left without a legion, and Legion XX was therefore transferred from Usk. This move necessitated a reorganisation further south, and Legion II Augusta, or part of it, was very probably moved to a new fortress at Gloucester. The Gloucester fortress is known to have been built at about this time, but its original garrison may have been intended to be Legion XIV Gemina, which returned briefly to Britain in 69–70. The position was strategically important, for a legion there could keep watch on South Wales (now without a legionary garrison) as well as on south-west England. After the final removal of Legion XIV in 70, Gloucester inevitably continued to be held, and Legion II Augusta is the only possible candidate; Exeter, however, was not completely evacuated for several years to come.

In 71 the new governor, Petillius Cerialis,

began the conquest of northern England; in this campaign Legion IX Hispana was moved forward from Lincoln to York and a newly enlisted legion, II Adiutrix, recently transferred to Britain as replacement for Legion XIV, took over the fortress at Lincoln. The next governor, Julius Frontinus, turned to the final reduction of Wales, and for this purpose concentrated three legions on the western front. Legion II Augusta was accordingly moved to Caerleon about 75 and not long afterwards Legion II Adiutrix built a new fortress at Chester. By 79 the conquest of Wales was complete, and four years later Legion XX was moved from Wroxeter to Inchtuthil by Agricola, to form the anchor of his Scottish conquests.

In the late 80s a serious military crisis on the Danube caused Legion II Adiutrix to be withdrawn from Britain; the legionary garrison fell to three and was never increased. Inchtuthil had to be abandoned together with much of Scotland, and the legions now settled down in what became their permanent fortresses. Legion II Augusta lay at Caerleon, Legion XX at Chester; Legion IX continued at York until replaced there under Hadrian by Legion VI Victrix.

This necessarily abbreviated account of military movements has illustrated the great wealth of legionary sites in Britain, and has shown how knowledge of them can help us to understand the progress of the Roman conquest. When Collingwood wrote his chapters of *Roman Britain and the English Settlements* in 1936 only six legionary sites were known (Caerleon, Chester, Gloucester, Lincoln, Wroxeter and York). The Fourth Edition of the Ordnance Survey *Map of Roman Britain*, published in 1978, shows eighteen, to which more can now be added. This great increase in our knowledge has been very largely contributed by aerial photography; but full understanding of the sites, and of the complexity of the history which they represent, will only come with excavation – a gigantic task. Meanwhile, this heritage deserves the most vigilant protection from the forces of premature destruction.

Particularly interesting is the evidence of Inchtuthil (20–22), a site of unique significance in the Roman Empire. Its recognition as a legionary fortress had not been made when Collingwood wrote. Sir George Macdonald had thought it merely 'the winter-quarters of a small army'. In the period since the Second World War not only has excavation recorded the most complete plan of a single-period fortress anywhere in the Roman world, but aerial photographs have revealed unparalleled detail of the construction camps occupied by the troops that built it; much also of great interest is now known both of the neighbouring military compounds in contemporary use and of other associated Roman works, such as the Cleaven Dyke, which exist in the vicinity.

A legionary fortress was surrounded by its *territorium*, the ownership of which was vested in the legate. Here lay the parade-ground, and often an amphitheatre (*ludus*) was provided where weapon-training might take place, as well as gladiatorial displays. **24** shows the amphitheatre at Caerleon.

So large and well-paid a garrison naturally attracted a large camp-following of manufacturers, merchants, and shopkeepers, whose settlement was known as the *canabae*. Since the land belonged to the legion, retired soldiers and others who wished to buy their homes had to do so further away, in settlements which were often advanced to the rank of *municipium*, or even *colonia*, as time went by. In Britain the only certain example of this is at York (**25**), where the *colonia* lies across the river from the *canabae* surrounding the fortress on the left bank of the Ouse. An early example of *canabae* is known at Longthorpe, where pottery manufacture and bronze-working were carried on at a site 0.5 km east of the fortress.

At fortress sites from which the troops moved on, the land was presumably made over eventually to the civil authorities or sold to private owners; but there was often considerable delay before the decision that the site was redundant could be taken. At Usk an auxiliary fort was built on part of the old fortress site. At Exeter and at Wroxeter the sites of the fortresses were in time developed as *civitas* capitals, the nucleus of the population presumably being derived from the *canabae*. At Colchester, Gloucester and Lincoln the fortress sites were used for *coloniae* of veteran settlers (at the last two only after a twenty-year interval since the time when the fortresses had been fully operational). But many other legionary sites reverted to agricultural use, as at Longthorpe, Lake, Osmanthorpe or Rossington Bridge. Fishbourne was made over to King Cogidubnus, who built his palace on the site of the military base.

References

S.S. Frere, *Britannia, a History of Roman Britain* (London, 1978). P.T. Bidwell, *The Legionary Bath-house and Basilica and Forum at Exeter* (Exeter, 1979); *Roman Exeter: Fortress and Town* (Exeter, 1980). W.H. Manning, *Usk, The Fortress Excavations 1968–71* (Cardiff, 1981). Colchester: P. Crummy, *Britannia* VIII (1977), 65–103. Lake: *Britannia* XI (1980), 391. Osmanthorpe: D. Riley, *Britannia* XI (1980), 330–2. For Caerleon, Inchtuthil, Longthorpe, Rhyn, Rossington and York, see entries below.

INCHTUTHIL, Tayside (20–2)

General view of site looking NW (**20**)

This panoramic view, taken on an exceptionally clear day, looks WNW over the level flood-plain of the Tay in the foreground, to the edge of the Highlands in the middle distance, and then over serried ranges of hills to the conspicuous peak of Schichallion (1076 m), a sacred mountain of the Picts, on the skyline, with the still higher mountains of the Ben Nevis group a little to the left at some 100 km distance from the camera. The Tay, the largest river to flow south-eastwards from the Highland front, emerges from the narrows at Dunkeld towards the left of the photograph, and then flows from left to right across the foreground. Beyond it in the centre of the view and clearly picked out by a curving belt of trees, lies the gravel plateau of Delvine, some 1.6 km from east to west, bounded by steep slopes that rise 10–15 m above the flood-plain. This plateau, which commands the opening of the Dunkeld gorge and affords wide views over the valley, was the site of the legionary fortress of Inchtuthil. At some stage, and very possibly in Roman times, the Tay followed a different course round the far side of the plateau, and indeed the river has eroded part of the north-east rampart of the fortress in the curve of trees at the right-hand end of the plateau.

Roman legionary fortresses not infrequently occupy a position on the hither side of a large river. The south-east rampart of the fortress can be seen as a narrow line just above the nearer belt of trees and the south-west rampart lies in an uncultivated oblong strip to right of a darker-toned field. The curving wooded left-hand tip of the plateau is occupied by a post-Roman promontory fort, and the two fields between this and the fortress, now divided by a belt of trees, are the site of construction camps (see below).

A mile beyond the further north-west side of the fortress can be seen the hamlet of Spittalfield, and at a little distance to the right of that, in a low ridge of hills within the shadowed area near the right-hand edge of the photograph, lies the Roman quarry whence came the conglomeratic Gourdie sandstone used for the fortress wall.

The fortress, partially examined in 1901 by the Society of Antiquaries of Scotland, and more fully excavated between 1952 and 1965 by Sir Ian Richmond and Professor J.K. StJoseph, was found to contain only timber-framed buildings, but the original turf and gravel rampart had been rapidly refaced with a stone wall. The fortress (22.25 ha, 55 acres) was begun probably late in 83 and was still incomplete when the garrison (almost certainly Legion XX Valeria Victrix) was evacuated in 86

20 Inchtuthil, Tayside (Perthshire); Roman legionary fortress and camps, general view of site, looking NW. NO 125396. APY 15: August 1966.

or 87. At about that time one of the British legions (II Adiutrix) had to be transferred to the Danube, a move which necessitated the withdrawal of the Inchtuthil legion to take over the vacant fortress at Chester. It is a curious reflection that had the garrison continued in occupation, Inchtuthil might have become the capital of Scotland just as the fortress foundations of Bonn, Vienna, Budapest or Belgrade have become modern capitals. However that may be, the site presents an archaeological prize which is all but unique: the plan of a single-period fortress of the first century.

Relationship of the fortress to the construction camp (21)

The greater part of the site was under corn when the photograph was taken. The south-west corner of the fortress can be seen on the right. In the field outside lies the north-east half of a large marching-camp or labour camp of *c.* 19.5 ha (48 acres). The whole north-east side of the camp is visible between the rounded angles of the ditch, showing as a dark line, while the width of the former rampart is indicated by the line of pits at its rear. A gate existed at the half-way point but is obscured

by the shadow of a tree. Towards the left of the photograph (to the right of a belt of trees) is seen the prominent crop-mark of a broad ditch running obliquely across the camp, which it post-dates. This was known to antiquaries as the 'Western Vallum'; the rampart lies on the north-east (the fortress side) of the ditch, so that the earthwork faces south-west and, in the absence of any gate or passage through it, cuts off the remainder of the plateau from the fortress. In fact, as aerial photographs show (22), this is the second of two presumably successive boundaries on this side of the fortress which seem to have demarcated the military zone when the camp was disused. Within the camp are seen numerous rows of pits running parallel with the north-east defences; two of the rows have pits so closely clustered as to suggest a street between. Excavation has revealed them to be rubbish pits; such pits are rarely found in marching-camps, and nowhere in such profusion or clarity. They suggest that this camp was occupied for a relatively long period, perhaps during the construction of the fortress, and if, as seems likely, they were dug each in front of a tent they

40

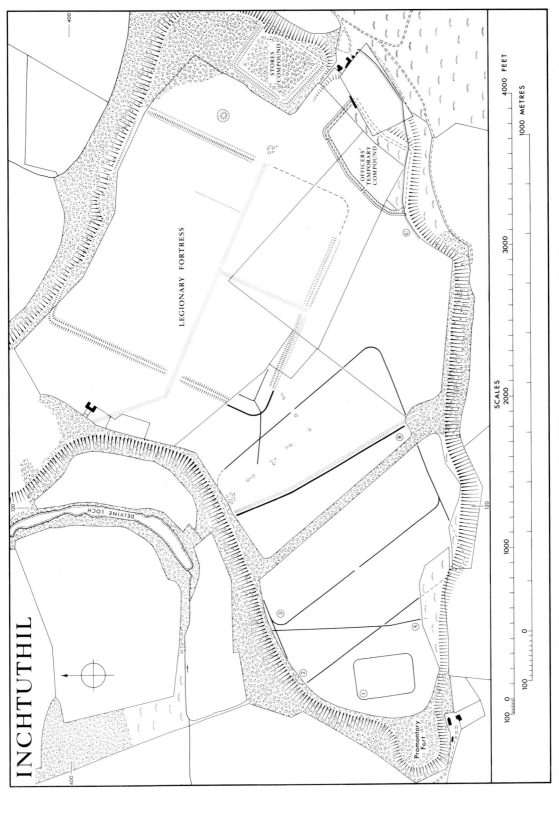

Fig. 6 Inchtuthil: general plan. Key: 1 small temporary camp; 2 first SW limit of large labour-camp; 3 later limit of labour-camp; A first boundary ditch; B 'Western Vallum'.

21 Inchtuthil; relationship of the fortress to the construction camp, looking NW. CDB 69: July 1977.

give an indication of the arrangement of the tented lines – an insight which is rare indeed. As at Masada, in Israel, the arrangement of the lines is quite different from those inside a permanent fortress. Between the suggested 'street' and the north-east rampart (in other words on the right side of the *via praetoria* of the camp) is a well-defined block of rows of pits *c*. 114 m (375 ft) square, but nearer the camera is an area with far fewer pits, suggesting different use. The rows run at right angles to the *via praetoria* (as laid down by Hyginus, *De munitione castrorum* 15–16), and on his calculations an area 375 ft square would hold six cohorts.

Western end of construction camp (22)

This view is at right angles to that of the previous plate and is of the next field to the west. In the background runs the line of trees which are on the

42

left of **21**, with part of the 'Western Vallum' beyond. In the foreground is seen the south-west ditch of the 19.5 ha camp with a central gap for its gateway, through which has been dug another straight ditch which is evidently the predecessor of the 'Western Vallum'. This ditch demarcates a somewhat larger military zone, and is evidently later than the first phase of the camp, since the ditch bends to pass through the south-west gate. In the centre of the plate lies the crop-mark of another ditch, parallel with the camp ditch in the foreground and with a corresponding gateway. Thus, there is evidence for a reduction in the size of the camp to 14 ha (35 acres) at a period when fewer troops than formerly were quartered there. Perhaps by this time a part of the force was occupying barracks within the fortress. Photographs show the whole length of the south-east ditch of the camp (Fig. 6), save for a short sector

22 Inchtuthil; W end of construction camp, looking NE. CDC 19: July 1977.

lying beneath the belt of trees. As there is no visible break in the ditch, the south-east gate must have lain under the trees: in other words the gate was not central but lay nearer to the north-east rampart than to the south-west one. Thus the gate on the north-east side is the *porta praetoria* and the camp faced towards the fortress. In the second phase, when the camp was reduced in size, the gates were all approximately central to their sides; but this may not have involved a major reorientation of the internal arrangements.

More rows of pits can be seen, and these run at right angles to those on **21**, being parallel to the *via decumana* through the rear gate. One of the 'streets' demarcated by closely placed pits appears to relate to the reduced camp, but two others run to the original rampart. These longer 'streets' extend for *c.* 213 m (700 ft), running from the outer rampart to the belt of trees, and thus appear to cross both the *retentura* and the *latera praetorii* of

the camp (the rear and central divisions); nor are there obvious gaps on the line of the *via quintana* (which should run parallel to the rampart in the foreground and divide the *retentura* from the *latera praetorii*). Clearly the pits are not evenly distributed throughout the camp: it seems probable that there were considerable open areas for the stockpiling of stores and materials, and that the sizes of the camps are therefore not necessarily related closely to the numbers of troops quartered there.

References

W. Roy, *Military Antiquities* (London, 1793), Pl. XVIII (plan). J. Abercromby and T. Ross, *Proc. Soc. Ant. Scotland* XXXVI (1902), 182–242 (1901 excavations). G. Macdonald, *J.R.S.* IX (1919), 113–62. Annual 'Roman Britain' reports, *J.R.S.* XLIII (1953)–LVI (1966). J.K. StJoseph, *J.R.S.* XLI (1951), Pl. VIII, 2 (oblique view of part of fortress showing barracks); *J.R.S.* LV (1965), Pl. X, 2 (different oblique view of camps).

23 Caerleon, Gwent; Prysg Field, W corner of the legionary fortress, looking SE. ST 335906. ABI 51: June 1960.

CAERLEON, Gwent, Prysg Field (23)

The foreground of the photograph shows the rounded corner of the fortress wall and rampart, with its corner-tower, and an interval-tower beyond. A cook-house was later built in front of the ground-floor entrance of each of the two towers, and a latrine block was inserted (left of the corner-tower) in the back of the rampart with space for about twenty seats over an open drain. Within the circuit of the *via sagularis* (perimeter street) are seen four of the six centurial barrack buildings of a cohort, arranged in facing pairs, separated by a metalled street. These four have been excavated and consolidated for display. At the near end are the large blocks occupied by the respective centurions; each block varies in the planning of its rooms. Beyond, are the *contubernia* of the men, rows of twelve double rooms with verandahs. The front room was used to house personal equipment and the rear one as sleeping-quarters. With eight men to the *contubernium* and eighty men to the century (Hyginus, *De munitione castrorum*, 1), only ten double rooms were necessary; the extra two may have been assigned to N.C.O.s

or other privileged staff, as for instance members of the legionary cavalry. The barracks are almost 74 m in length, and greatly exceed in size the barracks provided in the forts of the auxiliaries.

The stone barracks seen in the photograph were first constructed about the middle of the second century. Below most of them remains of an earlier phase (late first-century) have been found; but below at least one of the barracks farther to the left on this edge of the fortress such traces were absent, which suggests that some troops were for some time outposted, possibly at the legion's previous stations at Exeter or Gloucester, or possibly elsewhere. It must also be remembered that for much of the first half of the second century troops will have been away in the North, engaged on the construction of the two Walls and on various recorded campaigns. Only in times of peace was the complete legion assembled in its fortress.

References

G.C. Boon, *Isca* (Cardiff, 1972). *Britannia* II (1971), 246.

44

24 Caerleon; legionary amphitheatre, oblique view, looking E of N. ST 336904. BW 47: July 1948.

CAERLEON, Gwent, legionary amphitheatre (24)

Caerleon (*Isca*) was the fortress of Legion II Augusta from *c*. A.D. 74–5 onwards. The amphitheatre which was built outside the fortress in about 80 was placed on a rather restricted site lying between a bath-building and the defences of the fortress, marked by a line of trees just above the building. The reason for this cramped position is probably that much of the open area between the fortress and the river was still at this date occupied by a construction camp. The long and short axes of the amphitheatre measure 81.4 m (267 ft) and 67.7 m (222 ft) respectively, and the arena is 56.1 m (184 ft) long by 41.6 m (136.5 ft) wide, being very carefully laid out on geometric principles. The seating was of wood, supported on earth ramps contained within the stone walls;

the outer wall in the south quadrant is supported by buttresses (foreground) because of the fall of the ground here, but the rest of the external face was relieved by pilasters continuing the series in a purely decorative way. The building was repaired in the second century and again early in the third; more buttresses were added between the pilasters – a very large one is visible just above the main south-east (right) entrance. It has been suggested that these were necessitated by the presence of a timber-framed superstructure carrying the upper seating; the vibrations of a crowd transmitted through such framing might well have weakened the masonry.

The amphitheatre was excavated by Dr R.E.M. (later Sir Mortimer) and Mrs T.V. Wheeler in 1926–7 with money mainly contributed by the *Daily Mail*. Calculation shows that the seating capacity was amply sufficient for the entire legion;

25 York (*Eboracum*); site of the Roman fortress and *colonia*, vertical photograph: N is towards bottom right-hand corner. SE 6052. RC8-AI 30: April 1973. Scale 1:13500.

its purpose was doubtless partly for weapon-training, but the presence of small chambers round the arena (*carcares*) for gladiators or beasts shows that at special festivals the building was used for a different purpose. For two amphitheatres at urban sites, see **95** and **96**.

References

R.E.M. and T.V. Wheeler, *Archaeologia* LXXVIII (1928), 111–218, excavation report. G.C. Boon, *Isca, Roman Caerleon* (Cardiff, 1960) frontispiece (coloured reconstruction) and Pl. VIIIA (this view). G.C. Boon, *Isca* (Cardiff, 1972), 89–101, full discussion, with plans and Fig. 57 (oblique view of amphitheatre and fortress site). V.E. Nash-Williams, *The Roman Frontier in Wales* (2nd ed. by M.G. Jarrett, Cardiff, 1969), 29–33 with Pl. IIA (oblique view, printed upside down).

YORK *EBORACUM* (25)

York is an excellent example of the influence exerted on subsequent history by the skilful selection of sites which was so often exhibited by the Roman army. A fortress for Legion IX Hispana was built at *Eboracum* at the beginning of the Flavian period when, *c*. A.D. 71, Roman forces

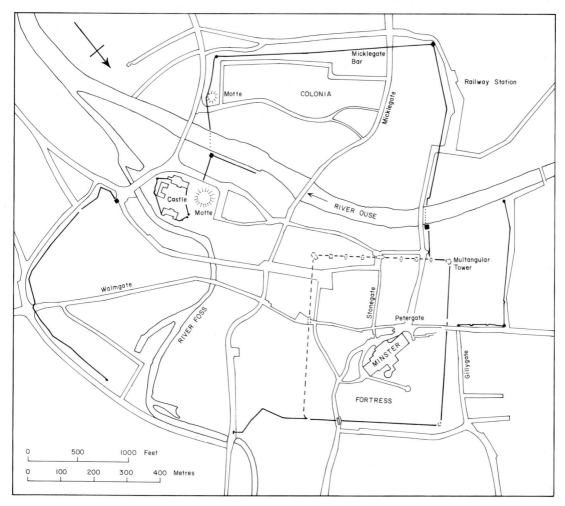

Fig. 7 York: interpretative plan to illustrate 25.

were advancing to the conquest of the Brigantes; it is clear that the choice of site was conditioned by a belt of glacial moraine which here provides a natural causeway across the wide and marshy valley of the river Ouse. The position was one of immediate strategic importance, separating the wild Brigantes from the more Romanized Parisi, and offering lines of penetration to north and north-west as well as north-eastwards towards the Yorkshire Moors. But it was soon apparent that the legion was not again to move forward to a fresh fortress site nearer Scotland, and that a permanent military base had become established. This was confirmed when in Hadrian's reign Legion VI Victrix took over the fortress from Legion IX on the transference of the latter to the Continent. York accordingly assumed even greater prominence in the North when its advantages as a centre of both road and river communications and as a seat of government became clear. An extensive civilian settlement sprang up near the fortress and expanded on both banks of the river. That on the left bank ranked as *canabae*, since it lay on legionary land; but in the second century the settlement on the right bank may have received a charter of self-government as a *municipium*: in the early third century it certainly gained the rank of a Roman *colonia*. In the fourth century York had one of the few Christian bishops recorded in Roman Britain.

On more than one occasion York was the scene of events of empire-wide significance. Here the Emperor Septimius Severus established his headquarters during his campaigns into Scotland (208–11), and here he died. A century later, in 306, Constantius I also died here and his son Constantine the Great was proclaimed emperor by the assembled army. In the early third century, when the province of Britain was divided, York became the seat of the governor of *Britannia Inferior*, and it

47

26 Longthorpe, Cambridgeshire; Roman military site, looking W. TL 157977. ADT 11: July 1961.

maintained its role as provincial capital and army headquarters during the various changes of the fourth century. Its importance at this time is illustrated by the grandiose rebuilding of the river-side defences with their monumental towers and gate.

In the post-Roman period York remained of continuing importance as the seat of an archbishopric, as capital of the Viking kingdom in north Britain, and as a market with extensive trade. This dominant position was maintained throughout the Middle Ages, while in modern times the city's development as a great railway centre and its continuing role in road communications have ensured abiding prosperity.

The photograph includes the sites of the Roman fortress and *colonia*, separated by the river Ouse, flowing from right to left. The fortress faced south-west towards the river. The Minster, overlying part of the Headquarters Building, is seen

lower right of the centre; the line of the north-west and north-east walls of the fortress can be seen a short distance to the right of, and below, the Minster respectively; the parts now visible are largely reconstructions of the medieval period. The early fourth-century multangular tower, marking the west corner of the fortress, lies at the edge of the open area with trees on the river bank. The *porta decumana* lay further north-west than the medieval gate in the north-east wall which has replaced it, and the course of the south-east wall has been built over; it turned back towards the river, on a line parallel with the north-west wall, from a point not far south-east of the medieval gate. Part of the *via principalis* is represented by Petergate, the street running from left to right just above the Minster, and the *via praetoria* by Stonegate, the street at right angles to this which approaches the south transept of the Minster.

The extensive civil settlement which later be-

48

27 Longthorpe; Roman military site, looking N. ADL 21: June 1961.

came a *colonia* lay on the opposite side of the Ouse. The medieval walls which are thought to coincide with their Roman predecessors can be seen running from the first road-bridge from the right round to Micklegate Bar and beyond. At York Castle, south of the fortress, an eleventh-century Norman motte can be seen occupying the peninsula between the Ouse and the river Foss, where Roman wharves have been discovered. A second motte lies across the Ouse. An extensive Roman cemetery was found in the area of York Station and others lay along the road beyond Micklegate Bar.

References

R.C.H.M., *Eburacum, Roman York* (London, 1962). L.P. Wenham, *The Romano-British Cemetery at Trentholme Drive, York* (London, 1968).

28 Rossington, South Yorkshire; **Roman vexillation fortress**, vertical photograph, N at top. SK 630991. K17-AI 157: July 1975. Scale 1:3900.

LONGTHORPE, Cambridgeshire (26–7)

The site lies 3.7 km south-west of Peterborough in a tactically strong position between the north bank of the river Nene (seen crossing the top left corner of 26) and the shallow valley of a small tributary (27, top). The twin ditches and entrance causeway of a very large fort or vexillation fortress are seen running east–west on the right of 26; they turn just within the field at the bottom and re-enter the light field near the middle of the field boundary. The gap for a gate on this side is clearly visible in 27. The turn at the end of the north side

may just be distinguished half-way across the darker field in the background of 26, but the rest of the west side has been destroyed by quarries now filled in (visible as a dark-toned area). The south side has suffered erosion on the slope down to the river, but the line of one ditch is visible on 26 where it was reutilised in a smaller single-ditched fort inside the larger.

The fortress covers 10.9 ha (360.5 by 301.95 m within the ditches), and the smaller fort 4.4 ha (201.3 by 219.6 m), areas of 26.9 and 10.9 acres respectively. The site was partially excavated between 1967 and 1973 and proved to have been occupied between *c.* A.D. 44–8 and A.D. 61. The fortress was shown to have contained a garrison consisting partly of legionaries and partly of auxiliary troops; the area, though much larger than that of a normal auxiliary fort, is not much over half the size of a full-scale legionary fortress; and the type, of which some 10 or 12 other examples have been discovered in recent years by aerial photography, has been called a vexillation fortress since it housed detachments. The buildings were timber-framed, set in shallow trenches cut in the Cornbrash (a rubbly limestone), and do not respond to aerial photography.

The smaller fort was shown to be later than the fortress, for its ditch cut through the sites of buildings belonging to the former. At 4.4 ha it is still a very large fort, over twice the normal size. Excavation failed to reveal a new set of buildings to go with it, and the most likely explanation is that the work represents an emergency reduction of the defended area. Moreover, the datable finds from the fort do not significantly extend the date range of those from the fortress. The probable historical context is that the fortress housed a vexillation of Legion IX which, together with its auxiliary cavalry, was disastrously defeated under its legate Petillius Cerialis in A.D. 61 by Boudicca. The remnants, we are told, regained their fortress; but serious losses may well have compelled an emergency reduction in the length of rampart capable of being manned while still allowing some existing buildings to continue in use. Soon after A.D. 61 the site was evacuated, and Legion IX constructed a new fortress at Lincoln.

Some 300 m east of the site excavation has revealed a contemporary military pottery-works. A fifth- to sixth-century Anglo-Saxon cremation-cemetery occupies part of the north-west corner of the fortress. In 1973 the land was taken over by a municipal golf course serving Peterborough new town, and parts of the area were buried beneath large dumps of earth; this put an end to archaeological investigation.

References

J.K. StJoseph, *J.R.S.* LV (1965), 74–6 with Pl. IX (vertical). S.S. Frere and J.K. StJoseph, *Britannia* V (1974), 1–129 with Pls. I–IV (vertical and oblique); *Britannia* VI (1975), 218. Pottery works: *Britannia* III (1972), 320–2; IV (1973), 291; VI (1975), 251–2. G. Dannell, *Durobrivae* III (1975), 18–20 with plan.

ROSSINGTON, South Yorkshire (28)

In the centre can be seen the ditches surrounding a large Roman military enclosure of 9.3 ha (23 acres) situated 6.8 km south-east of Doncaster.

The recognition of vexillation fortresses, of a size four or five times larger than a normal auxiliary fort but only about half the size of a legionary fortress, is a comparatively recent event in Roman archaeology, and only that at Longthorpe (26) has so far been examined, even partially, by excavation. Such fortresses are thought to belong mainly to the conquest campaigns of the first century and to represent the winter quarters of battle groups consisting probably of part of a legion with attendant auxiliary cavalry and infantry; later examples also exist, e.g. at Carpow on the Tay founded under Severus, and at Eining Unterfeld in Bavaria. Rossington lies west of the Trent and may represent an initial phase in the conquest of the Brigantes just before, or after, A.D. 70.

The double ditches along the east side and at the adjacent rounded south-east corner are clearly visible near the point of a wood. The other sides are marked by a single broad ditch which can be seen on the south side, on the west (left) side running across the apex of a triangular field north of the diagonal main road, and on the north side, which is less clearly visible crossing the north-east end of the same field. In the lower right-hand area of the photograph rather faint lines may be distinguished, running in two directions at right angles, obliquely to the modern landscape. These represent the ditches of an ancient field system, which other photographs show to be very extensive; the regular spacing of the ditches suggests an area of Roman land division. This recalls to mind evidence, admittedly sparse, for second-century veteran settlement in West Yorkshire (Frere, *Britannia, A History of Roman Britain* (2nd ed., London, 1974, 311 with n. 6).

References

J.K. StJoseph, *J.R.S.* LIX (1969), 104 with P. II, 1 (oblique view from E); *J.R.S.* LXVII (1977), 129. D.N. Riley, *Early landscape from the air* (Sheffield, 1980): field system.

RHYN, Shropshire (29)

That our knowledge even of such crucial historical factors as the dispositions of legionary forces in the first century is both deficient and liable to sudden revision is well illustrated by the discovery of Rhyn in 1975, where a fortress of 17.2 ha (42.5 acres) and another large fort, both previously unsuspected, came to light in the Welsh Marches. The site occupies a strong position on a gravel plateau between the river Ceiriog and a small tributary, some 2.5 km above the former's confluence with the Dee and at no great distance

29 Rhyn, Shropshire; Roman vexillation fortress and fort, vertical photograph, N at top. SJ 305370. K17-AI 186: July 1975. Scale 1:4400.

from where both rivers debouch from the mountains.

The double ditches of the fortress can be traced round the entire circuit (Fig. 8) save where, in a wood, the north-west corner has been eroded by the river, and where, at the centre of the south side, they fail to show in a white field. The fortress faces north; its gates are defended by *titula*, best seen at the west gate just below the wood. The south side is additionally protected by outworks consisting of a single ditch pushed forward some 30 m.

The fortress is partly overlapped on the east by another military work, which excavation has shown to be the later. This rectangular fort is defended on the north, south and west sides by a single narrow ditch that has given rise to a cropmark so narrow as to be barely visible on the photograph: the east limit, which must have lain near the edge of the plateau, above a small valley, is now obscured. The area within the ditch is about 4.5 ha (11 acres). Round the western half of this fort an outlying ditch forms an additional defence: at the west gate the ends of this ditch are staggered, an arrangement noted at Greensforge (55) and other first-century sites.

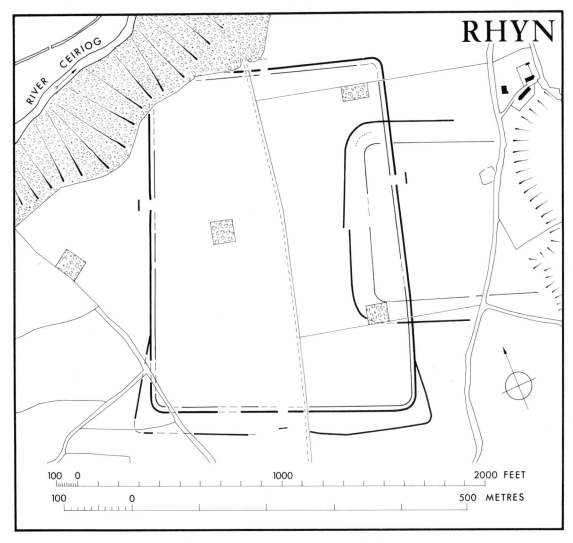

RHYN

Fig. 8 Rhyn: plan of military works.

Although not yet dated, the context of the vexillation fortress must lie within a few years of A.D. 50. It might be thought to represent an advanced base (*aestiva*) of Ostorius Scapula in his campaign of 48 against the Deceangli. Neither the gorge of the Dee at Llangollen nor the deeply entrenched valley of the Ceiriog offers reasonable approaches to the hinterland of North Wales (Fig. 9); but a line of 16 ha (40 acre) marching-camps, extending from Wall in Staffordshire to Corwen on the Dee west of Llangollen, suggests that a campaign directed either at the Deceangli or against Anglesey led a battle-group to penetrate the mountains in the region of Rhyn. The best course westwards would be along the ridge between the two valleys, an easy route but one where fields in permanent pasture give few opportunities for photographing crop-marks. Rhyn itself might represent an advanced base on this campaign (whatever its date). Alternatively the fortress might have no close connection with a particular campaign, rather representing an early division of garrison forces with the vexillation fortress at Leighton, south-east of Wroxeter, some 42 km away, before Legion XX was established at Wroxeter itself. That the second explanation is the more likely is suggested by the probability that on the evacuation of the fortress at Rhyn the site continued to be held on a smaller scale, on what was intended to be a permanent basis

References

J.K. St Joseph, *Antiquity* LI (1977), 55–60 with plan and Pl. VIII (this view); *J.R.S.* LXVII (1977), 145–9 with plan. Excavation: G.D.B. Jones, *Rhyn Park Roman Fortress* (Border Counties Arch. Group, 1978).

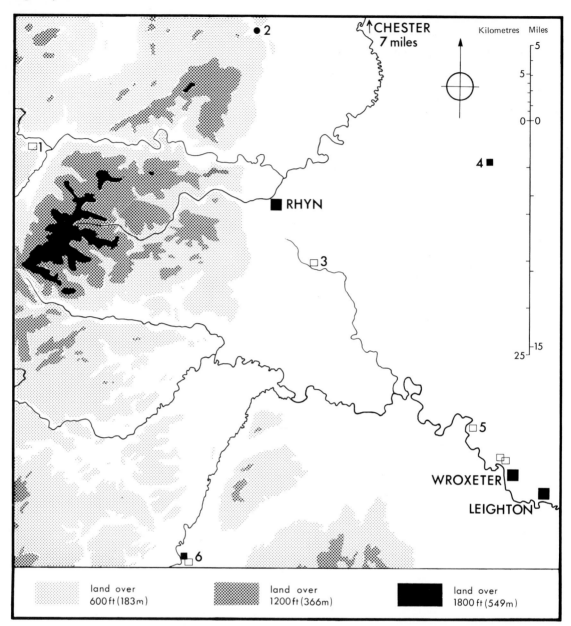

Fig. 9 Rhyn and the Northern Marches of Wales. Key: 1 Penrhos, near Corwen (camp); 2 Frith (Roman buildings and objects); 3 Whittington (camp); 4 Whitchurch (fort); 5 Uffington (camp); 6 Forden Gaer (fort).

CORBRIDGE (*CORSTOPITUM*), Northumberland (30)

Corstopitum lies on the north side of the Tyne, some 18 m above the water, on a low terrace overlooking the point where Dere Street crossed the river. The earliest military occupation comprised a large supply base or vexillation fortress lying 1 km west of the present site; it is attributed to the period of Agricola's advance into Scotland and no doubt preceded the establishment of the

road as now known. About 87–90, after the withdrawal from northern Scotland, a new fort was built on the present site to protect a bridge, and the earlier fortress was abandoned. From that time onward Corbridge remained a key position in the north, although both character and functions changed with time.

The fort itself always held a powerful garrison consisting first of an *ala* of cavalry and later of a cohort 1000 strong. It once suffered destruction by the enemy, *c*. 105, but lasted with various internal changes until *c.* 163, the date of the final evacuation of Scotland; however, during the second half of Hadrian's reign it may have been under care and maintenance only, the garrison having moved forward to a fort on the new Wall of Hadrian. During the period 90–163, therefore, the fort was fully operational when the Stanegate frontier was in use, or when the Antonine Wall was held, but does not seem to have been fully manned when Hadrian's Wall itself was garrisoned.

After 163 the character of the place changed; Hadrian's Wall was now once again the frontier, and a fort was no longer needed at Corbridge, which lies only 3.9 km south of the Wall. The defences were partially levelled and the buildings within were either adapted for other uses or replaced. Metal-working began to be a prominent activity.

Although there may have been another short intensive military phase under Septimius Severus, on the occasion of his invasion of the north, Corbridge during the third and fourth centuries developed as a town, but one having the character of a garrison town as well as that of a market centre for the surrounding district. A civilian *vicus* had already come into existence outside the second-century fort, and now additional population was attracted by the calls of industry and by the prosperity to be won by providing services for the frontier garrison. No doubt many old soldiers chose to retire there. At some stage the place received defences and eventually a town wall, enclosing some 16 ha (40 acres).

Some of the outlying areas of the town were investigated in the excavations of 1906–14, which lacked the rigorous dating techniques available today; but the central area of Corbridge, shown in the photograph, has been the scene of all work undertaken since excavation was resumed in 1934 and this has provided a framework for historical interpretation. Since 1933 the central area has been in the guardianship of the state, whose Ancient Monuments Department has gradually exposed and consolidated the structures. The modern building within the large Roman courtyard (right centre) is a temporary museum, and excavations on the site for a new permanent museum can be seen in progress (top centre).

Little is visible of the successive second-century forts whose east and west ramparts run left and right at the limits of the excavated area, at top and bottom of the photograph; the remains now exposed are almost all of dates later than 163.

The broad street running from top to bottom through the centre of the site represents a widening of the *via principalis* of the fort and a small part of the Antonine Headquarters Building and of the commander's house may be distinguished, respectively at the further and nearer ends of the courtyard. Of the *principia* only the shrine is visible, the sole portion of the building that was built in stone. The two long parallel buttressed structures just beyond the top left-hand corner of the courtyard are granaries of a later date; they occupy the site of two Antonine granaries belonging to the fort.

There is still disagreement about the date and purpose of the large courtyard building itself (known as Site XI), which used to be identified as a Severan military store building erected in connection with the northern campaigns of 208–11. It is probably, however, rather earlier than that and may have been built in the sixties or the seventies of the second century. The earlier buildings on the site were demolished but never completely levelled. As to purpose, the lack of essential features, such as *basilica* and offices, contradict suggestions that it could have been a military *principia* or the forum of a projected *civitas* capital; likely possibilities remain either a storehouse holding supplies for the Wall, or else a market building of the type thought to be associated, like similar structures at Nijmegen and Carnuntum, with trade across the frontier. However that may be, the building was never completed, and work appears to have been abandoned in haste, perhaps during a military crisis; that of A.D. 180 is a possible context. Only the rooms in the southern half were later finished to serve as shops and workshops.

That the assembly of stores continued to be a feature of Corbridge, even after the evacuation of the fort, is proved by the fact that the fort's two stone granaries continued to function and were now surrounded by a small compound whose wall is visible close beside them. At a later date the granaries were rebuilt on a larger scale and with stone floors, and an inscription of Severus is associated with them. Since the site was no longer that of a fort, the granaries and perhaps also the courtyard building must represent the establishment of a stores base, at which amongst other things the *annona militaris* (corn levy for the troops) was collected. The arrangement recalls the similar establishments known in the fourth century at Veldidena near Innsbruck and perhaps at Trier, and points to a continued official military foothold in the developing town. Between the granaries and Site XI a long narrow humped structure represents the base of a gravity-fed aqueduct leading to a fine stone fountain at the edge of the main street. This basin, too, was rebuilt in the early third century.

On the south (left) side of the main street can

30 Corbridge (*Corstopitum*), Northumberland; Roman town, supply base and underlying fort, looking WNW. NY 982648. CLQ 4: May 1980.

be seen further evidence of the military presence retained in the centre of civilian Corbridge, the site being chosen, no doubt, because it was still in government ownership. Here lie two walled compounds situated one on either side of a southward-leading street. Only the northern half of each compound is exposed, the remainder lying outside the area in official guardianship. Early in the fourth century the two compounds were united, the street being walled off at the north end and a gateway provided.

The compounds each contained a small headquarters building and were evidently designed for separate units. An inscription of Legion II Augusta from the West Compound, and other evidence for soldiers of both XX Valeria Victrix and VI Victrix at Corbridge, suggest that both compounds were used by legionary vexillations, one of whose main tasks was the manufacture of weapons and tools. Workshops and evidence for iron-working were found in the West Compound and probably exist in the other also, although most of the

buildings at present exposed there are living-quarters for officers and men and a store building. In the fourth century a potter was working in the East Compound. Each compound also contains *scholae* or guild-rooms where craftsmen could meet for religious ceremonies and for relaxation when off duty.

The wall surrounding each compound is 1.5 m thick; it follows a tortuous line along the north side in order to avoid a series of small temples which evidently already lined the main east–west street. These temples are of late second- or early third-century date and must have been the original source of the remarkable collection of reliefs and inscriptions collected from the site. These illustrate a great range of official and unofficial cults; the stones were reused in later structures and cannot be assigned to individual temples. Temple VI, outside the West Compound, had been demolished in the second half of the third century and a pottery store or shop was built on its remains; this was later destroyed by fire. Although its principal

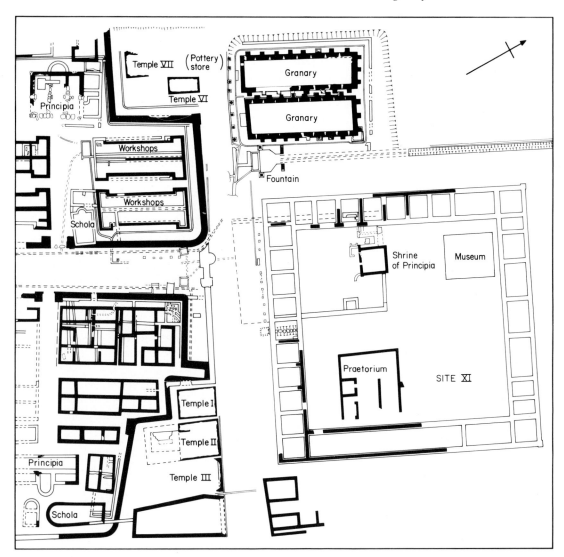

Fig. 10 Corbridge: plan of the area shown in 30.

trade was in contemporary mortaria the shop was also selling old stocks of late second-century Samian.

Running through both compounds on a line parallel with the main street a ridge can be seen with subsidences on each side, into which the third- and fourth-century buildings have sunk. At one time this feature was taken to indicate the position of the south ditch system of the underlying fort, but it is now known that these ditches must be sought much further south. The ridge marks the line of one of the repeatedly remetalled streets in the *praetentura* of the fort, which has supported later structures more firmly than the softer ground on either side.

The site is a fine example of the careful preservative work of the Ancient Monuments Depart-ment, and inspires the hope that one day a larger area may be taken into state guardianship for excavation and display.

References

I.A. Richmond, 'Roman legionaries at Corbridge, their supply-base, temples and religious cults', *Arch. Aeliana* (4th series) XXI (1943), 127–224. P. Salway, *The Frontier People of Roman Britain* (Cambridge, 1965), 45–59 with Fig. 5 (town plan). E. Birley, *Corbridge Roman Station* (Department of the Environment Official Guide, London, 1975). G. Simpson, *Britannia* V (1974), 327–39. J.P. Gillam, 'The Roman forts at Corbridge', *Arch. Aeliana* (5th series) V (1977), 47–74. J. Collingwood Bruce, *Handbook to the Roman Wall* (13th ed. by C.M. Daniels, Newcastle upon Tyne, 1978), 90–102. M. Brassington, *Britannia* VI (1975), 62–75. J.K. StJoseph, *J.R.S.* XLV (1955), 84 with Pl. XVII (oblique view looking NW). *Britannia* XII (1981), 322 (W rampart).

6

FRONTIERS

Roman frontiers were unlike modern ones, save only that customs duties had to be paid there and inspections of incomers made. The nature of the difference lay in the fact that the Roman Empire had no close neighbours of equal power or similar sophistication: beyond their borders the Romans always sought to maintain wide zones under their own control. These might take the form of client kingdoms in rather unequal treaty relationships, or else they might be areas patrolled by Roman forces, where severe restrictions upon native activity were enforced by Roman officers. The idea of equal partners on either side of a fixed divide was foreign to the thinking and experience of the Romans.

In the early years of the Empire, the world was still thought to be a place sufficiently small to offer the possibility of universal rule; Roman forces were poised in readiness for the advance rather than spread out in a defensive line. The disastrous loss of three legions in Germany in A.D. 9 caused a revision of ideas; by degrees the Rhine and Danube, which had been the springboards for the attack, became recognised as the *de facto* frontier, subject only to local adjustments from time to time. Thus by the end of the first century the re-entrant formed by the headwaters of the two rivers had been annexed to shorten the line, and an artificial frontier, no longer based on large rivers, had to be inaugurated. The word *limes*, indeed, which came to signify 'frontier', had originally meant merely a road, often one which led into hostile territory rather than along the Roman borders.

In Britain during the early years of the conquest there were several short-lived *limites* based on roads. The road itself, as for instance the Foss Way, or the road running from Wroxeter southwards towards Usk and Gloucester (6), was guarded by forts but formed merely the core of a military zone extending each side of it. In 81 Agricola created a *limes* of this sort, possibly only intended as a temporary measure, between the Forth and the Clyde; but little is known of its components. A year or two later he reinforced the road from Ardoch to the Tay with a closely spaced series of watch-towers; although some of these towers on the Gask Ridge lie over-far from the nearest fort, and despite the fact that the towers south-west of Kaims Castle differ somewhat in type from those north-east of it (p. 136), the system seems to be a real *limes*, designed to protect the area of Fife from infiltration from the north. Whether these towers were in contemporary use with the so-called 'glen-blocking' forts to their north-east is a question which may never be finally resolved; the system would be more comprehensible if it preceded or succeeded them, and both views have been advocated.[1]

After the abandonment of southern Scotland *c.* 105, a rather clearer *limes* was based on Agricola's old road between the river Tyne and Carlisle, and was probably extended along the coast of Cumberland. Additional forts were built so that they lay half a day's march apart, at *c.* 10 km intervals instead of the normal average of 21. Between them small forts and fortlets were established and probably some watch-towers. It is unfortunate that the details of this interesting system are still somewhat hypothetical because of lack of confirming excavation; but the line seems to possess close similarities to the land frontier begun in Upper Germany under Domitian twenty years earlier. The presence of so many troops along the road would facilitate control of native movement across the line, and would also provide the core of a quickly assembled striking-force when emergency arose.

Domitian had already built a wooden fence along a short sector of the German *limes*, but it was Hadrian whose new defensive policy favoured a continuous barrier along all sectors unprotected by a river. In Upper Germany he added to the existing road and watch-towers a palisade, through which entry could be made only at supervised gateways; but in Britain he was responsible for a far more expensive and powerful barrier, the Wall which still bears his name. This was placed a

1. See D.J. Breeze and B. Dobson, *Glasgow Arch. Journ.* IV (1976), 124–43 for the view that the towers date *c.* 88–87/90. See S.S. Frere in J Kenworthy (ed.), *Agricola's Campaigns in Scotland* (Scottish Archaeological Forum No. 12, Edinburgh 1981), 96 for the possibility that they may have been established in 80 or 81.

short distance north of the Stanegate on ground with a much more commanding view. For the first 72 km, from Newcastle to the crossing of the river Irthing, the barrier was planned to be of stone, 10 Roman feet wide; the final 50 km to Bowness on Solway was to be a rampart of turf, 20 Roman feet wide at the base. The reason for the change in material was apparently a virtual absence in the western sector of limestone needed for mortar. Thus speed of construction evidently outweighed other considerations; but later this sector was in fact rebuilt in stone. In addition to a wide ditch in front of the Wall, the original design provided for fortlets at every measured mile and for two towers evenly spaced between these Milecastles; but the fighting-garrison itself was still retained in the forts of the old Stanegate frontier to the south. The work of building was undertaken by the three British legions. The system is curiously rigid; little or no concession was made to topography, so that some towers and Milecastles occupy very unsuitable positions.

Some have sought the reason for the unique strength and monumental character of Hadrian's Wall in the emperor's desire for a lasting memorial for himself and for his policy of retaining the Empire within set bounds. The Wall is, however, rather too remote to justify such a claim; an explanation in practical military terms is preferable. There is evidence that very considerable and mounting hostile pressure was being exerted from both inside and outside the frontier line. This evidence is seen in the historical account of warfare in Britain at the outset of the reign, in the initial need to replace the Stanegate frontier by a new one, and later in the various costly modifications of design which were quickly found to be necessary. The Wall was to be built, at whatever cost, as a final solution to the problem of the British frontier.

Indications that the original design was insufficient for its purpose include the belated, though in the event rapid, transfer of the garrisons to new forts on the Wall itself, and then the laborious construction of the so-called Vallum, a deep wide flat-bottomed ditch (32) with banks set back on either side, along the whole distance behind the Wall; its purpose was to demarcate the military zone and to guard against rearward infiltration. Moreover, the Wall was soon extended to the east as far as Wallsend, on the estuary of the Tyne, while from the west end a system of Milefortlets and towers with spaced forts continued a long distance down the Cumberland coast, obviously to counter crossings from south-west Scotland. During the course of these various changes, the gauge of the stone wall was reduced

to 8 Roman feet for sectors so far unbuilt, perhaps to speed completion. Archaeologists name the original work the Broad Wall and the other the Narrow Wall.

The first series of forts to be built on the Wall itself comprised eleven in all; wherever topography allowed, these forts were placed astride the Wall so that three of their gates lay to the north. The intention was to speed the egress of troops in an emergency, but like several other features of the Wall's design this arrangement looked well in the design stage but proved less useful in practice.

Experience soon showed that this provision was excessive, and the gates not actually required were walled up. Before the end of Hadrian's reign additional forts had been added, but these were no longer set astride the Wall and were given only one gateway with direct access to the north.

The Hadrianic *limes* was laid out on the only possible geographical line in this area of Britain, and in the central sector was able to take advantage of the precipitous crags of the Whin Sill; but it suffered the disadvantage of lying too far south of the main centres of population in southern Scotland, which were not easy to control at such a distance. In the third century this disadvantage was overcome, after further punitive expeditions, by a system of outpost forts and by a wide-ranging force of light-armed troops and scouts, whose duty was to keep the population under direct observation.

Before this happened, and within only a few years of the completion of the Wall, there had been a dramatic change of policy following Hadrian's death. The new emperor, Antoninus Pius, a man of no military experience, felt the need to strengthen his position with a warlike achievement, and may have been under pressure to reverse his predecessor's unpopular policies. The difficulties inherent in the Hadrianic frontier were now well understood and – perhaps on the pretext of an attack on Roman territory – the decision was taken to eradicate them by reoccupying southern Scotland. Accordingly a new *limes* was constructed on the Forth–Clyde line, known today as the Antonine Wall.

There were many advantages in this move. The new line was only half as long as Hadrian's Wall and did not call for such extensive flank protection; and as it was to be made of turf the new Wall could be built very quickly. Moreover, the troublesome peoples of southern Scotland were now under direct supervision, while the main hostile element in northern Scotland, the Caledonii, lived too far away to be a direct threat. The resumption of friendly relations with the peoples of Fife is indicated by the rebuilding of Agricola's forts on the road northward as far as the Tay; these forts in effect formed a *limes* protecting Fife, as well as serving as outposts from which to detect any movement from the far north.

The builders of the Antonine *limes* made use of experience gained from Hadrian's turf wall; the new Wall was given a foundation layer of stones which improved drainage and provided sufficient stability for a rampart only two-thirds the width of Hadrian's to be built to almost the same height. The frontier line was also strengthened with a more massive ditch than that of Hadrian's Wall. The principal difference between the two Walls lay in the arrangement of their forts. The sixteen forts on Hadrian's Wall housed whole units spaced at intervals of *c*. 12 km. On the shorter Antonine frontier there were probably as many as nineteen forts, the majority housing only parts of units, spaced *c*. 3.5 km apart. Thus emphasis was placed on closer supervision in force.

There is, however, today growing evidence that this arrangement was an afterthought, and that the first design for the Antonine Wall was similar to Hadrian's, with perhaps six forts for whole units spaced at intervals of 12–14 km, the intervals between them being occupied by fortlets resembling the Milecastles in character. One of these fortlets, Wilderness Plantation, is shown in 40. This arrangement proved insufficiently powerful, and was soon changed.

The disadvantage of the Antonine frontier, exacerbated now that the initial miscalculation of the garrison necessary to man the Wall had been put right, turned out to be the strain imposed by the occupation of southern Scotland upon the manpower of the Roman army in Britain. Forts in the Pennines had had to be evacuated so that their garrisons could move northwards, and in 154 this lack of supervision seems to have facilitated a serious rebellion. Troops in Scotland had to move south to suppress it, and then, shortly after the Antonine system had been re-established, the call for reinforcements for fresh Continental wars compelled a second and final withdrawal. Thereafter Hadrian's Wall remained the frontier of Roman Britain, though now with improved arrangements for the supervision of the lands beyond the *limes*.

From the late second century a fresh threat to the province began to be felt, from the sea-raiders of northern Germany. Various measures for coastal defence in south-east Britain were taken during the third century, culminating in a new *limes*. Forts were built at a series of harbours from Brancaster in Norfolk round to Portchester near Portsmouth and Carisbrooke on the Isle of Wight, and in the fourth century they formed a special command under the Count of the Saxon Shore. The system was not created all at one time and there are variations in the types of forts, depending on their date of erection. The first fort at Richborough (44) certainly had earthwork defences, while the walls of Brancaster (46) and Reculver, both probably dating from the first half of the third century, have rounded angles and earth banks behind, in the manner of earlier forts. But several new forts were built in the 280s and Pevensey was added later still. These introduce a new late Roman design with thick free-standing walls having projecting towers at the angles as well as at intervals in between. Examples are illustrated at Richborough (44) and Portchester (45). They contained garrisons of infantry or cavalry with which to counter landings, but clearly also functioned in close association with the fleet.

These new forts illustrate how much the late Roman army had been thrown back on the defensive. The walls were far more high and massive than those of earlier forts, whose defences were primarily provided only against surprise, and whose garrisons were expected to fight in the open. The wall of Portchester is 3 m thick, that of Richborough even wider; at Pevensey the parapet-walk survives to show that it was almost 7.5 m above ground. The external towers mounted artillery in the form of arrow-firing catapults and were designed to provide enfilading fire and to keep attackers on the far side of the broad ditches.

In the second half of the fourth century further coastal defences were built in Yorkshire, comprising watch-towers which were probably the work of Count Theodosius as part of his restoration of the province in 369. They were placed as far as possible on high coastal cliffs to keep watch for Pictish war-boats, and must have cooperated closely with naval patrols. An example at Scarborough is illustrated (47).

References

S.S. Frere, *Britannia, a History of Roman Britain* (London, 1978). D.J. Breeze and B. Dobson, *Hadrian's Wall* (London, 1976). R. Bellhouse, *Britannia* XII (1981), 135–42 (Cumberland coast). S. Johnson, *The Roman Forts of the Saxon Shore* (London, 1976).

31 Haltwhistle Burn fortlet, Northumberland, looking WSW. NY 715662. ATV 44: December 1967.

THE TYNE–SOLWAY FRONTIER AND HADRIAN'S WALL.

I HALTWHISTLE BURN FORTLET, Northumberland (31)

The Roman road called the Stanegate, running from Corbridge to Carlisle, was originally laid out under Agricola; twenty years later, after Trajan's withdrawal of forces from Scotland, this road was more heavily garrisoned to become the backbone of a new frontier. The *agger* of the road can be seen in the left background approaching from the west, just to the right of the modern road B 6318. It crosses the steep gully of the Haltwhistle Burn by a typical series of sharp zig-zags and then approaches the left foreground, passing close beside the well-defined earthworks of a fortlet lying on the crest. The Haltwhistle Burn fortlet is one of a series alternating with forts along the road and is of Trajanic date. It appears to have

been held by a century of auxiliaries, their function being to patrol the road and guard the bridge or crossing.

On the hither side of the fortlet a modern lane runs north towards Hadrian's Wall which lies off the picture to the right. The lane crosses the corner of a small marching-camp of 1.12 ha (2.77 acres) whose gates are defended by *titula*. The camp has been labelled III by Bennett. To the right of the camp, on the other side of the lane, is a small earthwork (IV), only 0.09 ha in area and with but a single gate. In the foreground lies another camp (I) with *titula*, 0.89 ha in size but later reduced to 0.41 ha by a rampart across its centre. All these earthworks are thought to be practice camps, but III is large enough to have been operational and might perhaps be regarded as a construction camp associated either with the

32 Haltwhistle Burn area, Hadrian's Wall and the Vallum, looking E. NY 716665. BLL 25: January 1973.

fortlet or with the Stanegate itself. Camps I and IV are also seen on **32**.

II HALTWHISTLE BURN AREA, HADRIAN'S WALL AND THE VALLUM (32)

This view overlaps with **31** and shows in the right foreground Camps I, IV and part of III which belong to the Haltwhistle Burn group. Up the middle of the photograph runs the Vallum in splendid preservation. The name is a misnomer since the principal feature is a large ditch rather than a rampart, but its use has been sanctified by long tradition. The ditch is normally 6 m (20 ft) wide, 3 m deep and dug with a flat bottom 2.44 m (8 ft) wide; at a distance of 9 m from each edge is a turf-revetted mound containing the spoil from the ditch. The whole work thus possesses an overall width of 36.6 m (120 ft) or one Roman *actus*. The Vallum is not a strictly military work in the sense of being defensible, but rather a boundary difficult to cross, defining the rear of the military zone associated with the Wall. In the plate its straight, ruthless layout, going direct from point to point like a Roman road, contrasts strongly with that of the Wall itself twisting and turning

33 Housesteads (*Vercovicium*), Northumberland; panorama looking W. NY 790688. DS 28: July 1949.

along the summit of the crags. The intention that the Vallum should be continuous and uncrossable was illustrated by excavation in the marshy section near the quarry; here the sides of the ditch had been revetted with turves set on flagging in order to maintain their steep profile. At a later date, thought to be the moment when the Wall system became obsolete after the reconquest of southern Scotland in the early 140s, the Vallum was slighted. Gaps were cut through the mounds every 40 m, and causeways inserted across the ditch. A fine series of these gaps is seen in the South Mound in the foreground. Later still most of these causeways were removed; together with the earth thrown up during cleaning of the ditch the material created a

third bank, the so-called 'Marginal Mound' along the south edge of the ditch. The Marginal Mound shows clearly in the central portion of the photograph.

The Wall is here climbing onto the dolerite crags formed by the outcrop of the Whin Sill: the almost vertical north-facing escarpment gave it exceptional protection and a superb outlook. In the foreground lies Cawfields quarry which has destroyed a length of the Wall: the threatened extension of this quarry was the occasion that led to the Roman Wall and Vallum Preservation Scheme of 1931. Just above the top left corner of the quarry the walls of Milecastle 42 can be seen. Opposite the Milecastle there was the usual

34 Housesteads, Northumberland; Hadrian's Wall fort, looking W. NY 790688. CLY 13: May 1980.

causeway across the Vallum ditch: excavation has shown that this was not an original feature but was artificially created by filling in the ditch. The causeways at Milecastles together with the original causeways at forts facilitated the passage of patrols.

A Roman road known as the Military Way runs between the Wall and the Vallum. Its *agger* can be seen in the middle distance just left of the angle in the Vallum. Near the quarry the road is forced to cross the North Mound because the proximity of the ridge left too little space between Wall and Vallum, an indication that this road was a later feature of the frontier, not originally envisaged. The earliest milestones along it date to 213, but the road itself may have been built when the Wall was reconstituted as the frontier soon after 160.

A Roman water-mill was excavated in 1907–8 just off the bottom of the photograph close to where the Military Way crosses the Haltwhistle Burn; it was of third-century date. Unfortunately the site is now covered by a spoil heap from the quarry.

References

J. Collingwood Bruce, *Handbook to the Roman Wall* (13th ed. by C.M. Daniels, Newcastle, 1978), 30–32, 38–41, 175–9. J. Bennett in W.S. Hanson and L.J.F. Keppie (eds.), *Roman Frontier Studies 1979* (B.A.R. Int. Series 71 (1), Oxford, 1980), 151–72 with Pl. 11.2 (oblique view of camps and fortlet from the north). F.G. Simpson in G. Simpson (ed.), *Watermills and Military Works on Hadrian's Wall* (Kendal, 1976), 26–43.

III PANORAMA, HOUSESTEADS (*VERCO-VICIUM*),Northumberland (33)

In the foreground lies the fort of Housesteads, the subject of the next section (34). The central sector of Hadrian's Wall is magnificently and commandingly situated on the north-facing escarpment of the Whin Sill, described in the previous section. This sector is by far the most famous and most frequently illustrated, but it is important to remember that the Whin Sill extends for only 11 of the 80 Roman miles along which the Wall was built. The photograph looks west towards the area of 32, 8 km away. One-third of a Roman mile beyond the fort the stone walls of Milecastle 37 are seen attached to the rear of the Wall. Here a gateway pierced the Wall, though to very little purpose, as can be seen; the fact well illustrates the rigid and inflexible character of the original design for the frontier. The footpath left of the Milecastle very roughly marks the position of the Military Way; but the Vallum, here running near the foot of the slope towards the left of the photograph, is invisible, as is the Stanegate 1.7 km further south.

Reference

J.K. StJoseph, *J.R.S.* XLI (1951), 54–5 with Pl. V (this view).

IV HOUSESTEADS (34–5)

In 34, Hadrian's Wall approaches the north-west corner of the fort from the west through the belt of trees, and continues north-east from the north-east corner in the foreground. The Wall here is the so-called Narrow Wall, 8 Roman feet thick; but already before it was built there had been two successive phases of construction at Housesteads. In the first of these, the foundation for a stretch of Wall designed to the original broad gauge of 10 Roman feet had been laid along the crest of the Whin Sill and a turret attached to its rear had been built and occupied. Then came a change of plan. A decision had been reached to move auxiliary garrisons from the Stanegate further south into new forts on the Wall itself; so the turret was taken down and the fort erected. The foundations of the turret can be seen behind the centre of the fort's north wall. Normally forts of the first series to be placed along the Wall were planned to project through it with three gates to the north; here the steep escarpment prevented this and the north wall of the fort was built just below the crest along which the broad foundation had been laid. A north gate was indeed provided, approached by a ramp, and was of the same type with towers and

twin portals as the others; however, one of the portals was walled up even before arrangements for hanging its doors were installed. Clearly there was a lack of traffic up and down this slope, which could be bypassed at the Knag Burn gateway 100 m to the east (see below). The fort was at first free-standing, as its rounded northern corners show, and was only later joined by the Narrow Wall. The original north-east angle-tower was then found to be wrongly placed for such a junction; it was accordingly demolished and a new tower built a little further west to accommodate the Narrow Wall. There is evidence that all these changes took place within a very short time.

The fort of Housesteads (*Vercovicium*) of 2.06 ha (5.1 acres) was designed to hold a milliary cohort of infantry. In the third century the garrison was *cohors I Tungrorum milliaria,* and this regiment may have been stationed there as early as Hadrian's reign before being transferred to Scotland; but there is no direct evidence. During the third century there were two additional units present, the *cuneus Frisiorum* of cavalry and the *numerus Hnaudifridi,* an irregular formation of infantry; but the problem of the additional accommodation needed by them is unsolved.

The fort (34) gives an excellent impression of the orderly arrangement of a Roman auxiliary fort with its Headquarters Building (*principia*) in the centre, flanked on the north side by two buttressed granaries (*horrea*) and on the other by the large courtyard house of the unit's tribune; behind the *principia* lies a large hospital. The *principia* faces the *via principalis* at its junction with the *via praetoria* running to the gate in the foreground. The fort thus faced east in the direction of the Knag Burn (below the camera), near which a gateway (visible in 35) was provided through Hadrian's Wall to accommodate an existing traffic route. The front and rear areas of the fort were occupied by barrack buildings, ten in number, and by workshops; two barracks have been uncovered in the front, but are seen in their fourth-century state when rebuilt as two rows of free-standing 'chalets'. Just to left of the south-east angle-tower (left foreground) can be seen the rectangular building that houses the well-preserved men's latrine. This was flushed from nearby water-tanks and discharged through a drain running downhill beneath the fort wall.

Behind the fort the light-toned footpath leading from the *porta decumana* follows approximately the line of the Military Way. The land round the fort, particularly on the steep slope down from the south gate (left) and on the more level ground west of the fort, is heavily patterned with earthworks in the form of terraces, platforms and

35 Housesteads, Hadrian's Wall fort; vertical photograph. K17-X 5: February 1971. Scale 1:2800.

enclosures which show particularly well in **35**, a photograph taken in low winter sunshine after a light fall of snow. The platforms carried the houses of the civil settlement (*vicus*). Five of these buildings have been excavated and consolidated and are of the 'strip-type' normal in such villages. The sites of others can be distinguished, particularly in **35**, west of the fort and beside the road down to the Knag Burn. The terraces form part of an extensive series representing the remains of cultivation which in origin can be shown to be of Roman date but were still in use, and perhaps

extended, in medieval and later times. They have obliterated the Vallum which runs obliquely across the southward slope, passing the south side of the modern farm building and the most southerly of the *vicus* buildings lining the road running downhill from the *porta principalis dextra*.

Near the bottom right-hand corner of **35**, to the left of the approach path, lies Chapel Hill. In 1822 a Mithraeum was found in the small valley at its western end, and in 1960–1 the site of the circular temple of Mars Thincsus, from which inscriptions and sculpture had been recovered in

66

36 Chesterholm (*Vindolanda*), **Northumberland; Roman fort and** *vicus*, looking W. NY 771664. BLL 15: January 1973.

1883, was identified below its north slope. The temple lay close to a sacred spring enclosed within an apsed shrine; the spring itself can be seen on 35 near the point where the field wall on the north side of Chapel Hill makes a pronounced zig-zag. The excavations showed that a civil settlement had developed here south of the vallum in the second century, a time when civilians were debarred from the military zone north of it; but, except for the shrines, this area had declined in importance in the third century when the vallum was disused and a new *vicus* sprang up around the fort itself. Mars Thincsus was a Germanic deity whose worship was introduced by the new German units stationed here in the third century; the secret cult of Mithras, of course, which came from the East, had a wider appeal among the soldiery.

The site of Housesteads is owned by the National Trust, and the fort is in the guardianship of the Secretary of State for the Environment.

References

W.P. Hedley, *Antiquity* V (1931), 351–4 with Pl. II (R.A.F. vertical view of area). E. Birley, *Housesteads Roman Fort* (Department of the Environment Official Guide, London, 1952), plan; *Research on Hadrian's Wall* (Kendal, 1961), Fig. 25 (map). B. Jones, *Hadrian's Wall from the Air* (Manchester, 1976), 14 (oblique view from W). J.K. St Joseph, *J.R.S.* XLI (1951), Pl. V (our 33). S.S. Frere, *Britannia, a History of Roman Britain* (London, 1967), Pl. XI; (2nd ed. 1974), Pl. IV (our 33). J.K. St Joseph, *J.R.S.* LXIII (1973), 214–15 with Pl. XV (vertical under snow, our 35). D.R. Wilson in W. Rodwell and T. Rowley (eds.), *The Small Towns of Roman Britain* (B.A.R. 15, Oxford, 1975), 13 with Pls. XIIA, B (obliques looking W). Temple: R.E. Birley, *Arch. Aeliana* (4th series) XXXIX (1961), 301–19.

V CHESTERHOLM (*VINDOLANDA*), Northumberland (36)

Vindolanda lies on the Stanegate, 1.6 km south of Hadrian's Wall, but it was listed among the Wall forts in the *Notitia Dignitatum* and can be shown to have had a long history very different from that of other Stanegate forts.

In the photograph, the straight lane on the right represents the Stanegate: the course of the road is confirmed by two Roman milestones still in position, the first on the valley-bottom to right of foreground, the other beyond the top of the picture. The road is here negotiating the steep, deep valley of a north–south stream, the Bradley Burn; the fort occupies a commanding eminence on the west side of the valley, and in the hollow beyond lie the remains of an extensive *vicus*, where recent excavations have revealed a great deal of the plan and history of the settlement. To left of this can be seen a modern full-scale replica, facing south and not of course *in situ*, of a short length of Hadrian's Turf Wall.

Vindolanda is an example of a fort where the tactical position was so compelling that the site was never moved, and the photograph shows the considerable build-up within the defences caused by successive demolitions and reconstructions. Nevertheless excavation has proved that earlier versions of the fort did not conform exactly to the outlines of the visible remains.

Although the interior of the fort has been ploughed since Roman times, the raking sunlight falling on the ground surface covered with hoar-frost picks out grass-covered heaps of debris rising above the general surface and marking the outlines of buildings. In the centre lies the *principia*, excavated in 1932–5, and preserved for permanent display.

The original fort, of turf with timber-framed buildings within, may have been built *c.* A.D. 90 after some of Agricola's forts north of the Forth had been evacuated, but recent work has raised the possibility that the foundation may have been somewhat earlier, under Agricola himself. In Trajan's reign, after a further evacuation of Scotland, Chesterholm became an important element in the new Stanegate *limes*, and the fort may have been rebuilt to a different size. The remains of these early forts are deeply buried, and their size and plan are not yet known; they may have lain obliquely beneath the visible fort and traces of military or annexe buildings have also been found beneath the *vicus*. It was from these early levels that the remarkable wooden writing tablets and other timber remains were recovered, preserved in waterlogged layers below a great depth of later deposits.

When Hadrian's Wall was built, the garrison was moved from *Vindolanda*, presumably to one of the new forts on the Wall, and the site lay empty for 45 years. But after the second abandonment of Scotland, in the 160s, the eminence close to the stream was chosen for the site of a stone fort which faced south, as was established by the orientation of its *principia*, and extended a few metres farther north than the remains now visible. The fort as seen in the photograph is essentially a modification of this original stone fort carried out in the early third century, but with considerable further reconstructions undertaken from time to time; in one of these, *c.* 300, the Headquarters Building was rebuilt to face north towards the Stanegate. The buildings showing through the turf to the left of this *principia* have not been excavated; but in 1979–80 excavation in the right foreground of the fort confirmed that the buildings there are barracks of the fourth century, and revealed that later buildings datable after 360 had once existed above them, though now largely destroyed by the plough.

The civil settlement beyond the fort has yielded a well-known dedication to Vulcan erected by the *Vicani Vindolandenses*, thus confirming both the place-name and the status of the settlement as a *vicus*. This village developed during the later third century and is typical of such civil *vici* with its strip-buildings lining the streets and its evidence of metallurgical industry. The place began to decline in the late fourth century, but has yielded one tombstone thought to date from the fifth.

Beneath the *vicus* were found remains of an earlier settlement defended by a rampart. Although interpreted as a civil settlement established with the first stone fort, *c.* A.D. 160–5, the presence of defences and the character of the buildings, many of which are untypical of *vici*, may suggest that it was more likely an official administrative establishment. An inscription (*R.I.B.* 1696) shows that a *beneficiarius consularis*, an official from the governor's staff charged with police responsibilities, was stationed at Chesterholm for a period.

References

Robin Birley, *Vindolanda* (London, 1977) with Pls. IV–VI (oblique views looking W and S). G.D.B. Jones, *Hadrian's Wall from the Air* (Manchester, 1976), 15 (oblique view looking W). J. Collingwood Bruce, *Handbook to the Roman Wall* (13th ed. by C.M. Daniels, Newcastle upon Tyne, 1978), 156–62, with plan. P. Salway in K. Branigan (ed.), *Rome and the Brigantes* (Sheffield, 1980), 14–16 (discussion of *vicus* with plans).

37 Hadrian's Wall at Birdoswald, Cumbria, looking WSW. NY 616663. AVY 62: July 1968.

VI BIRDOSWALD, Cumbria (37)

The North Tyne, the Irthing and the Eden are the only rivers of any size to be crossed by Hadrian's Wall. In the photograph the Irthing is seen to flow at the foot of a steep and often wooded scarp; the course of the river here has shifted to the west since Roman times, and a turret and part of the abutment of the bridge on which the Wall crossed the river now stand isolated on dry land (at the bottom of the photograph). The remains are complicated by the presence of a Roman water-

mill at the bridge. Beyond it the Wall ascended the scarp, which was probably less steep before the river changed its course. At the top of the cliff is seen Harrow's Scar Milecastle (No. 49), under which remains of a Turf Wall Milecastle have been found. From this point westwards the original Hadrianic frontier was a rampart of turf; preparations for building the Broad Wall of stone, 10 Roman feet wide, terminated at the bridge or Milecastle, and when, a few years later, the Turf Wall was replaced in stone in this sector, it was a wall to the narrow gauge (of 8 feet) which was

69

38 Biglands, Cumbria, Cumberland coast; Milefortlet, looking SSE. NY 208618. CDH 85: July 1977.

built. Later still the whole of the rest of the Turf Wall was replaced in stone. For most of the 50 km to Bowness the stone wall took the same line as the Turf Wall, which was demolished to make way for it; but for almost 3 km westwards from Milecastle 49 the two works followed different courses.

The fort of Birdoswald can be seen to left of a farm which lies some 500 m beyond the Milecastle. The large size of the fort (2.14 ha, 5.3 acres) meant that there was little space to spare on the available level ground north of the river scarps. Like the majority of other first-series forts (p. 59) Birdoswald was placed astride the (Turf) Wall with the *praetentura* projecting to the north. A length of Turf Wall and ditch, together with a turret, was flattened to allow for the insertion of the fort. In the photograph the Turf Wall, closely attended by the Vallum because of the nearness

of the scarps, can be seen approaching the fort from the west; just outside a gate, a faint line in the meadow on the near side of the fort indicates its further course eastwards towards Milecastle 49.

A few years after the fort had been built, the inconvenience of having so restricted an area between the Wall and the river scarps, together with a new appreciation that three gates in front of the Wall were unnecessary (p. 59), prompted a reorganisation. A stone wall to the narrow gauge was built for almost 8 km westwards from the milecastle to the Red Rock Fault, the limit of limestone outcrops (p. 59), essential as a source of lime for mortar. This new wall ran to the northern angles of the fort instead of to the *portae principales*. In the photograph this Narrow Wall, recently consolidated by the Department of the Environment, and the ditch to north, can be seen

70

in the foreground; beyond the fort the Narrow Wall is obscured by a modern road, but the ditch can still be discerned. The rest of the Turf Wall was probably not replaced in stone until as late as 158–60; the new work was built to an intermediate gauge of 9 Roman feet.

The area shown in the plate is of great archaeological importance, for only in this short sector do the Turf and Narrow Walls take separate courses, a fact which facilitates the study of each in isolation. Excavations here in 1931–5 established the individual characteristics of the Turf Wall, its Milecastles and turrets, and determined the date of the replacement in stone.

References

J. Collingwood Bruce, *Handbook to the Roman Wall* (13th ed. by C.M. Daniels, Newcastle upon Tyne, 1978), 195–206, 211–27, with bibliography.

VII BIGLANDS, Cumbria (38)

The western termination of Hadrian's Wall is near the fort at Bowness on Solway, but the defensive *limes* continued down the Cumberland coast with the same spacing of fortlets at one-mile intervals, with two towers between, although now without a curtain-wall. The coastal road which here separates the foreshore from the agricultural land to the south is not infrequently flooded in places by the highest tides. Milefortlet 1 at Biglands lies 1676 m WSW of Bowness; its position just above the foreshore can be seen on the left of the photograph by the farm buildings of Biglands House, where the dark line of its surrounding ditch encloses an area of *c.* 40 by 50 m.

The fortlet, which lies only *c.* 4–5 m above high water, has been placed on a number of low storm-ridges composed of sand and gravel. The photograph gives a good impression of how in this western continuation of the Hadrianic system the coast itself took the place of a curtain-wall; the area lies beyond the lowest fords on the Solway, and crossings from south-west Scotland could only be made by boat.

Excavation in 1975, in advance of a new building, showed that the fortlet, which measured *c.* 35 by 29 m overall, had a turf rampart *c.* 7 m wide, later widened, and that it was occupied throughout most of the second century although with probable intermissions during the periods when the Antonine Wall was held. The garrison was very small, perhaps not more than 8–10 men. The north gate, facing the sea, was surmounted by a wooden tower from which a watch could be maintained.

Aerial photography followed by selective exca-

vation has also shown that in the sector between Bowness and the Moricambe estuary the Mile-fortlets were connected by a corridor *c.* 46 m wide defined by small ditches at front and rear. This arrangement, the equivalent here of the line of Hadrian's Wall, helps to explain why the Mile-fortlets, although so small, probably all have gateways at both front and back. The ditches were less than 1 m deep, and *c.* 1.5 m wide, and difficulty had been experienced in keeping them open in the soft subsoil of sand and gravel, for they had had to be recut. Clearly their purpose was to define a military corridor with its patrol track rather than themselves to form defences, but the system cannot have been long maintained. Farther south-west round the coast traces have been noted of a palisade, apparently taking the place of the forward ditch. The system was evidently conceived as part of the somewhat extravagant 'drawing-board' planning which characterises Hadrian's Wall as a whole in its initial phase.

References

J.K. St Joseph, *J.R.S.* XLI (1951), 56. T.W. Potter, *Britannia* VIII (1977), 149–85 (excavation report). G.D.B. Jones, *Britannia* VII (1976), 236–43 (linear ditches) with Pl. XXIIA (oblique view from south-east). J. Collingwood Bruce, *Handbook to the Roman Wall* (13th ed. by C.M. Daniels, Newcastle, 1978), 260–7. R. Bellhouse, *Current Archaeology* VII 3 (No. 74, Nov. 1980), 79–83 (Cumberland coastal system). T.W. Potter in W.S. Hanson and L.J.F. Keppie (eds.), *Roman Frontier Studies 1979* (B.A.R. Int. Series 71 (1), Oxford, 1980), 195–200 (Cumberland coastal system). R. Bellhouse, *Britannia* XII (1981), 135–42 with Pl. VIIIB (Tower 2B); *Trans. Cumb. and Westm. Antiq. and Arch. Soc.* LXXXI (1981), 7–13 (Milefortlet 20).

VIII BECKFOOT, Cumbria (39)

It is well known that the Hadrianic frontier in northern Britain comprised more than Hadrian's Wall itself, and that although the Wall ended on the west at Bowness on Solway, the line of Milefortlets and towers continued southwards along the Cumberland coast to guard against landings from across the Firth; at a slightly later date forts were added to this line. One of these forts was at Beckfoot. It lies close to the shore, towards which it faces, looking across to the hostile coast 12.5 km to the north-west; the site may previously have been occupied for a short time by Tower 14b, the measured position of which should lie here.

The fort was partly explored in 1879–80, but only when aerial photographs were taken in the dry summer of 1949 was the internal plan revealed. The photograph here shows the truly remarkable effect of drought upon a crop of oats. The

39 Beckfoot, Cumbria; Roman fort looking NW. NY 090489. DU 31: July 1949.

defences enclose an area of 1.3 ha (3.25 acres), a space appropriate to a garrison consisting of an infantry cohort, 500 strong: indeed a building-inscription set up by the Second Cohort of Pannonians, which was a regiment of this type and was probably in garrison during part of the second century, has been recorded. Finds suggest that the fort remained in occupation throughout the Roman period, and during this time there may well have occurred changes in internal planning, of which photographs provide hints.

The picture shows the broad system of four ditches, the line of the fort wall with the rampart behind and the internal streets, all in unusual detail. The *limes* road approaches the south-west gate and continues through the fort as the *via principalis*. The *praetentura* beyond this is divided into four blocks, the nearest of which on the left contains the outline of a buttressed *horreum* (store building) robbed of its stone; other photographs suggest that this is a late building overlying earlier foundations of a different type. A second matching *horreum* lies opposite on the near side of the *via principalis* in the central block, the rest of which is occupied by the Headquarters Building (centre) and commander's house (right); the area on the

40 The Antonine Wall; fortlet at Wilderness Plantation, Strathclyde (Lanarkshire), looking W. NS 597722. U 56: July 1947.

near side of the nearer *horreum* may be the site of the military hospital. A quingenary cohort of infantry would require six centurial barracks, which are normally found in facing pairs. Here there is room for all six in the *retentura* (foreground); but it is possible that only four lay in this position, supplemented by workshops or other long narrow buildings, and that at least in one of the periods of construction the other two barracks were placed in the *praetentura*. Crop-marks in the building-blocks nearest the far rampart give a hint of such an arrangement.

Outside the north-east corner of the fort (right foreground) are traces of a field system, suggesting the proximity of a civil settlement (*vicus*).

References

J.K. St Joseph, *J.R.S.* XLI (1951), 56 with Pl. IV, 2 (steep oblique from NE). R.G. Collingwood and I.A. Richmond, *The Archaeology of Roman Britain* (London, 1969), Pl. VB (oblique from NW). E. Birley, *Research on Hadrian's Wall* (Kendal, 1961), 214–16. J. Collingwood Bruce, *Handbook to the Roman Wall* (13th ed. by C.M. Daniels, Newcastle upon Tyne, 1978), 267–9 (with plan).

41 Balmuildy, Strathclyde; Antonine Wall fort, looking NNE. NS 581717. ADY 94: July 1961.

THE ANTONINE WALL

I WILDERNESS PLANTATION FORTLET, Strathclyde (40)

This fortlet lies in the western half of the Antonine frontier, approximately half-way between the forts of Balmuildy (to the west) and Cadder (to the east). Here the Antonine Wall itself has been almost entirely removed by the plough, but the line of its ditch appears as a dark band across the field. Excavation in 1965–6 was able to demonstrate that the fortlet was of one build with the Wall. The southern half of the rampart had entirely disappeared, but the photograph shows clearly the two ditches, 3.5 m wide and 4.3 m apart, that ran 5 m outside the rampart line. Their position suggests that the fortlet had a length of c. 28.5 m over the rampart; its width was established as 24.5 m. The fortlet had a narrow timber-revetted gate, 1.75 m wide, through the Antonine Wall, and (to judge by the causeway across the ditches) another of similar size through its south rampart. Few traces of structure survived in the interior.

At the time of the excavation the equidistant position of the fortlet from the forts at either side was reasonably interpreted as indicating a subsidiary post in the known dispositions along the Wall. But since then more fortlets have been identified – nine are so far known. Their disposition makes it clear that they belong to a primary phase of the design of the Antonine frontier, relating to widely spaced large forts; they were later abandoned when the decision was taken to substitute a series of smaller forts at shorter intervals.

References

J.K. St Joseph, *J.R.S.* XLI (1951), 61. J.J. Wilkes, *Glasgow Arch. Journ.* III (1974), 51–65 (excavation report) with plans and Pl. I (oblique view looking SW). L. Keppie in W.S. Hanson and L.J.F. Keppie (eds.), *Roman Frontier Studies 1979* (B.A.R. Int. Series 71 (1), Oxford, 1980), 107–12. *Idem, Britannia* XII (1981), 143–62 (general discussion of fortlets).

II BALMUILDY, Strathclyde (41)

With an area of 1.7 ha (4.2 acres) Balmuildy is one of the large forts on the Antonine Wall lying towards its western end at the crossing of the river Kelvin. The site has yielded two inscriptions recording construction under Lollius Urbicus by Legion II Augusta, but the garrison itself is unknown; these are the only epigraphic records of Urbicus on the Wall, but they prove that the system was begun, even if not completed, under

42 Rough Castle, Central Region (Stirlingshire); looking WSW. NS 844798. CDC 66: July 1977.

his governorship. Furthermore, Balmuildy is one of only two forts on this Wall to be defended by a stone wall rather than by a rampart of turf. It was extensively excavated in 1912–14; today the site has been much flattened by cultivation, but on the photograph the dark lines of its ditches, three on the west (left) and two on the east side, can be distinguished. The fort extends south of the modern A 879 road, its south-west corner lying beneath the trees beside the farm of Wester Balmuildy at bottom left.

The ditch of the Antonine Wall can be seen as a faint fold in the ground across the middle of two fields on the right as it approaches the north-east corner of the fort; it leaves the north-west corner at a sharp angle towards the north, to reach the river Kelvin some 85 m east of the modern road-bridge. The Military Way which accompanies the Antonine Wall crossed the fort from right to left

as the *via principalis* and then followed the Wall to the north; large stones from a bridge abutment and piers were found on the river-bed between the modern bridge and the line of the Wall.

The Antonine Wall itself is thought to have been built from east to west, and two considerations arising from the excavations show that the fort at Balmuildy had already been built before the Wall reached its vicinity. The first is that the north ditch of the fort, which is on line with the Wall ditch, is only half the size of the latter, as if dug independently. The second is that the north-west and north-east corners of the fort, which are rectangular, not curved, throw out short wing-walls as if to meet the frontier Wall; in fact, the latter runs in to the south of the north-east wing-wall to meet the fort wall behind it, and leaves the north-west wing-wall at a sharp angle. Evidently the fort and its wing-walls had been built before

75

the line of the Antonine Wall had reached this point. This evidence of construction early in the sequence of frontier works is consistent with the view, described above (p. 60), that Balmuildy, together with the other large forts, belonged to a primary plan for the Wall, which was soon modified.

The fort contained a small bath-building which stood alongside the east wall near the north-east corner; but later a second, larger bath-house was built in an annexe which lies to east of the fort. This building partly overlay the fort's ditches and evidently represents an afterthought. The site is now below the trees beside Easter Balmuildy farm.

References

S.N. Miller, *The Roman Fort at Balmuildy* (Glasgow, 1922). G. Macdonald, *The Roman Wall in Scotland* (2nd ed., Oxford, 1934), 312–24. A.S. Robertson, *The Antonine Wall* (3rd ed., Glasgow, 1979), 79–82.

III ROUGH CASTLE, Central Region (42)

The photograph shows one of the best-preserved sectors of the Antonine Wall with the small fort of Rough Castle and its annexes in the centre of the plate. The ground here falls gently northwards towards the Bonny Water, a small tributary of the river Carron; to the south there is a shallow trough of marshy ground. Beyond the fort the frontier line crosses a deep ravine cut by the Rowan Tree Burn, a small northward-flowing stream which must have presented considerable structural problems to the builders of the Wall. On the far side of the valley the great ditch, 12 m (40 ft) wide and perhaps originally 3.5 m deep, with the remains of the Turf Wall set back on its south (left) side, give a vivid impression of the strength of the *limes*. The Military Way which accompanied the Wall enters the picture near the line of tall trees, top left, and then divides, one branch following a zig-zag course across the valley to enter the fort at the *porta principalis sinistra*, the other skirting the south side of both fort and annexes.

The fort which is small, only 0.63 ha (1.6 acres) in extent including the ramparts, was excavated by the Society of Antiquaries of Scotland in 1903. The *principia* (Headquarters Building), a granary and the commander's house were in stone; the remaining buildings were in timber, as excavations in 1957–61 by the Inspectorate of Ancient Monuments confirmed. An inscription attests that the *principia* was erected by the Sixth Cohort of Nervii; if, as seems probable, this unit was in garrison, its men must have been divided between two or more forts since Rough Castle is not large

enough to accommodate a complete cohort. The bath-building was situated in the annexe just outside the *porta principalis dextra*; the position is marked by broken ground resulting from failure by the excavators of 1902–3 to back-fill their trenches. The annexe itself was altered in size at least once, and the south gateway had undergone alteration, but the 1957–61 excavations did not confirm Macdonald's interpretation of two successive widenings of the rampart; in particular, turf-work added to the inner face of the west rampart was shown to be an *ascensus*. These suggestions of long occupation are confirmed by the evidence of pottery excavated at the fort, which shows that occupation lasted from the early 140s until at least 163.

Excavation has shown that the fort is not of one build with the Antonine Wall but is secondary to it. Beneath the trees outside the nearest gate of the fort lies a small earthwork which has been interpreted as possibly one of the series of primary fortlets belonging, like that at Wilderness Plantation, to the original design of the frontier. No causeway remains across the ditch in front of this earthwork, but if one was ever present it could have been removed when the fort was built; if so, and perhaps in any case, the fort's own causeway (showing on the photograph as a light patch in the Antonine Ditch) must have been formed by secondary back-filling, but the point has not been satisfactorily settled by excavation.

In a triangular clearing in the woods, just beyond the outer end of this causeway, can be seen part of a remarkable defensive system consisting of ten parallel rows of small pits, members of each row overlapping gaps in the next. The system has close similarities with that depicted on Trajan's Column (Cichorius, Taf. XXV) and earlier used by Caesar at the siege of Alesia (*B.G.* VII 73), where they were nicknamed *lilia* (lilies) by his soldiers; but no traces of timber stakes – the basis of the comparison with the lily – were found at Rough Castle. When disguised by foliage or rough grass these pits would throw into serious disarray an attacking party attempting to approach across them. It is a curiosity that *lilia* pits, otherwise so rare in the Roman world, should be discovered at Rough Castle only 10 km south of Bannockburn, where they were used with such devastating effect in 1314.

References

Sir George Macdonald, *The Roman Wall in Scotland* (2nd ed., Oxford, 1934), 217–38. R.C.A.H.M. *Stirlingshire* I (Edinburgh, 1963), 100–2 with plan. A.S. Robertson, *The Antonine Wall* (3rd ed. Glasgow, 1979). I. MacIvor *et al., Proc. Soc. Ant. Scotland* CX (1978–80), 230–85.

43 The Antonine Wall at Croy Hill, Strathclyde; looking W. NS 7477. GN 64: July 1951.

IV CROY HILL, Strathclyde (43)

The ditch of the Antonine Wall, a formidable military obstacle, is seen running up the centre of the picture. The turf structure of the Wall itself has here been flattened, but it stood to the left of the ditch; on the forward side of the ditch the low upcast mound of quarried material can be seen here and there. The small fort of Croy Hill stood at the little clump of trees left of the ditch in the middle distance. Beyond it the Wall continues to climb to the summit at 147 m (482 ft above Ordnance Datum) where there are two 'expansions' of the turf wall which are thought to have been intended as beacon platforms. From there the Wall descends sharply to the village of Croy in the distance. Beyond lies Bar Hill with its fort on the summit. The picture provides a good idea of the tactical position of the Wall on the forward slope of an east–west valley, possessing good command of ground and excellent views north.

Just this side of Croy Hill fort the diggers of the Roman ditch encountered an outcrop of very hard basalt, and there is a short stretch of 25 m, visible to the right of the trees, where the ditch was never dug. On the low knoll 90 m beyond the fort stood a fortlet now recognised as one of a regular series (like the Milecastles of Hadrian's Wall); these, together with a few widely spaced large forts, constituted the first design of the Antonine Wall. Later, the fortlets were abandoned and occasional small forts, of which Croy Hill is an example, were inserted in the gaps between the large ones. The well-known small military enclosure underlying Croy Hill fort can now be explained as the construction camp of the builders of the original fortlet.

References

Sir George Macdonald, *The Roman Wall in Scotland* (Oxford, 1934), 141ff., 258ff. A.S. Robertson, *The Antonine Wall* (3rd ed., Glasgow, 1979), 64–9. Ordnance Survey 1:25000 Map, *The Antonine Wall, Britannia* IX (1978), 413–15 with plan of fort and fortlet.

44 **Richborough** (*Rutupiae*), **Kent; Saxon Shore** fort, looking S. TR 3260. SU 28: June 1956.

COASTAL DEFENCE

I RICHBOROUGH, Kent (44)

The site stands on a bluff above the west side of the river Stour, at a height of *c.* 16 m, the highest ground for several kilometres in any direction. The river now meanders in complicated fashion as far south as Sandwich, before turning north to its mouth in Pegwell Bay. Over the centuries there have been very considerable changes in the coastline, and some 3 km of sand and gravel flats now separate Richborough from the sea. In Roman times, Thanet may well have been all but an island with an arm of the sea extending westwards where the Stour now flows: the coastal configuration farther south may have ensured that Richborough was a reasonably sheltered harbour. The photograph illustrates an important Roman monument of many periods, maintained under state guardianship after extensive excavations between 1922 and 1938.

In historical sequence the features visible are:

(1) Right centre within fort wall: a short length of double ditch crossed by a causeway: this is part of the base created by the invading army of

Claudius in A.D. 43. The defensive system, which runs for 640 m north–south, defended a promontory of considerable size but now greatly reduced by erosion. The ditches have never shown as crop-marks even outside the later fort, presumably because they were soon packed with demolished rampart material and are now deeply buried.

(2) Immediately beyond the cruciform structure on its large rectangular base the outline of two timber granaries, each *c.* 37.5 by 8 m, are marked. These belonged to the military supply base maintained here from *c.* 44 to 85. At least eleven of these large store buildings existed. Just inside the gate of the stone fort another contemporary timber-framed building has been similarly marked out. It was 16.75 m long by *c.* 8 m wide and had an open front to the south; it may have been a shop.

(3) The cruciform foundation on a rectangular concrete base. This is all that remains of a great triumphal monument in the form of a four-way arch which was erected *c.* 85–90 when the stores depot was given up. The monument,

78

which may have attained a height of *c.* 26 m, stood at the head of Watling Street (the road to London) at the entry to Britain, and presumably commemorated the conquest. The cruciform arms are the roadways through the arch; the structure itself rested on four piers now robbed from the angles. The piers were carried on the great concrete foundation which is 38.4 m long by 24.7 m wide, and 9 m deep.

(4) Inside the north-west corner of the triple ditches and partly cut by them is a masonry building of the second century. It originally consisted of three attached shops with a colonnaded portico in front on the south side; only the most easterly shop now survives. There was a very large front room and two parallel wings behind, one containing two, and the other three rooms. At about the same time the masonry building in the north-east corner of the later stone fort (bottom left) was erected. Although mostly lost to erosion, enough remains to establish a large courtyard building which replaced a succession of earlier similar buildings going back to the middle of the first century. The building is clearly an official one, and sufficiently important for the ditch system of the earth fortlet to have been modified to respect it; a *mansio* or rest-house of the public post, in which official travellers could be accommodated, is the most likely identification.

(5) The triple ditches of the mid-third-century earth fortlet which enclosed only half a hectare, immediately surrounding the great monumental arch, which it served to protect. The summit must have commanded a wide view, forming an invaluable look-out. The question whether the structure incorporated a beacon or other aid to navigation cannot now be answered, but this is likely enough. This was just the time when the menace of Saxon piracy was beginning to become serious. The *mansio* was retained in use.

(6) The large (2.43 ha) stone-walled fort of the Saxon Shore, erected *c.* 280–90. The ditches and rampart of the small earth fortlet were levelled and the monumental arch demolished; the concrete platform was occupied by the Headquarters Building (*principia*) of the new fort. The outside wall of the building can be seen near the edge of the platform. The fort had a stone wall *c.* 3.35 m thick, which still stands in places to a height of 7.6 m and was provided with projecting rectangular towers, one of which on the north side (foreground) covers an angled postern. The main gate faced Watling Street on the west side; whether or not there were other gates is unknown. The whole of the east side of the fort, facing the presumed site of the harbour, has been eroded, and fallen pieces of wall can be seen beside the railway line in the left foreground. Outside, there were two large ditches except on the west side where for a short length three were cut (one of them presumably on a mistaken line and soon filled in).

Within the fort, the *mansio* was demolished and a small bath-building was erected on its site; this is visible in the middle of the *mansio*, resting at a higher level. A building that looks in plan like a small classical temple can be seen facing the south-west corner of the *principia*, and a second larger one partly overlies the Claudian ditches; these may have been *scholae* or buildings for military religious guilds. Few traces of barracks were recovered; they appear to have been in timber, possibly laid directly on the contemporary surface, and to have been separated by spreads of gravel. Near the north wall and towards the north-west corner of the fort (invisible on the photograph) is a tile-built basin which is thought to be the baptistery of a Christian church built of timber in the fifth century. The site of a later church, of the Anglo-Saxon and subsequent periods, can be seen at the north-east corner of the earth fortlet.

References

B.W. Cunliffe, *Fifth Report on the Excavations at Richborough, Kent*, (Oxford, 1968). S. Johnson, *The Roman Forts of the Saxon Shore* (London, 1976), 48–51.

II PORTCHESTER CASTLE, Hampshire (45)

Portchester Castle (probably the *Portus Adurni* of the Notitia Dignitatum) is a fort of the Saxon Shore situated at the head of Portsmouth harbour, where its low-lying position on the very strand shows that the garrison was intimately concerned with naval strategy and with the command of this almost land-locked harbour. A fleet based there could control the Solent, with the approaches to the Isle of Wight and to the great inlet of Southampton Water. The continuing importance of the position is attested by the Norman castle built by Henry I in the north-west corner of the fort; the castle was much altered in the time of Richard II to serve as a royal residence, and under Henry V it became a base for the Agincourt campaign.

Outside the fort, behind and to right of the keep, can be seen a curving earthwork; once thought to be of Iron Age origin, it has been shown by excavation to be post-Roman and almost certainly of the fourteenth century. The

45 Portchester Castle, Hampshire; Saxon Shore fort, looking NW. SU 625046. AR 7: June 1948.

walls of the fort itself, enclosing 3.34 ha (8.25 acres), and their hollow U-shaped external towers, are of late third-century date although much patched or reconstructed in medieval times. The church in the south-east corner is all that remains of a house of Augustinian Canons founded in 1133.

The evidence suggests that this Saxon Shore fort was an addition to those of the system grouped at the Straits of Dover, and that it was constructed by Carausius, who had made himself Emperor in Britain in 286. A fleet based here could intercept northern sea-raiders who had broken through the cordon in the Straits, while also undertaking the local defensive tasks already outlined; military units also housed within the fort could round up enemy forces whenever they landed. A short break in the occupation in the 290s, suggested by the evidence of coins, might have been occasioned by a redistribution of forces by Carausius when the loss of his continental territories had dislocated the strategy of concerted naval measures from both sides of the Channel.

As a result, a naval squadron at Portchester might no longer have been thought vital. However, the local aspect of defence must still have been pressing, and it is more probable that the cause was the destruction of the garrison in the struggle between Allectus and Asclepiodotus in 296. Whatever the reason, the fort was reoccupied soon afterwards and continued in occupation until the early fifth century with some reorganisation occurring about 340. That the interior contained no masonry buildings may seem surprising. Accommodation was provided in timber structures raised up on sill-beams resting on the surface; subsequent disturbance has rendered them very difficult to recognise in excavation. During the middle of the fifth century Saxon settlers took over the place, and it remained a centre of settlement thereafter, becoming a *burh* in the early tenth century as part of defensive measures taken by Edward the Elder against renewed sea-borne raids.

Even after the medieval castle had become outmoded as a centre of power, the site continued in sporadic official use. In the early sixteenth

46 Brancaster, Norfolk; Saxon Shore fort (*Branodunum*), vertical photograph, N at top. TF 7844. K17-AM 64: June 1976. Scale 1:4100.

century a huge buttressed naval store-house, 72 m long, was constructed in the left-hand quarter of the enclosure; in dry seasons its plan is clearly visible as a parch-mark in the turf. Later, in the seventeenth, eighteenth and early nineteenth centuries the site was used as a prisoner-of-war camp.

Portchester is one of the best surviving examples of the Saxon Shore forts and gives an excellent impression of the changes in design introduced in Roman military architecture after the disasters of the middle of the third century. Much more emphasis is laid on the defensive capacity of the curtain, which was 3.05 m (10 ft) thick and at least 6.1 m (20 ft) high; and the projecting towers provide a good field of fire for the catapults mounted in them. Only two major gates were provided; the north and south walls are pierced solely by posterns.

References

B.W. Cunliffe, *Excavations at Portchester Castle* I (London, 1975), excavation report, Roman; II (1976), Saxon; III

(1977), medieval. A.L.F. Rivet and C. Smith, *The Place-Names of Roman Britain* (London, 1979), 441–2. O.G.S. Crawford, *Antiquity* XII (1938), 478–9 with Pl. I (oblique view looking NE showing site of naval store-house).

III BRANCASTER, Norfolk (*Branodunum*) (46)

The third-century fort which occupies the centre of the photograph is visible on the ground as a raised platform *c*. 175 m square. The defences, consisting of a wall backed by a rampart, are now levelled: their remains have helped to retain a considerable depth of soil over the interior, thus accounting for the dark tone on the photograph. Ramparts are not often found in late Roman forts of this type, and the presence of one here, together with the absence of projecting towers, probably indicates that the fort, like that at Reculver, was earlier than the main series. The gates, however, lie at the centres of their respective sides, a feature of late Roman castrametation.

The fort, of some 2.55 ha, is surrounded by a wide hollow, but indications on the photograph

47 Scarborough (Castle Hill), North Yorkshire; Roman signal-tower, looking NE. TA 052892. BTB 6: June 1975.

suggest that this masks more than one ditch. Within the ditch system is seen the prominent light-toned band of the rampart, in front of which the position of the wall, which has been largely robbed of stone, is visible here and there as a narrow dark line. The rampart is interrupted by four breaks, *c.* 12 m wide, for gates, but the gate-houses themselves have been robbed of their masonry.

Near the centre of the south half of the fort is seen the Headquarters Building (*principia*) with its courtyard, cross-hall (*basilica*) and apsed shrine (*aedes*). The position of this building shows that the fort faced north towards the sea. Other substantial buildings can be seen in the north-east quarter of the fort.

North of the west half of the fort can be seen the narrow double ditches of a rectangular enclosure with rounded corners; this has been taken for an earlier fort, but its low-lying and inconvenient position, together with the absence of a causeway across the south ditches, throws doubt on the identification.

To the east of the fort the course of an approach road from the south can be traced by the dark lines of its side-ditches *c.* 10 m apart. It is intersected by the modern A 149 road, and continues towards the top of the photograph. North of the modern road, the Roman road is joined and crossed at right angles by a wider road not so regularly laid out, and a rectangle is defined by a parallel field-road that extends east for *c.* 120 m from near the north-east corner of the fort. However, the impression of a regular layout is belied since this field-road diverges to the north-east and then bifurcates. Many small ditched closes can be seen around these roads to east of the fort, and further south as well. A similar system, not visible on this photograph, covers the area west of the fort, and has been sampled by excavation. Timber buildings were found there and the earliest occupation was of second-century date, before the fort came into existence. The fort, which is not exactly aligned to the east–west road, appears to have obliterated the road in part, and must thus be later. The enclosures, extending over *c.* 23 ha, suggest that a prosperous settlement had developed, probably in connection with a harbour that may later have served the fleet.

Two tiles bearing the stamp of *cohors I Aquitanorum* have been found west of the fort, where they had been reused; in the *Notitia Dignitatum* the garrison is listed as the *Equites Dalmatarum*.

References

J.K. StJoseph, *Antiq. Journ.* XVI (1936), 444ff. (excavations); *J.R.S.* LXVII (1977), 157–8 with Pl. XVII (vertical). D.A. Edwards, *East Anglian Archaeology* II (1976), 258–9, Fig. 69 (plan), Pls. XXI–XXV. S. Johnson, *The Roman Forts of the Saxon Shore* (London, 1976), 34–37 with Fig. 21 (oblique). D.A. Edwards and C.J.S. Green in D.E. Johnston (ed.), *The Saxon Shore* (C.B.A. Research Report No. 18, London 1977), 21–9 with plan and six aerial photographs.

IV SCARBOROUGH (CASTLE HILL), North Yorkshire (47)

About the year 370 a number of signal-towers were built on high headlands along the Yorkshire coast with a view over large bays. Their provision is thought to be part of the measures taken by Count Theodosius to re-establish and strengthen Roman power in Britain, after the serious troubles of 367. Much of the province had been overrun by barbarian raiders, many of whom were Picts from the North who by taking to the seaways had found a method of bypassing Hadrian's Wall. Increased coastal defence was a necessity.

Erosion of the cliffs has damaged several of the towers; at Scarborough some three-quarters of the site survives, but the Roman remains are partly obscured by the foundations of a late Saxon chapel and by structures forming part of the medieval castle. The Roman tower, built at about 77 m above sea-level, was surrounded by a ditch 5.8 m wide which is crossed on the west side by a causeway: in the photograph the ditch on the north side is invisible because unexcavated. A berm 9.14 m wide separated the ditch from a perimeter-wall which has small projecting semicircular towers at the corners and a single entrance facing the causeway. Though only 1.37 m thick above its foundation, this wall could have been made properly defensible by a wooden fighting-platform supported on brackets. The wall enclosed a courtyard 29 m square, in the centre of which rose a large tower 15.24 m (50 ft) square at the base though reduced by successive offsets as it rose. The upper part of the wall was *c.* 1.67 m thick, and the building contained two rows of three stone bases apparently to carry timber pillars supporting the first (and probably further) floors. A seventh and central base may have been designed to support a staircase. The bases are invisible on the photograph. It is usually supposed that the structure was strong enough to rise to a height of 30 m, which would provide a greatly extended view as well as command of the outer defences including the bottom of the ditch. Such a tower could not, of course, contain a garrison sufficiently strong to oppose a landing in force, but there would certainly be sufficient accommodation within the tower for a unit large enough to defend its own walls. Among the purposes of such stations would be the early sighting of the approach of raiders and the provision of adequate warning and shelter to the local population; but it is also probable that they formed part of a wider system whereby news of the course and size of hostile fleets could be passed on to naval or mobile land forces in time for them to intercept or oppose a landing. This conclusion seems all the more likely when we reflect upon the somewhat barren nature of the immediate hinterland of the towers, which can hardly have supported a large population: some connection between the known series of towers and the estuary of the Humber is very probable, but the evidence is likely to have been lost by coast erosion.

There are considerable similarities between the Yorkshire towers and contemporary *burgi* along the Danube frontier in Hungary, some of which possess internal pillars and a perimeter wall (though lacking angle-towers); an even closer parallel is the *burgus* at Asperden in Lower Germany, also of the reign of Valentinian I, which lies behind the actual frontier. It is probable that some of these *burgi* served to protect stores of corn in addition to their other functions. A somewhat obscure building-inscription from the tower at Ravenscar seems to refer to the two elements of the structure as *turris* (tower) and *castrum* (fort) respectively, and does not use the term *burgus* although this is widely attested on the continent.

There is evidence that some at least of the Yorkshire towers continued in service to the end of the fourth century or a little later, and two have yielded human bones in contexts which suggest violent death at the hands of attackers.

References

R.G. Collingwood in A. Rowntree, *The History of Scarborough* (London, 1931), 40–50 with Fig. 20 (photograph) and Fig. 30 (plan). W. Hornsey and J.D. Laverick, *Arch. Journ.* LXXXIX (1933), 206 (plan) in excavation report of similar tower at Goldsborough. Asperden: *J.R.S.* LIX (1969), 185; *J.R.S.* LXI (1971), 196 (comparative plans). Ravenscar inscription: *R.I.B.* 721, R.G. Goodchild, *Antiq. Journ.* XXXII (1952), 185.

7

FORTS OF THE AUXILIARIES

As with legionary sites so with the forts of the *auxilia* Britain is rich, not only in the mere number of examples which are present but also in their variety and degree of preservation.

Organisation

The auxiliaries differed from legionaries in lacking Roman citizenship, a benefit normally awarded them only at the end of service; but they also had a different organisation. Three types of unit were raised from among those warlike groups of provincials who supplied auxiliary troops; these consisted of cohorts of infantry (*cohortes peditatae*) or of infantry with a mounted contingent (*cohortes equitatae*) and *alae* of cavalry. For most of the first century all three types of regiment had a nominal strength of 500 (they are termed quingenary units); but during the Flavian period some units were doubled to milliary strength, and both then and later new units were sometimes enlisted at this larger size. The actual strength in all types of unit was, however, rather less than the nominal.

A quingenary cohort of infantry consisted of six centuries, but as the centuries, like those in the legions, probably contained only 80 men, the total complement was only 480 (excluding officers) rather than 500. An equitate cohort had four troops (*turmae*) of horsemen in addition to its six centuries. Milliary cohorts were not exactly double this strength; they had ten centuries of infantry, to which eight *turmae* were added in *cohortes milliariae equitatae*. A quingenary *ala* had 16, and a milliary *ala* 24 *turmae*. The *turma* was considerably smaller than the century – probably only 30–32 men – so that two *turmae* were normally assigned to a single barrack. Milliary *alae* always remained rare; Britain had only one, a unit which had been enlarged to this size early in the second century.

Auxiliary soldiers were normally expected to serve for 25 years, after which they were granted honourable discharge and a bronze diploma attesting their award of citizenship. The total numbers of auxiliaries at least equalled the total of legionaries. Although in time of war they often served alongside the legions, in peacetime they soon came to be stationed separately in their own forts, in scattered garrisons along the frontiers or along the roads behind them. Occasionally it can be proved, particularly in the first century, that where garrisons of exceptional strength were needed, two or more auxiliary units or parts of units could be placed in the same large fort. Examples of large forts which must have contained mixed or multiple garrisons are Baylham House (51) and Dalswinton (74). Hod Hill (48) had a garrison of both infantry and cavalry. Conversely some small forts, as for instance on the Antonine Wall and at Crawford (10), housed only part of a cohort or *ala*, which was divided between two or more stations. Very occasionally a detachment of legionaries and an auxiliary unit would garrison the same fort together; but this was probably not often done, because the legionaries were too valuable to be dissipated in small groups, and in any case differences in the scales of pay might make for discord. Newstead in one of its periods furnishes an example, as possibly also does Hod Hill.

Some auxiliary units, particularly the archers, remained expert in their national weapons; but for the majority it was probably only slowly during the first century that specific equipment differing from that of the legionaries became normal. Although the high standards of legionary training and achievement were not expected of them, the auxiliaries nevertheless steadily developed their efficiency and reliability; Agricola at Mons Graupius could hold back his legions and win the battle with his *auxilia*; earlier still, in 47, Ostorius Scapula had defeated the Iceni with a force of auxiliaries.

Of lower status than the auxiliaries there had always existed forces of allies and of tribal levies which could be called to the assistance of Roman armies in time of war. Towards the end of the first century some of these were organised on a more regular basis and were known as *numeri* (at first a colloquial term descriptive of any small force). These new units could be used for some of the routine tasks formerly undertaken by auxiliaries, where only small numbers of men were required. On the Upper German frontier *numeri* of Britons are known; they occupied forts of only 0.6 ha (1.5 acres), in which the accommodation suggests a complement of 120–130 men. At a later date somewhat larger *numeri* came into being there. In Britain no *numerus* is actually attested before the third century, but their size would have been ideal for garrisoning some of the small forts which otherwise must have been held by detachments of auxiliaries. After the reign of Severus, various evidently small *numeri* of *exploratores* (scouts), Raetian javelin-men and German light-armed troops joined the auxiliary garrisons of some forts on the frontier; but how they were accommodated is unknown.

Fort sizes

The amount of accommodation required by each type of auxiliary unit naturally varied, and this fact is reflected in the sizes of their forts. Thus quingenary cohorts of infantry are often found in forts of 1.2–1.4 ha (3–3.5 acres), while quingenary *alae* and milliary cohorts have forts of 2–2.56 ha (5–5.6 acres), although garrisons of milliary size could sometimes be given forts of only 1.7–1.8 ha (4.2–4.5 acres).

It is thus theoretically possible, by a consideration of the defended area, to form some estimate of the size, if not always the type, of unit in garrison even where no epigraphic evidence exists. For this purpose undoubtedly the most informative measurement is that of the internal area – that part of a fort actually occupied by the accommodation; for ramparts and perimeter streets vary very much in width. However, so many forts remain unexcavated, and therefore unable to yield the required detail, that it is more convenient to remain content with the second best and to work from the dimensions most readily acquired, rather than to refrain from attempting estimates because so few internal areas are known. For this reason fort areas quoted are based on overall measurements from rampart-front to rampart-front, or wall-front to wall-front. There are other factors also which show that only rough-and-ready results can be expected from this type of calculation. Very few forts have been completely uncovered, so as to show the accommodation in its entirety and in full detail; of those which have been, a surprising number reveal some anomaly of garrison, such as either too few or too many barracks for any particular type of unit. Detachments seem often to have been outposted on other duties. Nevertheless even approximate estimates of numbers can be very useful.

A further curious fact is that such forts in Britain as can certainly be assigned to the various types of unit are consistently smaller, by *c.* 30%, than their counterparts in Roman Germany. The contrast illustrates the differing traditions of practice which developed in provincial armies, and shows that there was no overall standardisation laid down by central authority.

Location

In his account of Agricola's first northward campaign, Tacitus tells of native states being enclosed with garrisons and forts (*multae civitates . . . praesidiis castellisque circumdatae*, Agricola 20). This system of cordon control, in which movement was controlled by means of strong-points connected by roads which could be patrolled, had already proved effective in Wales, and it explains the observed distribution pattern. Forts tended to lie 19–29 km (12–18 miles) – a day's march – apart; only on frontiers was there normally a closer spacing (p. 58). They were almost always close to a road, but only exceptionally does the road actually traverse the fort. They often lay close to rivers, where they were assured a water supply and could protect a bridge. In mountainous country they were often placed where several valleys meet, so that observation could be maintained in more than one direction. Unlike prehistoric fortifications, they were seldom placed (as at Hod Hill, 49) on really high ground; but a good tactical position was almost always chosen, often on a slight eminence overlooking lower ground between the fort and the hills (10). Something of the contemporary environment can often be deduced from observations of this sort.

Ground-plan

The layout of a fort was that of a fortress in miniature. At the centre lay the *principia* (Headquarters Building), flanked by the *praetorium* (commander's house) and the granaries (*horrea*) (34); some forts also had a hospital. The *via principalis* ran across the fort from gate to gate in front of these buildings, and was met on the axis of the *principia* by the *via praetoria* leading to the main gate and flanked by barracks. Behind the *principia* the *via decumana* ran to the back gate, and it too was flanked by barracks. Many of these elements can be seen in the photographs which follow. The shape of the barracks tended to evolve with time; from the Antonine period the space occupied in earlier barracks by the verandah fronting the men's *contubernia* was often absorbed into these quarters; and in the fourth century, at least on Hadrian's Wall, a new type of barrack, divided into free-standing 'chalets', makes its appearance (34).

Within this general form individual forts show considerable minor variations of arrangement, and extra buildings for workshops and stables are to be expected. A fort is said to 'face' down its *via praetoria*; in theory this direction should be either eastwards or towards the enemy; in practice it was normally the direction of the most significant topographical feature, whether that was an approach road, a river-crossing or even a port.

The ditch system

The fort was protected by ditches, regularly cut and curving carefully at the angles, but of no outstanding width or depth. The usual number of ditches is 2–3; some forts possess more numerous ditches (e.g. Whitley Castle (70) or Ardoch (79)), but the extra ones are often accounted for by the defences having been redesigned or by special local conditions (e.g. on the west side of Whitley Castle (70), where the neighbouring hill approaches close). At some forts, for instance Glenlochar (76), Newstead or Strageath, evidence has been obtained for reinforcement of the ditch system by such 'obstacles' as dry thorn barricades or wooden fences. Caesar (*B.G.* VII, 73) describes how sharpened stakes, nicknamed *cippi* ('grave-stones'), were fixed in the bottom of a ditch. In general the purpose of the ditches was to impede attack within killing-range of javelins hurled from the rampart. At two forts, Hod Hill (48) and Cawthorn Fort D (62), special skills were devoted to the creation of defensive zones of great subtlety. They were based on the conception of the Punic ditch (*fossa punica*) which rises more steeply on one side than on the other and is liable to cause a man in a hurry to miscalculate his leap; escape from the prepared zone is impeded.

Ramparts

The rampart during the first century was normally of turf. The front rose at an angle as steep as possible (often 65–70 degrees), while the back stood vertically for 1.2–1.5 m before taking a more gentle slope. Sometimes the rampart was wholly of turf, reinforced at horizontal intervals of a metre by layers of branches which held it together; sometimes only the front and back were of turf, material from the ditches being used in the core. When not used for this purpose the product of the ditches was neatly spread beyond them. Care had obviously to be taken over the technique of rampart construction: Livy (X, 5) tells of a rampart which fell forward into the ditch through the weight of those standing upon it. A valuable supplement to knowledge gained from careful excavation is provided by scenes on Trajan's Column showing turf ramparts actually under construction or newly finished; details seen there, such as timber merlons or the log corduroys forming the rampart-walk, would otherwise be matters only of inference.

Turf ramparts of these types are numerous in Britain but rare on the Continent, where the earth-and-timber kind was normal; this had vertical revetments of timber to retain the core. This difference, like that in relative size mentioned earlier, is a mark of diverging traditions; but some earth-and-timber ramparts do occur in Britain. The constant transfer of officers and even of units must have kept the army in Britain in touch with Continental developments. One of the reasons for the preferred use of turf in Britain was that so many of the forts were, like those depicted on Trajan's Column, constructed in the course of campaigns. Turf was readily available; timber in quantity would have taken time and effort to procure. Turf-work therefore became standard practice. On the Continent the majority of forts lie on frontiers where they could have been built at leisure.

Walls

The earliest example of a stone wall being added to a previous turf rampart in Britain is at the Inchtuthil fortress; but from Trajan's reign onwards stone walls were often – although by no means always – provided. As with town walls (p. 148), a rampart was always placed behind the wall even at forts where there had been no turf predecessor. The practice saved building a massive wall as well as providing solidity and facilitating arrangements for access to the wall-top. Only in the new coastal forts of the late third century (p. 60) was the practice discontinued.

Gates and towers

In turf forts gatehouses and towers were of timber. The principal gates had double portals normally flanked by towers; minor gates might be surmounted by a tower. Agricolan forts often had their gates set back, behind the incurving ends of the rampart: the ditches curved in to match. The Flavian fort at Strageath (80) had three gates of this sort, but in the later forts on the same site the design was changed. Inset gates of very similar type had existed at the Neronian fortress of Vetera in Lower Germany and were not an innovation; but together with other more experimental designs of gate they may illustrate Agricola's interest in the professional details of fort construction and his encouragement of new ideas – a suggestion which may find additional support in the unusual 'Stracathro-type' entrances at some contemporary marching-camps (p. 131). He was able to boast to his son-in-law that no fort of his had suffered capture or been forced to surrender.

Gateways of this inset type outflank the approach to the portals, and they merely improve on the design more normally found in timber gateways, where a forecourt is created by advancing the front of the towers. When stone gateways came to be built this design was far less frequently followed; many were built flush with the rampart. Stone gateways were less inflammable, and the army perhaps more confident. Only in forts of the late Roman period are gateways once again regularly protected by projecting towers.

It is not certain whether timber gate-towers were clad in planks or were left entirely unenclosed; scenes on Trajan's Column certainly suggest that open towers were normal. Yet planks would be required at least on one side of the ground floor to retain the turf of the rampart, and a completely enclosed ground floor might well have been thought necessary to shelter men on guard-duty from the rigours of the British climate. At Inchtuthil nails withdrawn from planks by a claw-hammer were found in a guard-chamber at the *porta principalis sinistra* and remains of a pile of planks in another at the *porta praetoria*. Burnt planking was also found near the *porta decumana* at Strageath (though this gate had no guard-chambers), while at Fendoch there were structural indications of an enclosed guard-chamber at the *porta principalis dextra*.

When rebuilding or reoccupation of a fort occurred, the site was not normally changed, especially when no alteration in area was called for, as at Strageath (80). When larger garrisons arrived at Dalswinton (74) and Whitley Castle (70) the original forts were merely extended, after throwing down one rampart. This was also done in one of the phases at Bainbridge (65). Sometimes, however, when a unit of a different size took the place of the original garrison, a new fort was built beside the old; at Greensforge (55) there was insufficient room to enlarge the existing fort; at Gelligaer (Glamorgan) a smaller fort in stone replaced the turf fort on a neighbouring site. But often, especially in Wales, a reduction in size was effected by excluding and slighting part of the old fort, as at Tomen-y-Mur (61).

Annexes

Many forts possess a fortified annexe, as at Ardoch, Bainbridge, Dalswinton and Strageath (79, 65, 74, 80). An annexe was always used for military purposes, such as the protection of stores, transport and workshops which it was inconvenient to place within a fort. A military bath-building might also be found in an annexe. Annexes did not, however, house civilian settlers. This conclusion is supported by the contrast shown on the two Walls. On the Antonine *limes* the forts are generously provided with annexes; the absence of annexes from forts on Hadrian's Wall is thought to be accounted for by the presence of the Vallum, which excluded civilians from the area and removed the need for individual annexes. At Bainbridge (65) the annexe was for a period incorporated into the fort, and later divided from it once more. At Llanfor (59) the large pre- or early Flavian fort is accompanied by a fortified enclosure standing a little apart, in which the foundation trenches of a large timber granary can be seen. Here the enclosure is better classified as an independent stores base than as an annexe; but the difference in purpose is perhaps not great.

Parade-grounds

Another feature which was probably once normal in the vicinity of a fort was the parade-ground (*campus*). Actual remains of these do not often survive. Their position can sometimes be deduced from the discovery of altars dedicated to Jupiter, as at Maryport (Cumbria) or Birdoswald; a new altar was dedicated annually, and at Maryport the old ones were buried, apparently on the edge of the parade-ground. All the more impressive is the visible parade-ground at Hardknott (66), where a large area (152 by 121 m) has been levelled on the mountainside and a tribunal constructed at one edge. Another parade-ground, 123 by 98 m, can be identified at Tomen-y-Mur (61). It has also been suggested that the old hill fort of Hod Hill (49) became an exercise area for the cavalry stationed in the Roman fort there. Dedications to the *Campestres*, goddesses of the training-ground, by cavalry units may furnish further clues to the location of these areas.

The training and drill which go to make a good unit are well suggested by remains of this sort, as also by the banked enclosures resembling miniature amphitheatres which survive at Tomen-y-Mur and perhaps at Forden Gaer (58); these may have been intended for weapon-training. Attention must also be drawn in this context to the practice camps discussed on p. 136.

Vici

In the course of time settlements of merchants and camp-followers (*vici*) grew up in the vicinity of forts, for soldiers, with their regular pay, offered an attractive market for goods and services. In southern Britain such settlements often developed into permanent towns or villages after the garrisons had moved on, but in Wales and the North the history of a *vicus* often seems to be much more intimately connected with the presence of the nearby garrison. *Vici* were not infrequently

48 Hod Hill, Dorset; Roman fort, looking S. Soil-marks. ST 854108. BZ 39: April 1949.

abandoned when a fort was evacuated, as if the garrison was the sole *raison d'être* of the settlement, even after a considerable period. There is evidence from inscriptions (*R.I.B.* 899, 1616, 1700; *J.R.S.* XLVII (1957), 229) that the inhabitants possessed a communal organisation with limited local powers of administration. Such 'military' *vici* are further discussed on p. 150.

Aerial photography has contributed much to the study of forts, not only by displaying their setting and state of preservation more comprehensively than even the best map can, but also by recording details of plan and construction to a degree only otherwise obtainable by large-scale excavation. But its special contribution has been the multiplication of discoveries. This can be best appreciated in the form of a table setting out the numbers of forts and fortlets in Wales and the North which were marked on successive editions of the Ordnance Survey *Map of Roman Britain* published in 1931, 1956 and 1978. Almost all the increases are sites discovered from the air.

	Wales and the Marches	North of Hadrian's Wall (excluding the Antonine Wall)	Total
1931	29	21	50
1956	29	45	74
1978	56	61	117

The total has more than doubled, and to these figures should be added the numerous military sites discovered since the Second World War in England south of Hadrian's Wall. It is an impressive achievement.

References

R.G. Collingwood and I.A. Richmond, *The Archaeology of Roman Britain* (London, 1969), Ch. III. V.E. Nash-Williams, *The Roman Frontier in Wales* (2nd ed. by M.G. Jarrett, Cardiff, 1969). D. Breeze and B. Dobson, *Hadrian's Wall* (London, 1976). M.J. Jones, *Roman Fort Defences to A.D. 117* (B.A.R. 21, Oxford, 1975). C. Cichorius, *Die Reliefs der Traianssäule* (Berlin, 1900). A.P. Gentry, *Roman Military Stone-built Granaries in Britain* (B.A.R. 32, Oxford, 1976).

Timber granaries: W.H. Manning, *Saalburg Jahrbuch* XXXII (1975), 105–29. Timber gateways: W.H. Manning and I.R. Scott, *Britannia* X (1979), 19–61. Cavalry training-grounds: R.W. Davies, *Arch. Journ.* CXXV (1968), 73–100.

HOD HILL, Dorset (48–9)

The Roman fort stands in the north-west corner of a large Iron Age hill fort of 22 ha (55 acres). The vast scale and traditional style of the native earthworks contrast instructively with the slighter but more scientifically designed Roman defences. Ploughing of the Roman fort began in the nine-teenth century, and many finds (now in the British Museum) came to light. These and dis-coveries made in the excavations of 1951–8 date the construction of the fort to the period of the Roman conquest of Dorset soon after A.D. 43, and show that it was held for only a very few years. The defences enclose 4 ha but of this area 0.4 ha was useless for building purposes, being taken up by a wide strip of Iron Age quarry-pits (seen very clearly in 49), from which material had been dug to heighten the prehistoric rampart. The space actually occupied by buildings extended over 1.82 ha (4.5 acres).

The two Roman sides of the fort's defences comprised a rampart of chalk and turf fronted by an elaborate ditch system designed to keep the hand-thrown missiles of an enemy at a distance, and to create a killing-zone within the range of Roman javelins once the outer ditch was crossed. Each of the causeways leading to the two main gates is – unusually in Roman permanent works – defended by a detached length of bank and ditch known as a *titulum*. These served to break up a rush on the wooden gates standing at the inner ends of the causeways, and to cause attackers to veer left or right, so exposing their unshielded flanks to Roman missiles. To the left of each gate-position a widening of the turf rampart is seen; these are thought to indicate ramps leading up to catapult platforms. A Roman arrow-firing catapult (*ballista*) had an effective range of *c.* 200 m, that is to say from the south gate as far as the hill fort rampart in the background of 48; and the two platforms are so placed as to fire at the unshielded right side of foes approaching the causeways.

The photograph (48) shows that both causeways are lined with double ditches which narrow the causeway as it nears the gate. This effect is not easy to appreciate quickly on the ground because of the workings of perspective; but it would result in the jostling into the side-ditches of the outer members of a tightly bunched attacking party.

The outer ditch lies some 27 m from the rampart, just within javelin-range, and the ditch is so shaped as to be easy to jump from outside but difficult to gauge for a leap in the reverse direction (*fossa Punica*). The spoil has been levelled over the interval, and the next ditch though only 2.25 m wide has a channel 45 cm deep at its base but less than a foot's length wide; a fall here could break an ankle.

Despite long-continued ploughing the street system of the fort is clearly visible (48) in the freshly ploughed soil. The fort lacks a regular back gate (*porta decumana*) though a small gate has been provided through the north-west corner of the Iron Age rampart in order to allow water-parties access to the river Stour at the bottom of the hill. The main range of buildings fills plots occupying the full available width behind the *via principalis* which runs north–south across the centre of the fort. The *via praetoria* joins this at right angles from the east. Thus the street plan is T-shaped; and although here this may be explained by the special topography, it does nevertheless seem to be an early feature, matched at the Claudian forts of Great Casterton, Lincolnshire and at Valkenburg in the Netherlands. The fort faces eastward towards the easiest approach route.

In the interior the outline of building-plots is visible in the soil. The central plot opposite the end of the *via praetoria* contained the Headquarters Building (*principia*) in front, and one of the two *praetoria* (commander's houses) of the double garrison immediately behind it. A broad white band outlines the site of the two buildings, but they cannot be distinguished individually. Thus this soil-mark and others like it do not represent collapsed wall material but rather the position of gaps or of access paths. It is not easy to match the marks on the photograph with the plan of the buildings as established by excavation. This has shown that on the near side the *principia* was flanked by six narrow stables *c.* 57–58 m long, and that beyond it lay six somewhat shorter barracks, also end-on to the street, with three transverse buildings behind them. The garrison contained both infantry and cavalry, but the theory that the former were legionaries is not now so secure as when first propounded. It was based on the types of armour and weapons found. But recent research suggests that in the middle of the first century there was as yet no clear differentiation between the equipment used by legionaries and that used by auxiliary infantry. Today, therefore, only the presence of *ballistae*, indicated both by the em-placements near the gates and by the discovery of typical projectile heads, remains to prove the presence of legionaries, for these catapults are not attested in the hands of auxiliaries before the third century. Possibly only a small specialist

49 Hod Hill; Roman fort, looking W. UM 91: April 1957.

group of legionaries was present to man the *ballistae*, the main infantry garrison consisting of a cohort of auxiliary infantry. This conclusion better suits the extremely cramped accommodation provided for the infantry, which is unparalleled on legionary sites.

We may be sure that it was immediate tactical and political considerations which placed the Roman garrison on the summit of this high hill (143.5 m, 471 ft) with its distant water supply. Roman forts normally lie in valleys. The river Stour, however, sweeps the base of the steep slope to the west (right), 100 m below. The latrine block stood just inside the south gate, and it is accordingly thought that its contents were taken to the river down the far slope, and that fresh water was brought up from further upstream by parties using the gate in the near right-hand corner. One water-storage tank was found.

A circular ditch partly overlain by the *via praetoria* presumably surrounded a Bronze Age burial-mound which occupied the summit of the hill until flattened by the Romans.

49 shows the relationship of the Roman fort to its Iron Age predecessor. The latter had two gateways; one, the West Gate, lies in the left background and gave access to the river; the other (the Steepleton Gate) lies in the foreground (extreme right) and faces the direction of easiest access. From the Steepleton Gate an Iron Age street leads into the foreground of the hill fort among a large number of hut-platforms, more of which survived in good preservation before wartime ploughing. Today only a triangular sector, distinguished on the left of the photograph by its slightly darker tone, remains unploughed. Some of these hut sites were excavated in 1951–8, and one proved to be of great interest because of the number of *ballista* bolts found in its remains. The position of these pointed to a remarkable accuracy of firing. The *ballista* itself had been fired from the south-east, presumably from just outside the defences in the left foreground of the photograph, and the close positioning of the missiles implies the use of a siege-tower overlooking the rampart. A tower over 15 m (50 ft) high would have been needed, but this would be well within the capacity of a legion to build, towers almost twice this height being attested, e.g. at Masada. There was no indication that the Steepleton Gate itself had

50 Stanway (Gosbeck's Farm), Essex; Roman fort, looking N. TL 963227. BXN 14: June 1976.

been burnt in an assault, so probably the hill fort surrendered once bombardment had driven the defenders from the ramparts.

After the forced evacuation of the native population, the Steepleton Gate continued to be used by the Romans; but it became choked with mud. A new access way (the 'Ashfield Gate', bottom centre) was therefore cut through the old ramparts, and causeways were inserted across the ditches outside and across the quarry-pit hollow within. An impression of neat economical engineering still remains.

The interior of the hill fort may now have become an area for exercise and manoeuvre by the Roman garrison; a harness-pendant belonging to the cavalry was found among the hut sites, at the point where it must have been lost, for the ground there has never been disturbed by ploughing.

References

J.R.S. XL (1950), Pl. VIII, 1 (our **48**). O.G.S. Crawford and A. Keiller, *Wessex from the Air* (Oxford, 1928), Pl. I (vertical). I.A. Richmond, *Hod Hill* II, *Excavations . . . between 1951 and 1958* (London, 1968). R.C.H.M., *Dorset* III Pt 2 (London, 1970), 263 with Pl. 198.

51 Baylham House (*Combretovium*), **Coddenham, Suffolk; Roman forts**, looking N. TM 114526. CMF 33: June 1980.

STANWAY (GOSBECK'S FARM) Essex (50)

The fort lies 500 m WNW of the temple at Gosbeck's Farm (136) some 4 km south-west of the fortress and *colonia* at Colchester. Its tardy discovery at such a well-known site underlines the value of repeated reconnaissance. The west side adjoins a curving hedge which follows one of the pre-Roman ramparts demarcating the Gosbeck's area, and this bank may well have been utilised as the western rampart of the fort, somewhat as the Roman fort on Hod Hill (49) exploited the defences of the hill fort in which it stood. The land around Gosbeck's Farm shows many crop-marks relating to the pre-Roman occupation, and this particular field is no exception. The fort itself is nearly square and covers 2.2 ha (5.5 acres). The south-east corner has been destroyed by a modern road, but the single ditch is clearly visible on three sides. Within and very close to it lies a palisade trench for the front of the rampart, and another *c.* 3–3.5 m away for its rear revetment, but these lines are too fine to show clearly on a printed reproduction. They indicate a box rampart, with vertical front and rear, of a type rare in Roman Britain although well-known on the Continent. Behind the rampart and close to it runs a line of pits, which extends round most of the perimeter.

52 Baylham House; Roman forts, looking SE. CMF 28: June 1980.

The north gate is represented by four post-holes, set two on either side of the causeway.

The *via principalis* running from north to south is demarcated by pits or large post-holes, and on its left at the centre of the fort faint traces of a timber Headquarters Building can be seen, with central courtyard and five rooms to the rear. There are indications also of the walls of barracks in the *praetentura* (right). It is noteworthy that as at Valkenburg I, in the Netherlands, there is no *via* or *porta decumana* behind the *principia*, and that the street plan is a simple T. This is a characteristic of other pre-Flavian forts such as Great Casterton and Hod Hill.

The fort has not been dated by excavation, but its position, facing the native sanctuary and distant from the *colonia*, suggests a date of 43 or soon after. A garrison sent to protect the colony either in 49 on its foundation or in 61 after its temporary eclipse would surely have been located nearer at hand. The siting of the fort strongly suggests concern with the native centre from which the legionary fortress, even if it had troops to spare during a time of active campaigning, was somewhat remote. How long the fort continued to be held after the establishment of the fortress is another unanswered question.

References

D.R. Wilson, *Britannia* VIII (1977), 185–7 with Pl. XIII (this view). P Crummy, *ibid.*, 88, map showing location. J.K. StJoseph, *J.R.S.* LXVII (1977), 126–7 with plan. Timber-faced ramparts: M.J. Jones, *Roman Fort Defences to A.D. 117* B.A.R. 21 (Oxford, 1975), 82–3.

BAYLHAM HOUSE, Suffolk (51–2)

Combretovium, in the valley of the small river Gipping 10 km NNW of Ipswich, was an extensive settlement on the Roman road from Colchester to Caistor by Norwich, at a point where branch roads lead westwards towards Cambridge and north-eastwards towards the coast. The civilian settlement lies north of the area shown in 51 and 52, just beyond the top of 51. The comparatively narrow floor of the valley is composed of gravel, and photographs, taken in a spring drought, show with exceptional clarity in the parched meadow grass the greater part of the ditch systems of two Roman forts. The site had been discovered some years before by Mr R.H. Farrands. The photographs show not only the two forts, both of substantial size, but also the course of the Colchester–Caistor road as it continues northwards up the valley from the crossing of the river. The road runs through both forts, a fact which suggests an early date for each, at a time when long-distance movement was largely confined to military traffic.

In 51 the old and new courses of the modern A 140 Ipswich-to-Norwich road appear at the top right-hand corner. The large fort lies in the centre of the picture; its north side, marked by the dark lines of triple ditches, can be seen just below the second hedge from the top of the photograph. Near a large isolated tree the ditches turn south at a well-rounded angle and can be traced across the field as far as a thick hedge. The west side is largely obscured, but the curve of the inner ditch at the north-west angle is visible near the corner of the same field, and the line of the western defences continued below the outbuildings and garden of Baylham House. The smaller fort lies inside the larger and has four ditches; these show on both photographs more faintly. The north side runs from the most northerly outbuilding of Baylham House to a rounded north-east angle, with the east side lying half-way between Baylham House itself and the east side of the large fort. Ditches curving from the south-west corner can be seen south of the house, and since there appear to be four ditches at the angle they probably relate to the smaller fort. Where then is the south side of the large fort? If it too was in line with the four ditches, and the lie of the land precludes a course much further south, may we deduce that the smaller fort is later than the larger, and made use of parts of two pre-existing sides? The behaviour of the roads suggests the opposite, namely that the large fort is an extension of the small one.

The principal line of road extending right across 51 follows a curiously sinuous course, as if the line were determined by pre-existing features. The course so clearly visible now may not, indeed, everywhere be the original line. From the south the road bends slightly to cross the quadruple ditch system, presumably at a gate, and then runs straight through the small fort, beyond which it bends north-east and forks; the western (left) branch continues obliquely through the gate of the large fort, but the right-hand road is cut by the fort's ditches and had clearly become obsolete when they were dug. The smaller fort would therefore seem to be the earlier; it has an area of 2.1 ha (5.3 acres). The larger fort is about 5.8 ha (14.5 acres) in size and may perhaps be recognised as a small vexillation fortress. A context in the aftermath of the Boudiccan rebellion might be suggested, as at Ixworth (53); if so, the smaller fort would belong to the Claudian period and its fate during the rebellion would be interesting to establish. Whatever the sequence, few Roman permanent military works of the period of the Conquest are known in East Anglia, and the remains at Baylham House are an important addition to their number.

References

Proc. Suffolk Inst. of Arch. XXVII (1958), 179; XXVIII (1961), 91. R.H. Farrands, Colchester Arch. Group, *Annual Bulletin* No. 20 (1977) with map; *ibid.* No. 21 (1978), 2–3.

IXWORTH, Suffolk (53)

Triple ditches are clearly visible defining the south angle and the greater part of the two adjacent sides of a large Roman fort, south of a small tributary of the Little Ouse 9.5 km north-east of Bury St Edmunds. Two of the three ditches of the north-east side can just be distinguished across the top of an oblong meadow to right of some large sheds and below a white rectangle surrounding a swimming-pool. The ditches on the south-east are interrupted at a gate which from its position must be the *porta principalis sinistra*. The photograph suggests that the western ditch system is close to, if not beneath, the main A 143 road (left). Thus the fort measures *c.* 193 by 215 m (630 by 710 ft) within the ditches and covers 4.0 ha (10.0 acres).

Parch-marks indicating streets, pits and ditches suggest that the fort is overlaid by a civilian settlement that extends some distance to the east. One street enters at the site of the *porta praetoria* (bottom) but seems partly to override the ditches there; within, it makes a junction with the street from the other gate-position before veering off to the north. Faint traces of what may be the

53 Ixworth, Suffolk; Roman fort, vertical photograph (N at top left corner). TL 931698. K17-AL 119: June 1976. Scale 1:2900.

original streets of the fort can be seen near this junction. The street which leaves the right-hand gate soon bends northwards before being destroyed by a recent quarry for sand. Beyond this disturbance there is a junction with a second road running obliquely as if to pass the east corner of the fort's ditch system; on either side of this road regularly disposed ditches of small contemporary fields may be recognised. The fort is of unknown date, but was probably constructed as part of the measures to control the Iceni after the rebellion of Boudicca in A.D. 61. The civilian settlement may owe its existence to an important local pottery industry.

References

J.K. StJoseph, *J.R.S.* XLIII (1953), 82; *J.R.S.* LIX (1969), 127–8 with Pl. II, 2 (oblique view of S field); *J.R.S.* LXVII (1977), 128 with Pl. XVI, 1 (this view).

KIRMINGTON, South Humberside (54)

The site, in the Wolds of north Lincolnshire, is strategically well-placed in the mouth of a gap

which is still an important route for traffic moving east and west across the Wolds. The photograph suggests at least two successive phases of occupation. The dark lines of the substantial double ditches and rounded corners of what appears to be a large Roman fort of *c.* 3.4 ha (8.5 acres) extend southwards (left) beneath the perimeter track of a wartime airfield, which just enters the left margin of the picture. This fort is overlain by a number of metalled roads showing as lines of parching and associated with a native Romano-British settlement attested by pottery finds. There are also a number of ditched drove-ways together with closes defined by smaller ditches, which extend widely both inside and outside the defences. Whether these, or some of them, precede the fortification is not clear, but Iron Age pottery has been recovered from the surface. Traces of two rectangular buildings can be seen near the right margin.

In its irregularity of plan, the settlement, which extends over an area at least 450 by 450 m, closely resembles the Romano-British settlements in the Fenland (see Holbeach, **132**), and the supersession

54 Kirmington, South Humberside; Roman fort and settlement, looking W. TA 057113. BZM 72: July 1976.

of a military site by a civilian settlement can be paralleled at Ixworth (53).

References

D.N. Riley, *Britannia* VIII (1977), 189–91 with partial plan and Pl. XIVA (oblique looking NE). J.K. StJoseph, *J.R.S.* LXVII (1977), 138–9 with Pl. XVI, 2 (oblique looking SE).

GREENSFORGE, Staffordshire (55)

Greensforge, lying south-west of Wolverhampton and some 23 km south of the Watling Street, on a Roman road connecting Gloucester and Worcester with Kinvaston, was clearly an important military centre on the western front in the middle of the first century A.D., as a group of large marching-camps in the vicinity bears witness. The core of the site is a low promontory narrowing to the south between the river Stour on the west and a minor tributary. Here a small marching-camp of only 0.33 ha and the rounded corner of another (of which the rest has presumably been ploughed out) seem to be among the earliest features; however, the more extensive remains are those of two forts (Fig. 11). The first lies in the dark field on the left and only at the north-east corner do its two ditches cross the road. The second, also having two ditches, is larger and occupies the centre left of the picture. There is an attached annexe on the east. The rampart of this fort is known to be built of gravelly subsoil between turf cheeks. That both forts were held at the same

55 Greensforge, Staffordshire; Roman military earthworks, looking NNW. SO 864886. ABR 31: June 1960.

time is hardly conceivable.

The first fort, with an area of 1.6 ha (4.0 acres), is of a size appropriate for a cohort of infantry 500 strong, and it occupies the tactically strongest part of the peninsula, being additionally protected both by two broad overlapping ditches (to right of the road in the foreground) and by a second ditch of two straight lengths, some 45 m further out, which cuts off the end of the promontory. At a later date a decision was evidently reached to increase the garrison at Greensforge, but there was no room to enlarge this fort. A bigger fort, now of 2.2 ha (5.54 acres), was accordingly constructed on more spacious ground outside the original perimeter. This fort is of a size suitable for an *ala* of cavalry or possibly a mixed force of more than one unit of auxiliary infantry.

This suggested sequence explains the observed facts. If the larger fort had been the earlier, it could have been reduced in size in the normal manner with far less labour than was demanded by the construction of a whole new fort. Both forts are of early date; the larger one has yielded a sherd of Claudian samian. By the sixties at the latest the army will have moved on to new positions nearer Wales.

By the time the second fort had been built there had been opportunity to construct a road to it; roadside ditches approaching this fort have been recorded on photographs of the fields beyond the far edge of our plate. The overlapping earthwork outside the smaller fort is a rare feature, found in Britain at a few pre-Flavian and Flavian forts (Canon Frome, Llwyn-y-Brain, Newton on Trent, Rhyn, Castledykes). Here its design can be criticised for allowing an attacker to present his shielded side to the rampart; but the gap is almost 20 m away from the fort gate, a distance approaching extreme missile range, and the advantage of barring a direct rush down the level plateau was no doubt thought preponderant, and preferable to the more orthodox arrangement of such ditches.

56 Buckton, near Leintwardine, Hereford and Worcester; Roman fort, looking N. SO 390734. YP 76: June 1959.

References

J.K. StJoseph, *J.R.S.* XLIII (1953), 84–5 with Pl. IX, 2 (oblique view of large fort from NE); LV (1965), 84; *Antiquity* XL (1966), 300–3 with plan and Pls. XLVI (this view) and XLVII (oblique view of both forts from SW). G. Webster, *Trans. Birmingham Arch. Soc.* LXXX (1965), 82–3 with Pls. 10 (oblique of part of large fort from NW) and 11 (oblique of small fort from SW), both by W.A. Baker, and map showing road. S.S. Frere, *Britannia, a History of Roman Britain* (London, 1967), Pl. 14A (panorama from NW by W.A. Baker).

BUCKTON, Hereford and Worcester (56)

The area round Leintwardine was evidently of considerable strategic importance in the first and second centuries as a meeting-place of valleys that offered the best routes westwards through dissected hilly country. An early military road running south from Wroxeter through the Church Stretton gap (6) to Gloucester and Usk may have served as a frontier for a few years in the middle of the first century, and provided a spring-board for further advance. From Leintwardine the valley of the river Teme leads directly west and then north-west towards central Wales, with an alternative route afforded by the valley of the Clun to the north (Fig. 12). The upper valley of the Teme is commanded by a substantial hill fort on Coxall Knoll 2.5 km west of Buckton, and among the hills 4 km further west lies another powerful native fortification, Caer Caradoc. That the Teme valley at least was used as an invasion route by Rome is testified by the discovery of a very large marching-camp of 25.9 ha (64 acres) at Brampton Bryan (SO 379723), and by another of substantial size (10 ha, 25 acres) at Walford (SO 393722); a third of only about 1.5 ha (3.7 acres) lies near the Buckton fort and may be its construction camp.

It is, however, the garrison forts which emphasise the district's strategic importance. Earliest, perhaps, is the hill fort of Brandon Camp (SO 400724), inside which aerial reconnaissance revealed (and

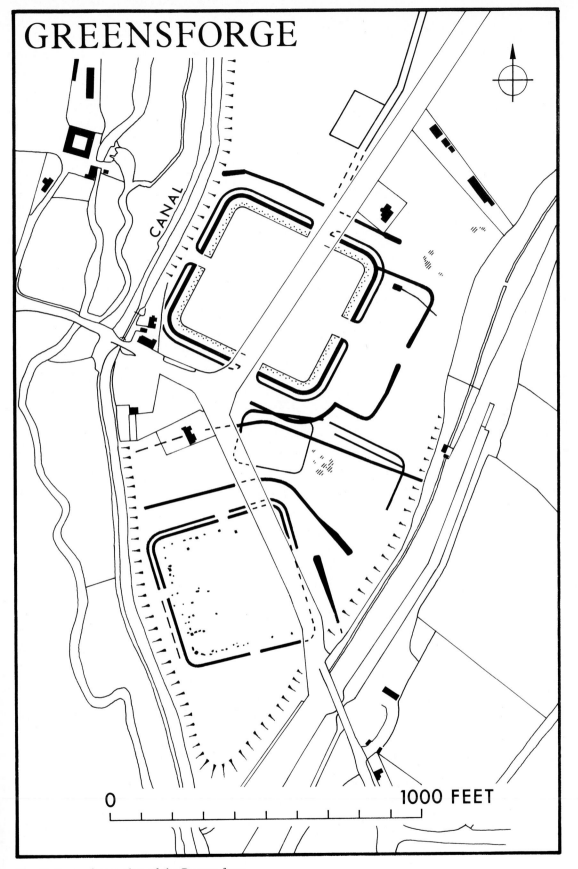

GREENSFORGE

CANAL

0   1000 FEET

Fig. 11 Greensforge: plan of the Roman forts.

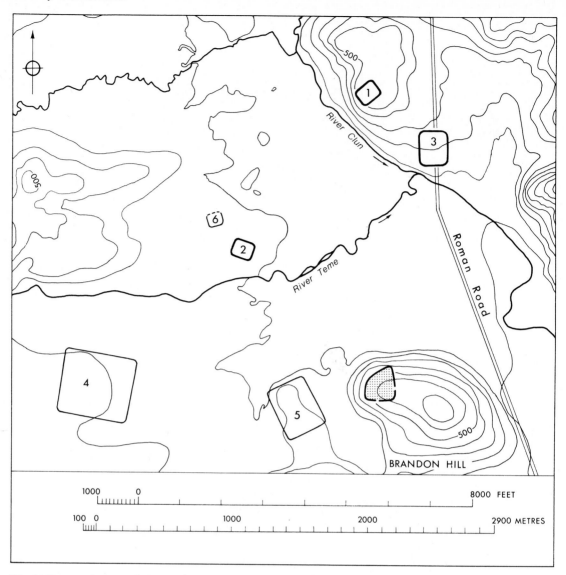

Fig. 12 Roman sites near Leintwardine. Forts: 1 Jay Lane; 2 Buckton; 3 Leintwardine; unnumbered, Brandon Camp. Camps: 4 Brampton Bryan; 5 Walford; 6 Buckton. Contours are at intervals of 7.6 m (25 ft).

excavation in 1981 confirmed) a very large timber granary and other timber-framed military buildings. The site yielded Neronian samian, and may perhaps be regarded as a forward stores base for one or other of the campaigns in the late 50s. The fort at Jay Lane, north-west of Leintwardine, which was discovered from the air by W.A. Baker in 1960, is the earliest fort of normal character to be recognised in the area; the few pieces of pottery which it has yielded are of Neronian to early Flavian date. This fort, which covers 1.97 ha (4.9 acres), stands well above the valley floor, at a height of 150 m above Ordnance Datum, commanding extensive views both north and south along the road and also over much ground to the west.

The fort of Buckton succeeded Jay Lane with little if any interval soon after 70, and the move may perhaps represent measures taken by Julius Frontinus in preparation for his invasion of Wales. It is 2.36 ha (5.9 acres) in size and lies on level but lower ground at 123 m above Ordnance Datum. The first fort here had a rampart of turf, and timber-framed buildings within; in a second period a stone wall and gates were added to the rampart and new timber buildings replaced the old. Occupation ceased *c.* 130–40, possibly so that troops could be released for the Scottish campaigns.

The photograph shows the street plan of the south half of the fort together with the dark belt of the rampart and the parch-mark of the wall.

57 Trawscoed, Dyfed (Cardiganshire); Roman fort, looking N. SN 671727. CBH 33: September 1976.

The fort faces east (right). The *via principalis* issues from the south gate (foreground), where projecting towers flank a twin-portalled gateway, and is continued by a road towards the Teme. Both the plan and what little is known of the barracks suggest that the garrison was an *ala* of 500 cavalry.

About 160, massive defences were erected at Leintwardine itself on the site of an existing roadside settlement; they enclosed 4.55 ha (11.3 acres). Despite the fact that a trunk road runs through the site and that the size is unusual for a fort, the character of the defences and the provision of a bath-house argue that it was a military work; it is perhaps best explained as a stores base. Occupation continued until the late fourth century, but perhaps with an increasingly civilian character. Little is known of the interior because of modern buildings and much erosion.

In conclusion, the Leintwardine district may be said to display a remarkable assemblage of military works, noteworthy for the changes of site chosen for successive garrisons. This must be connected with changes in the size of forces employed and of

the tasks they were set. The base at Brandon Camp has a good view up two valleys towards the west and over the flat ground on which Buckton lies, but much of the course of the road is out of sight. This consideration reinforces the opinion that the occupation was of a special and temporary character, while the large size of the interior (3.3 ha) and the length of the perimeter presuppose a considerable force. The Jay Lane fort was placed in the most commanding position despite the uneven ground, with excellent outlook towards hostile territory and along the various valleys, and it provided good surveillance of the road in both directions. The emphasis is on sound defensive location. The fort at Buckton is on low-lying but level ground with immediate surveillance of the river-crossing and easy access to water, but otherwise with a greater concern for mobility and for the offensive. Neither fort lies near the known course of the road, and both must have been served by diversions. Possibly the earliest fort of all has still to be found.

58 Forden Gaer, Powys (Montgomeryshire); Roman fort, looking N. SO 208989. AYT 57: July 1969.

References

J.K. StJoseph, *J.R.S.* LI (1961), 123–5 with Pl. IX, 1 (this view). S.C. Stanford's excavation report, *Trans. Woolhope Naturalists' Field Club* XXXIX (1968), 222–326 (with aerial photographs by W.A. Baker). V.E. Nash-Williams, *The Roman Frontier in Wales* (2nd ed. by M.G. Jarrett, Cardiff, 1969),91–5 (with map and plans). J.K. StJoseph, *Antiquity* LIII (1979), 51–5 (Brandon Camp with map of district, our Fig. 12). *Britannia* XIII (1982), forthcoming, Roman Britain report, for excavations in Brandon Camp.

TRAWSCOED, Dyfed (57)

The fort at Trawscoed, discovered by observation on the ground in 1959, lies on the east bank of the Ystwyth some 12.5 km south-east of Aberystwyth. The later discovery of a fortlet at Erglodd and a large fort at Penllwyn, both situated between Trawscoed and the long-known fort at Pennal, shows that the Roman north–south road ran well inland of the west coast of Wales on its way south to Llanio.

The whole circuit of the defences at Trawscoed is plainly visible. The fort, which has an area of 2.4 ha (5.05 acres), is obliquely bisected by the modern B 4340 road, half of it lying in parkland and half in a ploughed field. The dry summers of 1975–6 produced parch-marks which revealed much detail of a street plan with unusual features. The fort faces west (left) towards the river as the position of its *via principalis* shows; east of this lie two *viae quintanae*. The greater part of the circuit of the *intervallum* street is also visible. Trial excavation in 1962 showed that the fort was occupied in the late first and early second centuries, and that its east rampart had been widened in a second structural phase. A timber building, perhaps a barrack, lay next to the eastern *intervallum*. Beyond the dark belt marking the ditch system on the north side runs an external street parallel to the defences, from which a road leads north in extension of the line of one of the *viae quintanae* on a course parallel with the main road to Penllwyn, seen as a broad parch-mark. This system of roads suggests the presence of an extensive *vicus*.

References

J.K. St Joseph, *J.R.S.* LI (1961), 128 with plan and Pl. IX, 2 (oblique view looking NE); *Antiquity* XXXV (1961), 272 (with same plan and plate (XXXIX b)); *J.R.S.* LXVII (1977), 153–4 with Pl. XIV, 2 (vertical view). V.E. Nash-Williams, *The Roman Frontier in Wales* (2nd ed. by M.G. Jarrett, Cardiff, 1969), 113–16.

FORDEN GAER, Powys (58)

Forden Gaer is a large Roman fort of 3.25 ha (8 acres) on the right bank of the river Severn between Wroxeter and Caersws, lying close to a ford (prominent in later history) across the river at Rhydwhyman and at the point where the valley floor begins to widen after the 14 km narrow reach past Newtown. The site is unusual among forts in Wales both for its size and for its long occupation. Only small-scale excavations have taken place there, in 1926–9, yielding results that are far from easy to interpret. The earliest fort seems to have been of the Flavian period, and occupation continued, with various reconstructions, until the late fourth century, although the fort never received stone defences. The Romans may have penetrated this part of the Severn valley, at least as far as the fort at Llwyn-y-Brain near Caersws, even earlier, and a pre-Flavian fort may be expected at or near Forden Gaer, but so far has eluded discovery.

The fort and its surroundings have been observed from the air over thirty-three years (1945–77); the photographs taken on these flights have proved invaluable for the study of the site, but even after a third of a century reconnaissance may yield new information. The fort stands on the flood-plain of the Severn in a low-lying position at the head of a long tongue of land between that river and its tributary the Camlad. In extreme conditions the ground around the fort is liable to flood, and since 1945 flood-water has twice been recorded drowning hollows in the fields, especially to the east, and partly filling the hollow of the fort ditches. Other floods may well have passed unrecorded on air photographs and of course the regime of the Severn may have changed since Roman times. The photograph was taken from the south when the whole site was under corn, at a time when the angle of lighting was such that the view gives no idea of the relief of the earthworks. They form in fact an impressive upstanding platform and rather suggest that they might in part have been deliberately raised to ensure that the interior of the fort was above flood-level.

The fort is surrounded by a broad hollow which aerial photographs show to mark the course of three ditches. Outside this a low bank of clay is present along the east and south and part of the west sides, though today much denuded. In the photograph this bank is visible on the south as a light-toned band. The flood-plain hereabouts is largely of gravel and loam, so much of the clay may have had to be imported. The bank has been supposed to be the rampart of the earliest fort; but the area enclosed is too large and too irregular for this to be likely, and the suggestion that the bank was designed as a protection against flooding has much to commend it.

Careful study of the whole sequence of aerial photographs in the Cambridge Collection taken over years suggests that the rampart round the north-west (far left) angle and along the northern third of the west side is somewhat more massive than that forming the remainder of the west side, and indeed that it projects slightly further west, appearing to override the innermost of the three ditches. This variation evidently struck the Ordnance Surveyors, accounting for the odd shape of the earthwork as depicted on large-scale Ordnance Survey maps, where the effect is exaggerated (O.S. map, Salop XLVI SE, 6-inch scale, 1903 edition). The difference is hardly explicable solely in terms of nineteenth-century agricultural operations. Moreover, the westernmost of the north–south streets, though clearly visible on photographs for the southern two-thirds of the fort, is much less clear thereafter, as if it had there been destroyed or buried beneath later deposits. The significance of these facts is not easy to assess. Whether at some late period an area near the north-west angle amounting to about one-sixth of the whole fort was separately defended is an interesting question that can be answered only by excavation.

Outside the western defences near the southwest angle is a standing stone (the Hoar Stone), perhaps a Bronze Age monument.

The street system, shown by parch-marks, has unusual features and must represent at least two periods, in one of which the streets were laid out obliquely to the visible defences. The central street, starting from the angle of a wood, appears to run right across the fort, crossing the expected position of the *principia*. This recalls a similar feature at Newton Kyme (63) and may indicate a late Roman rearrangement of the interior. To the

59 Llanfor, Gwynedd (Merionethshire); Roman supply base, steep oblique view looking NE. SH 938363. CBB 33: August 1976.

east of it and perhaps also to the west run parallel streets. The street nearest the western (left-hand) defences is by no means parallel with the others, and it evidently extends southwards beyond the fort, inclining slightly to the east on approaching the Severn. It seems to be overridden by the fort's rampart and to be cut by the ditches. Possibly this is an early road to Llwyn-y-Brain which was diverted when the fort was built. Gaps at the centre of the north and south ramparts mark gate-positions, but there are none in the long sides for the *portae principales*. Possibly their absence is the result of fourth-century alterations. Considerable reconstruction of the ramparts occurred perhaps *c.* 160 after a fire, and again in the fourth century.

An explanation is needed for the choice of site – not a particularly defensible position on such low-lying ground, 81 m above Ordnance Datum, liable to flood. The existence nearby of a ford across the Severn is hardly reason enough, since the river could have been bridged in many places. The ridge 600 m to the north and 91 m high, lying west of the farm known as The Gaer, would seem to offer a better position well above flood-level,

with more commanding views, especially north-wards down the Severn, the very direction in which the same ridge blocks the view from the known fort. If the first Roman forces to penetrate so far west had sought a site for a fort hereabouts, a better position than this (about SO 206995) would be difficult to find; further examination might prove rewarding.

Reconnaissance around Forden Gaer has recorded numerous other crop-marks over the years. The line of the Roman road leading ENE, eventually to Wroxeter, is clearly visible for 600 m as far as the crossing of the Camlad. Although heavily ploughed, the road still rises above the level of the ground on either side, as if it had been laid upon a substantial *agger*, a very reasonable precaution against flooding. Crop-marks of a narrow ditch forming a rather elongated rectangle may provide a clue to agricultural enclosures to the east. Whether a dumb-bell-shaped hollow near the Roman road and *c.* 200 m north-east of the fort (visible at the top right-hand corner of the photograph) was indeed adapted as a small amphitheatre or as a *gyrus* for the training of cavalry mounts, as has been suggested, is more

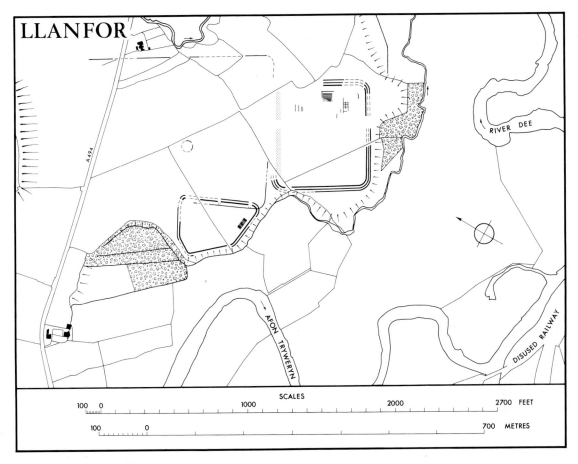

Fig. 13 Llanfor: general plan.

open to question. Together with other undulations in the gravel plain around the fort, this hollow fills with water in exceptionally wet weather.

Close to the north side of the Roman road, though not aligned to it, and some 600 m from the fort, a rectangular enclosure *c.* 70 m long defined by two ditches appears on some photographs; the angles are sharp. Date and purpose are unknown. In the very next field to the north other crop-marks suggest an Iron Age settlement with pits and round houses, while photographs of the field north of the fort (under grass when **58** was taken) have recorded overlapping crop-marks indicating prehistoric and perhaps post-Roman occupation.

This account will have made clear the crucial importance of Forden Gaer and of its surrounding area as a source of knowledge relating to the Roman period in Wales. That further damage to the site by ploughing should be halted until this potential has been exploited is quite evident. Large-scale excavation will be necessary for full recovery of the complicated history of the site.

References

G.C. Boon in V.E. Nash-Williams, *The Roman Frontier in Wales* (2nd ed. by M.G. Jarrett, Cardiff, 1969), 85–8. J.K. St Joseph, *J.R.S.* XLIII (1953), 85; LXIII (1973), 235–6. P. Crew, *Bull. Board of Celtic Studies* XXVIII (1980), 730–42 with plans and Pls. Ia, Ib, IIa (oblique views).

LLANFOR, Gwynedd (59)

Llanfor lies in central North Wales 1.3 km north-east of Lake Bala. Here in the dry summers of 1975 and 1976 parch-marks in permanent pasture revealed a hitherto unknown fort of large size (3.6 ha, 8.9 acres), with a separately fortified enclosure or supply base beside it, together with other works (Fig. 13). The site, which lies near the confluence of the rivers Tryweryn and Dee, on level ground about 5 m above the flood-plain, commands the valley floor and has a good all-round outlook.

Llanfor is situated only just over 8 km from the long-known fort of Caer Gai, which was occupied, as excavation has shown, from about 75 or 80

105

until *c.* 120. The forts are too close to be contemporary and the establishment of Llanfor is certainly the earlier; but only excavation will reveal whether it represents the earliest Flavian occupation of the region, or whether, as is more probable, it is a foundation of late Claudian or Neronian date, and attests a penetration of Wales at that time far deeper than had been suspected.

59 shows the supply base which is associated with the fort; the fort itself lies just off the picture at top right. The enclosure is an irregular polygon adjusted to the size and shape of a small promontory, and is defended by double ditches on its east and north sides. Only a single ditch is now visible on the sides which face the flood-plain, but on other photographs there is a hint of a second ditch, perhaps now largely ploughed away, on the edge of the scarp. The area enclosed is *c.* 1.2 ha (3 acres). On the long east side the double ditches are interrupted for three gates, of which two are clearly visible. At the central gate can just be seen the four post-holes which carried the gate structure and perhaps a tower above it; at the south (right-hand) gate only two of (originally) four post-holes are visible. These two gates are of the type, with only a single portal and perhaps a tower above, which was sometimes employed for minor gates. Unfortunately the site of the third, most northerly, gate is unclear, though the break in the outer ditch lies quite close to the north angle.

The broad sinuous bands that cross the two fields from right to left are areas where the grass has retained its verdure, perhaps because of a slightly greater depth of soil. In a light-toned patch between the two lowest bands in the right-hand field, and not far from the enclosure ditch, may be discerned some twenty closely spaced, parallel fine dark lines. They run at right angles to the line of the ditch and on the photograph somewhat resemble a fingerprint. These marks are not in line either with the modern hedgerow or with the agricultural grain of the field; they certainly represent the foundation trenches of a large timber granary which is at least 28 m long and 9 m wide – a *horreum* approaching legionary size. Towards the top of the photograph and a short distance to right of the hedge, are two closely spaced circular or penannular marks, perhaps 8–10 m overall, while just beyond the limit of the photograph yet another circular ditch, *c.* 21 m in diameter and interrupted for an entrance, probably surrounds a signal-station or watch-tower. It lies too close to the fort to be considered contemporary.

Finally, a thin continuous dark line just within and parallel to the double ditches on the east side of the enclosure represents the ditch of a marching-camp, which cannot be contemporary and is presumably earlier than the supply base. The ditch turns north just outside the sharp angle of the enclosure; other photographs show lengths of its south and east sides and demonstrate that the area of the camp was at least 11.7 ha (29 acres), indicating a powerful campaign force.

References

J.K. StJoseph, *J.R.S.* LXVII (1977), 149–50 with plan and Pl. XIV, 1 (panorama looking SW over fort and enclosure). Caer Gai: V.E. Nash-Williams, *The Roman Frontier in Wales* (2nd ed. by M.G. Jarrett, Cardiff, 1969), 54–6.

CAERHUN (*KANOVIUM*), Gwynedd (60)

The fort of *Kanovium* lies on a navigable reach of the Conway, at the point where the river ceases to be tidal, and where the coastal road from Chester to Caernarvon made its crossing. The site has long been known and was extensively excavated in 1926–9 (except for the north-east quarter, now occupied by a church and graveyard); but the dry summers of 1975 and 1976 revealed new and important information about the *vicus*. The fort itself (centre foreground) covers 1.97 ha (4.86 acres) and, to judge by the accommodation provided, housed a *cohors equitata* 500 strong. A small annexe, invisible on the photograph, is known to have been attached to the eastern half of the southern defences. Outside the south gate (*porta principalis dextra*) a road can be seen as a light-toned strip curving slightly to the left to avoid the annexe. West (left) of this road the photograph reveals a previously unknown walled enclosure attached to the defences; this is probably of post-medieval date. The road leads southwards along the Conway valley, eventually reaching Tomen-y-Mur (61).

Just north-east (right) of the fort, and immediately above a large tree, can be seen the parch-marks of part of the military bath-building, which was excavated in 1926–9; above this again the photograph shows a second building, perhaps a *mansio*, apparently situated in a walled enclosure which extends as far west as the road leaving the *porta principalis sinistra*. This road runs north-east, roughly parallel with the river and is seen to traverse an extensive *vicus*, previously unknown, which is marked by long narrow strip-buildings on either side of the road. Other parch-marks east of this may indicate the position of a harbour.

Note: The prominent marks somewhat resembling a multivallate hill fort in the field north-west of the Roman fort are caused by a hay crop in process of being gathered in.

60 Caerhun (*Kanovium*), Gwynedd (Caernarvonshire); Roman fort and *vicus*. Vertical photograph, N at top. SH 776704. K17-AI 182: July 1975. Scale 1:3200.

References

P.K. Baillie Reynolds, *Arch. Camb.* 1926–36 (excavation reports, also reissued as *Excavations on the site of the Roman fort of Kanovium at Caerhun, Caernarvonshire* (Cardiff, 1938)). V.E. Nash-Williams, *The Roman Frontier in Wales* (Cardiff, 1954), 23–7 with Pl. XIIIB (ground panorama from E); *ibid*. (2nd ed. by M.G. Jarrett, Cardiff, 1969), 56–9. J.K. St Joseph, *J.R.S.* LXVII (1977), 151 with Pl. XV, 1 (this view).

TOMEN-Y-MUR, Gwynedd (61)

Tomen-y-Mur is in North Wales 3.5 km south of Ffestiniog; it lies at a height of 291 m in a most exposed position astride a broad spur having a fine view in almost all directions. The site was occupied by two successive Roman forts and by the motte (or tomen) of an early medieval earth-and-timber castle. The original fort, extending to 1.7 ha (4.2 acres), was founded in the Flavian period and defended by an earthen rampart and double ditch. The garrison may have been a part-mounted quingenary cohort or possibly two cohorts of infantry. Later, perhaps *c.* 120, a smaller unit (such as a normal infantry cohort) was transferred to Tomen-y-Mur and the fort was reduced to 1.34 ha (3.3 acres); this was achieved by abandoning much of the *retentura* of the old fort and building a new rampart fronted by a wall at a little distance behind the Headquarters Building. The line of this is marked on the photograph by a field wall

61 Tomen-y-Mur, Gwynedd (Merionethshire); Roman fort, looking WNW. SH 706386. CBE 27: August 1976.

extending each side of the tomen. Beneath this castle mound considerable structural remains of the new Roman rear gate may well have been preserved.

It has been stated in the past that there are no indications of internal buildings in stone, but this photograph clearly reveals immediately in front of the tomen parch-marks caused by the stone foundations of the *principia*; presumably this building replaced an original structure in timber. In

the *praetentura* are other parch-marks, some of which probably relate to metalled streets running between barracks, but, in addition, there are indications of at least two long narrow stone structures.

From the *porta praetoria* (foreground) a road led south-east to a finely preserved bridge abutment at the crossing of a small stream at the bottom of the photograph. About 30 m to the right of the road, where the grass has parched white, lie the

62 Cawthorn, North Yorkshire; Roman camp and forts, looking NE. SE 785901. K 27: August 1945.

remains of a bath-building uncovered over a century ago. Beyond the fort and just to right of an imaginary line extending the field wall running out from the tomen the earthworks of two small practice camps can just be distinguished. Besides the features just mentioned, a small amphitheatre or *ludus*, a partly levelled area of 1.3 ha perhaps for a parade-ground, and a number of tombs lie outside the fort to the north-east, beyond the limits of the photograph.

It is not uncommon in Wales to find forts reduced in size by the construction of a new length of rampart to exclude part of the original circuit, and where dating evidence is available the reduction of garrison which this implies is normally associated with extensive redeployment of forces necessitated by the construction and manning of Hadrian's Wall. The renewed advance into Scotland which occurred twenty years later under Antoninus Pius may have been responsible for further draining of troops from Wales and the evacuation of several forts including Tomen-y-Mur.

References

V.E. Nash-Williams, *The Roman Frontier in Wales* (Cardiff, 1954), Pl. XVIII (wide panorama looking SE). *Ibid.* (2nd ed. by M.G. Jarrett, Cardiff, 1969), 111–13 with map, plan and Pl. XB (oblique view looking SW). E.G. Bowen and C.A. Gresham, *History of Merioneth* I (Dolgellau, 1967), 230–5 (with map). J.K. StJoseph, *J.R.S.* LI (1961), 130–1 (practice camps).

CAWTHORN, North Yorkshire (62)

The photograph shows a remarkable group of four Roman military works arranged side by side on a waterless plateau above the crest of a steep north-facing scarp, 6 km north of Pickering. They were labelled A–D by Richmond. In the foreground lies a fort (D) of 1.4 ha defended by a turf rampart and widely-spaced ditch system of Punic form; there are three gates only, for in the north side, on the very crest of the slope, the *porta praetoria* is lacking. This fort impinges at its southeast corner on the rampart and ditch of a long narrow irregularly shaped temporary camp (C) which possesses three gates defended by external *claviculae*, all of them on the eastern side. Further to the north-east lies a second fort (A) with substantial bank and ditch extending over 2.65 ha (6.56 acres). Attached to the east side of A is a further rectangular fortification (B) extending into the top right-hand corner of the photograph. This was evidently intended, not as an annexe, but as an enlargement of A, since the east rampart of A was flattened to give access; moreover the gates of A were originally defended by *titula* which have been overlaid by double *claviculae* on the west and south sides corresponding with the double *claviculae* provided for B. The combined area of A and B is 4.57 ha (11.3 acres). There is thus evidence for at least two periods, and it has been suggested that C (with all three gates facing A) was the construction camp for A, and that A + B was occupied by the force which later built D, to which a lightly metalled track was laid round the north side of C. Excavation failed to find indications of permanent timber-framed buildings in either A or D, but in both A and B there are indications of tented lines in the form both of low turf mounds which would give protection from the weather, and of 'dug-outs'. The troops occupying C (who are assumed to have built A) were evidently a far smaller force than that which occupied A + B; but that both were legionary is suggested by the presence of turf platforms for *ballistae*, for at least in the first two centuries A.D., only legions were equipped with *ballistae*.

Cawthorn has long been held to comprise a practice ground where on two occasions legionaries from York were exercised in the skills of fort construction. The date, suggested by the *claviculae* and also by the pottery found, lies within the Flavian or Trajanic periods (A.D. 80–120). This theory has been to some extent undermined by the recent discovery of a Flavian fort at Lease Rigg, *c*. 15 km to the north, near Whitby, on the Roman road which passes Cawthorn. The existence of this fort seems to demand another near Cawthorn

to fill the interval between Lease Rigg and the fort at Malton which lies *c*. 18.5 km yet farther south. Renewed excavation is called for, especially in the interior of D which was little explored, in order to search more thoroughly for permanent structures. One fact militates strongly against the idea of occupied forts being placed in this position, namely the absence of an adequate water supply. Water would have had to be fetched in barrels by pack-animals from the Sutherland Beck flowing at the foot of the steep slope to the north.

Whether or not either fort (A or D) was ever operational, the group as a whole is of unique interest and strengthens the view that construction camps are to be expected near permanent forts. In the 37 years since this photograph was taken, much of the area including the whole of Fort D and Camp C has become overgrown with scrub and fir trees, so that the earthworks are much less readily visible than formerly, either from the air or on the ground.

References

W. Roy, *Military Antiquities* (London, 1793), Pl. XI. I.A. Richmond, *Arch. Journ.* LXXXIX (1933), 17–78 (excavation report with plans and plates, including Pl. XVIII, vertical view of D). *J.R.S.* XXXIX (1949), Pl. XIV, 2 (this view).

NEWTON KYME, North Yorkshire (63–4)

Little is known from excavation at this site which lies 15.5 km WSW of York, beside the river Wharfe; but finds suggest occupation in the late first to early second century and again from *c*. A.D. 300. The photographs show two superimposed forts, the second over twice the size of the first. The earlier fort is seen in 64, where the double ditches of the south and part of the east sides show as dark lines which meet at a rounded corner. Outside its south gate the approach road bends through a few degrees, running obliquely under the axial street of the later fort and being cut by the defences of the latter. 63 shows that the later road rejoins the approach road, making a sharp bend immediately outside the south gate of the large fort. There is no clear indication that a road left either fort northwards to cross the river; a Roman road from Tadcaster to Aldborough known as the Rudgate crossed the river *c*. 200 m further west.

Fort II is exceptionally large at *c*. 4 ha (almost 10 acres) and seems to be unusual in having its *via principalis* running on the long axis of the plan. This can be paralleled only at Forden Gaer (58). The fort has a very wide inner ditch and a narrow outer one, visible on the west, south and east sides. A dark line on the inner side of the inner

63 Newton Kyme, North Yorkshire; Roman fort, vertical photograph, N at top. SE 456454. K17-AI 163: July 1975. Scale 1:2500.

64 Newton Kyme; Roman fort, oblique view, looking N. CEI 85: August 1977.

ditch is probably caused by the trench from which the masonry of the fort wall has been robbed. A new *via principalis* has been laid down slightly east of the old one, kinking slightly outside the demolished defences of Fort I and then continuing to the new south gate on a course a little oblique to the early approach road below it.

Both sides of the axial road can be seen to be closely built up with strip-buildings of a distinctly civilian character; and this fact raises the question whether there was a third phase here, after the second fort had been evacuated of its garrison, when the defended area was taken over by a *vicus*. Should this prove to be so, the axial street may belong to this settlement rather than to the second fort, which may after all have possessed a conventional street plan.

South of Fort II a ditched drove-way leads westwards (left) and other ditched enclosures are visible thereabouts; some of them are at an angle to the line of the road and may therefore represent the boundaries of earlier fields. They are crossed by the light lines caused by modern ploughing. Other photographs show that the south-west angle of Fort II cuts across a square enclosure

having sides of *c.* 40 m. The north–south road (Road I) leads south to join the Rudgate. A second road (Road II) approaches from the south-east, from the direction of Tadcaster, entering **63** beneath the modern lane from Newton Kyme village (bottom right). Its metalling is the cause of a narrow light line crossing the field to the south-east corner of the fort. Perhaps this original alignment was replaced by Road III (see below) when Fort II was built.

On the south side of Road II an oval enclosure some 12–15 m across can be clearly distinguished; it is surrounded by three closely spaced and roughly concentric dark lines which may represent robbed walls. The comparatively small size of this structure suggests that a large tomb is the most likely explanation. A row of much smaller ring-ditches perhaps five in number, three of them having central burial-pits, is aligned to yet another metalled road (Road III) that runs eastwards from Road I just south of a modern lane. South-east of these tombs, and in the same field, a prominent dark curving line forms part of the circumference of a henge monument of late Neolithic date. That this earthwork, so close to the fort, even now

65 Bainbridge (*Virosidum*), **North Yorkshire; Roman fort and annexe**, looking NW. SD 937902. CIF 45: January 1979.

survives in low relief raises the question whether, like Maumbury Rings (96), the henge was reused as a military *ludus* or amphitheatre.

References

J.K. St Joseph, *J.R.S.* XLIII (1953), 87 with Pl. XI, 1 (different oblique view); XLV (1955), 82; LV (1965), 77–8; *Antiquity* LIV (1980), 134 Pl. XVIII (vertical photograph). *Current Archaeology* VII, 3 (No. 74, Nov. 1980), 71 (oblique view of henge-monument from SE by D. Riley).

BAINBRIDGE, North Yorkshire (65)

This fort (probably named *Virosidum* in Roman times) lies in Wensleydale, occupying a narrow glacial mound – the Brough – which rises steeply above the east bank of the small river Bain near its confluence with the Ure. The site is in the heart of the Pennines, conveniently placed to guard a Roman road running across the range from Lancaster past Bainbridge to Catterick, not far from the point where it may have been crossed by a subsidiary route leading northwards from Ilkley past Grassington (134) in Wharfedale to Bainbridge, and thence north-eastwards to Reeth in Swaledale and on to Greta Bridge.

The site was first occupied under Agricola, but the size and shape of the early Flavian post built by him are still unknown. The buildings of that period so far discovered are on an alignment oblique to that of the visible fort, but the early defences have not been located. The recent discovery at Wensley, only 14 km to the east, of a turf-and-timber fort hardly less than 1.2 ha (3 acres) in size and probably of this early period may suggest that the Agricolan post at Bainbridge was no more than a fortlet. Alternatively the fort at Wensley may prove to belong to the period *c.* 120–60 when Bainbridge was unoccupied, and might then represent a wider spacing of garrisons.

The fort so clearly visible in the photograph was built in the Flavian–Trajanic period, *c.* 90 or 105, to the shape of a parallelogram, though not far from a square, 1.06 ha (2.63 acres) in extent.

66 Hardknott Castle (*Mediobogdum*), **Cumbria; Roman fort.** General view, looking WSW down Eskdale. NY 219015. F 24: July 1945.

The site thereafter was occupied throughout the Roman period (except between *c.* 120 and 160), and was reconstructed on several occasions; in consequence stratification 2 m deep has accumulated inside the ramparts.

The photograph, taken when the ground was under a covering of snow, shows the *via principalis* crossing from left to right, with the Headquarters Building behind it; outlines of other buildings are also visible, being indicated either by trenches dug to rob the walls of stone or by the scars of excavation. From the *porta principalis dextra* (left) a terraced road leads left towards the crossing of the Bain. In the background an elaborate system

of ditches bars the narrowing crest of the ridge to seizure by the enemy.

In the centre foreground can be seen outlines of a fortified enclosure attached to the east face of the fort, together with indications of buildings, amongst them what may be a bath-house. This enclosure was first built in the Severan period and must be the *bracchium caementicium* ('stone-built outwork') referred to in an inscription of 205–8 (*R.I.B.* 722); it was rebuilt later in the third century. For part if not all of that century, the enclosure actually formed an extension to the fort, for the earlier east wall dividing them had been taken down; the wall was rebuilt on the

114

67 Hardknott Castle; Roman fort. Oblique view from the NW. BAW 91: February 1970.

original line at the beginning of the fourth century, when the position of the east gate (*porta praetoria*) was shifted slightly northwards to its visible position. The attested third-century garrison was the Sixth Cohort of Nervii, a unit which required no more accommodation than was available in the fort before its extension; presumably, therefore, additional troops had been drafted in.

Bainbridge well illustrates the thoroughness of the grip imposed upon Brigantian territory by Agricola during his northern advance. The hill country was subdivided into blocks by roads guarded by forts holding strong positions – a system of cordon control. Although by the third century the Brigantian hillsmen are thought to have accepted Roman rule, the fort at Bainbridge continued as a garrison centre until the fifth century, nor is there much sign that in all this time any sizeable civil settlement developed here. The position of the site, deep in the Pennines, shows that local security rather than frontier defence in

depth was always its predominant purpose. The garrison did of course also serve as part of the strategic reserve.

References

R.G. Collingwood, *Proc. Leeds Philosophical Soc.* I (Pt 6, 1928), 261–84 with Fig. 1 (plan). W.V. Wade, *ibid.*, VII (Pt I, 1952), 1–19 with Fig. 1 (same plan); *ibid.* VII (Pt 3, 1955), 153–66 with Fig. 2 (plan). B.R. Hartley, *ibid.* IX (Pt 3, 1959), 107–31 (excavations). *J.R.S.* LIX (1969), 207 with Figs. 29–32 (*principia* plans). A. Raistrick, *The Romans in Yorkshire* (Clapham, 1960), central Pl. (vertical view).

HARDKNOTT CASTLE, Cumbria (66–7)

General view of fort, looking WSW

The fort of Hardknott (*Mediobogdum*) guards the western approach to the Hardknott and Wrynose Passes over which the Roman road crosses from Ravenglass on the coast to Ambleside at the head

68 Old Carlisle (*Olenacum*), Cumbria; Roman fort and *vicus*, looking W. NY 260464. BPB 19: November 1973.

of Lake Windermere, where it divided to Brougham and to Watercrook, thus bisecting and cordoning the difficult country of the Lake District. The Roman road is approximately on the line of the modern one which is seen climbing the approach to the pass on the left of the photograph. The outline of the fort can be seen on the right of the road on the nose of the promontory, but in this view the interior is not yet cleared and consolidated. Nearer the camera and marked by a large dark rectangular patch of vegetation is a feature of great interest – the fort's parade-ground which has been carefully terraced and levelled into the irregular hillside. It measures *c.* 152 by 121 m (500 by 400 ft). At the middle of its north (right) side a largely natural knoll marks the commanding officer's *tribunal*. Such features must once have been common but are very rarely now to be identified with such clarity.

Oblique view from the NW

In this view the Roman road is in the background, and the strength of the position can be appreciated. The fort is square in plan, measuring 114 m (375 ft) each way, an area of 1.3 ha (3.23 acres). The fort was founded under Hadrian, and an inscription of his reign found at the *porta praetoria* (top) records the garrison as the Fourth Cohort of Delmatae, an infantry regiment 500 strong. The fort has a stone wall and the photograph also shows a double granary (left), the Headquarters Building or *principia* (centre) and part of the commander's house (*praetorium*). On the conquest of Scotland in the 140s the garrison was evacuated, but the fort was rebuilt *c.* 163 by the governor Calpurnius Agricola, after the land north of Hadrian's Wall was given up. Between the fort and the road can be seen the military bath-

69 Old Carlisle; Roman fort, looking E. DS 58: July 1949.

building, a simple row of rooms with a detached circular *laconicum* behind.

References

J.R.S. XXXIX (1949), Pl. XIV, 1 (oblique panorama looking E up the pass). I.A. Richmond in National Forest Park Guide *Hardknott* (H.M.S.O., 1949), 11–19 with map, plan and Pl. as last and another oblique view looking N. D. Charlesworth, *Trans. Cumb. and Westm. Antiq. and Arch. Soc.* LXIII (1963), 148–52 (granary); R.P.Wright, *ibid.* LXV (1965), 169–75 (inscription).

OLD CARLISLE (*OLENACUM*), Cumbria (68–9)

The fort, of 1.82 ha (4.5 acres), lies in the middle of the Cumberland plain, north of the Lake District mountains and *c.* 16 km south-west of Carlisle. Throughout most if not all of its existence the garrison was an *ala* of cavalry 500 strong. The history of Old Carlisle is not known in any detail as the site has not been excavated. The fort was probably established either under Trajan or under Hadrian and thereafter held to the end of the Roman occupation. Indeed, there is some reason to suspect that it continued as a centre of importance in the fifth century. Cavalrymen enjoyed a higher rate of pay than that of infantrymen, and a large civil settlement round the fort may be a result of this relative affluence.

Although most of the ground immediately to south and west of the fort has at one time been ploughed, the meadow in which the site now lies has long been under permanent pasture, and in consequence the minor earthworks both inside and outside the fort survive in relatively good condition and constitute a precious example of this type of field monument. Despite the fact that the earthworks are not formed by the walls themselves, but by trenches dug along the walls by stone-robbers, they yield a tolerably informative plan.

The platform of the fort is plain to see, and the rampart and ditches stand out boldly. The site lies at an altitude of 67 m on a bluff protected on its west and north sides by the steep ravine of the Wiza Beck, some 15 m below; but on the other two sides, where the ground is more level, extensive traces of a *vicus* are seen. Buildings even extend to the small flat area outside the north gate (69, left), but not, apparently, to the western promontory. The Roman road from Papcastle to Carlisle enters 68 at the top left-hand corner: from there to the bridge over the Wiza Beck it is overlain by the modern A 595 road. On the nearer side of the

117

70 Whitley Castle, Northumberland; Roman fort, looking S. NY 695487. BEW 17: February 1971.

beck, the modern road bends to the left and its predecessor emerges, lined thickly on both sides with small, closely packed building-plots. These probably represent strip-buildings end-on to the road, as is normal in such roadside settlements. Another road left the *porta praetoria* of the fort (near side), to join the main road just beyond the farm in the foreground, and this too is heavily built up. From the main Roman road a side street climbs northwards towards the south-east corner of the fort and can be seen to serve numerous houses. This street passes across the east front of the fort, and may be the start of a road noted in the eighteenth century as running northwards, probably in fact making for Drumburgh on the Solway coast. On a level area some 75 m south of the left-hand gate (the *porta principalis dextra*), half-way between it and the main road, lie the outlines of a large courtyard building which is doubtless a *mansio* of the posting system. No bath-building is to be seen; the baths may have been built on lower ground west or north of the fort. There are traces of an ancient rock-cut aqueduct leading along the valley on the near side of the stream and only just above it; this may possibly represent a water supply for a bath-building placed somewhere on the floor of the valley.

Within the fort, the *principia* can be seen in **68** on the far side of the *via principalis*, and what may be granaries lie beside it on the right. As **69** shows, the front and rear divisions of the fort each exhibit eight long narrow building-plots parallel to the *via principalis* and arranged four each side of axial streets. These are appropriate for the eight barracks and eight stable-blocks which an *ala quingenaria* would require.

References

R.G. Collingwood, *Trans. Cumb. and Westm. Antiq. and Arch. Soc.* (2nd series) XXVIII (1928), 103–19. E. Birley, *ibid.* LI (1952), 16–39. P. Salway, *The Frontier People of Roman Britain* (Cambridge, 1965), 114–19 with map. J.K. St Joseph, *J.R.S.* XLI (1951), 54 with Pl. IV, 1 (our **69**). S.S. Frere, *Britannia, A History of Roman Britain* (London, 1967) Pl. 14B; (1978 ed.) Pl. 6A (our **69**). N.J.

71 Risingham (*Habitancum*), Northumberland; Roman fort, looking S. NY 890862. AQO 90: January 1967.

Higham and G.D.B. Jones, *Arch. Journ.* CXXXII (1975), 24–5 with Fig. 2 (schematic plan) and Pl. IIIA (oblique view looking S). D.R. Wilson in W. Rodwell and T. Rowley (eds.), *Small Towns of Roman Britain* (B.A.R. 15, Oxford, 1975), Pl. XIA (our **68**).

WHITLEY CASTLE, Northumberland (70)

The complexity and fine preservation of the defences of Whitley Castle are matched in the Roman Empire only at Ardoch (**79**). The fort (1.2 ha, 3 acres) lies some 19 km south of the fort of Carvoran on Hadrian's Wall on a Roman road connecting that fort with Kirkby Thore (*Bravoniacum*). The ground rises steeply to the west of the fort (right side of photograph) and extra ditches have been provided on that side. Round the rest of the perimeter four ditches run as far as the *portae principales*, but on the remaining north-east side the defences appear to be weaker despite the fact that the approach there is at least as easy as on the other sides. The remains of a bath-house were excavated *c*. 1810 just outside the *porta principalis*

sinistra; the scars of the excavation can be seen near the left corner of the fort. The building stands in the way of the outer defences coming from the right, which might be taken to suggest that the baths had been built before the outer ditches were added. In fact, however, there are various indications that the fort had originally been smaller than it later became, and that the bath-building was intended to lie beyond the original north corner. The character of the rampart south-west of the *portae principales* differs from that in the *praetentura* (left); it is much more massive and upstanding. The photograph shows the denuded remains of what may be the line of the original north-east rampart just left of the *via principalis*.

The position of part of the *principia* (Headquarters Building) and various other structures (at least one of them a barrack) can be seen as shadow marks in the unploughed rough pasture in the right-hand half of the fort; there is no *porta decumana* or back gate. The evidence from a small

119

72 Newstead (*Trimontium*), Borders (Roxburghshire); Roman fort and campaign base. Vertical photograph, N at top. NT 570344. K17-AS 30: July 1977. Scale 1:4600.

excavation in 1957–8 suggested that the fort was established in the middle of the second century and continued in occupation until the middle of the fourth.

Much of the surrounding ground displays traces of ridge and furrow cultivation, but in the foreground are faint indications of small rectangular plots which may belong to the *vicus* of the fort. The bath-building was probably supplied with water through a leat coming from the small ravine in the foreground. What may be the sinuous course of this aqueduct can be seen near the central field walls. The straight line of the Roman road can be faintly discerned passing to left of the fort.

References

J. Hodgson, *History of Northumberland* (Newcastle, 1840), 74 (with poor plan). J. Collingwood Bruce, *The Roman Wall* (2nd ed., London, 1853), 325. J.K. St Joseph in W.F. Grimes (ed.), *Aspects of Archaeology in Britain and Beyond* (London, 1951), Pl. XVI (oblique view looking NE). N. Shaw, *Arch. Aeliana* (4th series) XXXVII, (1959), 191–202 (excavation report).

RISINGHAM (*HABITANCUM*), Northumberland (71)

The fort of Risingham lies on Dere Street some 20 km by road north of Hadrian's Wall, to which it served as an outpost during the third and fourth centuries. The site lies in a comparatively sheltered position in the wide valley of the river Rede; part of the north-west corner has been eroded by the river, which now flows in a bed further north.

A fort was first placed here in the Antonine period during the reconquest of Scotland *c.* 140–2, and was garrisoned by a part-mounted cohort of Gauls. No remains of this fort are visible, and even the exact size is unknown, save that it extended further west than the visible fort; the latter was built in the early third century and was occupied continuously thereafter until 367.

On the right a multiple ditch system is crossed by a causeway leading to the west gate. But on the east (left) side the appearance of ditches is deceptive, for the visible features are remains of ridge-and-furrow cultivation, and excavation there revealed no traces of ditches below. An expanse of marshy ground on this side was perhaps considered sufficient protection. On the south (far) side traces of multiple ditches do survive, much modified by ridge-and-furrow, especially towards the right, as discontinuity with the west ditches makes clear.

But although part of the ditch system has been ploughed, the interior of the fort has not. Low raking light of a winter's afternoon, falling on ground whitened by frost, has picked out the low relief of features still present on the surface though previously unnoticed. None reflect the ordered layout of a normal fort. Some are the result of old unfilled excavations, but the rest may represent a less regular building-plan of the fourth century or possibly even a post-Roman settlement within the walls.

Certainly the visible fort, which covers 1.8 ha (4.4 acres), underwent considerable reconstruction and replanning, both of the defences and in the interior. The south (far) gate is original, but the west gate was found by excavation to be a single-portal aperture cut through the wall in the early fourth century. The position of the original *portae principales* further south is unknown. The new gate was part of a complete reorganisation of the interior, during which a new *principia* was built facing west down the street leading to the new gate; the latter thus became the *porta praetoria* in a very anomalous position. The late *principia* was partly explored in the 1840s and was left unfilled with dumps of earth around it. A cruciform area was uncovered which can still be seen; the cross-hall (*basilica*) extends north–south with the shrine (*aedes*) on the left. The rest of the surrounding building was left undug. The original Headquarters Building must have lain more centrally and have faced either north or south.

In 1840 part of a small bath-building was uncovered in the south-east (top left) corner, but its remains cannot be distinguished on the photograph. Some of the features in its vicinity recall the late 'chalet' type of barracks known at Housesteads and Great Chesters.

References

I.A. Richmond, *Arch. Aeliana* (4th series) XIII (1936), 184–98; The Romans in Redesdale: *Northumberland County History* XV (1940), 66ff. J. Collingwood Bruce, *Handbook to the Roman Wall* (13th ed. by C.M. Daniels, Newcastle upon Tyne, 1978), 289–94. J.K. StJoseph, *J.R.S.* LIX (1969), 107 with Pl. III, 1 (this view).

NEWSTEAD (*TRIMONTIUM*), Borders (72)

Newstead with its four successive large forts played a key role in Roman strategy for controlling southern Scotland. The site lies on a bluff above the south bank of the river Tweed, in a position to protect the bridge which carried Dere Street across the river, and is overlooked from the south-west by the three peaks of the Eildon Hills (8), from which its name *Trimontium* was derived. The fort was extensively excavated between 1905 and 1910, after which imported soil was spread over the site to a depth of 1 m in order to restore the ground to cultivation; this covering also served to protect the archaeological remains from the plough, and it is remarkable that after this treatment they show so clearly in the photograph.

The earliest fort, built by Agricola to an unusual plan, is buried too deeply to be visible. What can be seen is the street plan and buildings of the Antonine I and II forts, which extend over 5.9 ha (14.7 acres). The *via principalis* crosses the fort from north to south to right of a line of trees, and on its east (right) side lie the barracks occupied first by a vexillation of legionaries and later by the cavalrymen of an *ala milliaria*.

The fort was an important staging-point for traffic using Dere Street and was accordingly furnished with some unusually large fortified annexes to house the convoys and the no doubt numerous resident camp-followers. To the west lay an annexe of 2.8 ha with multiple ditches, clearly seen to left of the fort. To the east was an annexe xv of 8 ha, defended by double ditches seen near the right margin of the photograph. South of the fort lay a third annexe, of 5.9 ha, again with

73 Birrens (*Blatobulgium*), **Dumfries and Galloway; Roman fort,** looking W. NY 218752. UX 9: May 1957.

double ditches which are visible near the centre at the bottom margin, where they are seen to be interrupted by a gap through which ran the Flavian version of Dere Street. Farther to the right, the Antonine version of this road, making for the visible *porta principalis dextra*, can just be traced on either side of an abandoned railway. The photograph also reveals the finer dark lines which mark the ditches of various marching-camps: no less than seven are known near the fort. Three on converging courses can be seen within the east annexe, and one of them is incorporated in the defences of the Flavian version of the east annexe.

Datable finds show that the fort remained in occupation as an outpost of Roman control in the second half of the second century long after the rest of southern Scotland had been given up. The existence to south of the fort (but hardly visible in this photograph) of the most southerly of the series of enormous camps of 66 ha (163 acres) suggests that it was at Newstead that Severus mustered his army of invasion in 208, and the fort has yielded a few sherds of samian pottery which may be contemporary.

References

J. Curle, *A Roman Frontier Post and its People* (Glasgow, 1911). I.A. Richmond, *Proc. Soc. Antiq. Scotland* LXXXIV (1949–50), 1–38. R.C.A.H.M. (Scotland), *Roxburghshire* II (Edinburgh, 1956), 312–20 with map and plans. Samian: B.R. Hartley, *Britannia* III (1972), 40.

BIRRENS (*BLATOBULGIUM*), Dumfries and Galloway (73)

Birrens lies beside the Roman road through southern Scotland which runs north-westwards from Carlisle to Annandale. The site is 16 km from the edge of the low-lying flood-plain of the Esk and 14 km from the Annan valley at Dryfeholm near Lockerbie. Burnswark (18) lies 4.7 km to the north-west. The fort occupies gently sloping ground protected on two sides by streams, the Mein Water (left) and its tributary the Middlebie Burn. During the second century, in periods when Scotland was unoccupied, it served as the most northerly western outpost of Hadrian's Wall and as part of the normal garrison network when the Antonine Wall was held. The fort was the first to be explored in the long programme of excavations of Roman sites begun by the Society of Antiquaries of Scotland in 1895; since then, further excavation has been undertaken in 1936–7 and in 1962–7.

The photograph shows the platform of the fort; the south side has been eroded by the Mein Water. The north side is defended by an impressive series of six ditches which recall the unusual multiple ditch system of Whitley Castle (**70**); they have been eroded on the east (near) side by the Middlebie Burn. Beyond the fort can be seen a second large defended area on a somewhat different alignment. The existence of this enclosure has been known since the time of General Roy, who drew a plan of it in the mid-eighteenth century, but despite additional more accurate detail revealed by aerial photography in 1939 and in later years, it has never been examined by excavation, all effort having been concentrated on the visible fort; date and purpose consequently remain undetermined. The wide surrounding hollow visible on the ground is caused by a system of triple ditches, and a second system of triple ditches has been noted within. The enclosure may well have served as an annexe to successive second-century forts, but the possibility remains that it was originally the site of a Flavian fort. However, interpretation must take account of the fact that the area of the enclosure is crossed obliquely by the line of the Roman road, which is also oblique to the second-century forts.

The visible fort lies over the site of a minor Flavian enclosure with a single small ditch enclosing perhaps 0.53 ha (1.32 acres). Although claimed as a fortlet, this could equally well be a small marching-camp; it appears to be of Agricolan date and, if a fortlet, could well have been replaced in the second Flavian period by a full-sized fort. The principle of economy of hypothesis nevertheless suggests that the two triple-ditched enclosures relate as annexes respectively to the known Hadrianic and Antonine forts, despite their differing alignment.

In Hadrian's reign a cohort fort covering 1.68 ha (4.12 acres) was built over the fortlet as part of the outpost system north of Hadrian's Wall; this fort had a turf rampart and timber buildings save for the central range, which was in stone. In the Antonine period it was replaced on the same site by the visible much larger fort, which probably had an area of 2.07 ha (5.2 acres); the buildings were now all of stone. In the first Antonine period the garrison was *cohors I Nervana Germanorum*, which was replaced in Antonine II by *cohors II Tungrorum*; both were milliary and part-mounted. The new garrison had to rebuild the interior of the fort, which had been destroyed by fire; the

wealth of finds in the debris suggests that enemy action rather than a Roman demolition party had been responsible. If so, the destruction of the fort may have some bearing on events at Burnswark (**18**). Another link between the two sites is the three lead *ballista* balls discovered in the fort, for such lead *glandes* are otherwise extremely rare in military sites of the period.

In the field to the north of the fort crop-marks suggest the presence of another annexe, and in the same area they have revealed the existence of a large timber building which is probably a *mansio* of the posting system.

References

W. Roy, *Military Antiquities* (London, 1793), Pl. xxiv. D. Christison *et al.*, *Proc. Soc. Ant. Scotland* xxx (1896), 81–199 (1895 excavations). E. Birley, *ibid.* lxxii (1937–8), 275–347 (1936–7 excavations). A.S. Robertson, *Birrens (Blatobulgium)* (Edinburgh, 1975), (1962–7 excavations), with review article by D.J. Breeze in *Britannia* viii (1977), 451–60. O.G.S. Crawford, *Antiquity* xiii (1939), 285–6 with Pl. vb (oblique view looking E by C.G.M. Alington). J.K. StJoseph in S.N. Miller (ed.), *The Roman Occupation of South-Western Scotland* (Glasgow, 1952), 85–7 with Pl. xxxiv (oblique view looking E by C.G.M. Alington); *J.R.S.* xli (1951), 57–8; *ibid.* xlviii (1958), Pl. xi, 2 (this view).

DALSWINTON, Dumfries and Galloway (74)

Like the fort at Glenlochar (**75**) Dalswinton was discovered in the drought of 1949. It lies in south-west Scotland in a position overlooking the flood-plain on the east side of the river Nith, 10 km north-west of Dumfries (Fig. 14). The photograph clearly shows that the site is occupied by two successive forts of different sizes, each possessing an attached annexe on the north-east (distant) side. These two annexes overlap, and a third annexe is attached to the south-east (right-hand) side of the larger fort. Excavation in 1954 demonstrated that the earlier fort was the smaller. Both are nevertheless of exceptional size, Fort I being 3.48 ha (8.59 acres) and Fort II 4.16 ha (10.29 acres), and both belong to the first century. Fort I was established by Agricola, perhaps in 82 or 83, and must have contained a garrison consisting of two auxiliary units, both of them probably part-mounted, or possibly of a single *cohors milliaria equitata* if regiments of this size existed so early. The second fort, dating to the period after Agricola's recall when the Romans had abandoned Scotland north of the Forth, is large enough to house a milliary *ala*; but since the only such regiment known in Britain, the *ala Petriana*, was not expanded to milliary size until the opening years of the second century, more probably the fort housed two distinct cavalry regiments, each 500 strong. It

74 Dalswinton, Dumfries and Galloway; Roman fort, looking NE. NX 932849. DV 9: July 1949.

may have been the perceived advantages derived from such a powerful striking force that persuaded the Roman command to expand the *ala Petriana* once the time came to evacuate Dalswinton. At any rate both garrisons were, in their differing ways, of exceptional strength, and they point to the great strategic importance of Dalswinton, which corresponds in south-west Scotland to the key site of Newstead on the Tweed.

The photograph clearly shows the triple longitudinal division of the *praetentura* of the second fort (foreground) by narrow streets defining barrack positions; this fort faced south-west towards the river Nith, behind the camera. But the photograph also shows the wider parch-mark of the *via principalis* of Fort I, running from front to back beneath a large tree and passing across the causeway of the north-east gate of this fort, above the centre of

the picture. The position of this street demonstrates that Fort I faced south-east down the valley.

The position is well chosen, with the north-west flank protected by the steep-sided gully of a minor tributary and the south-west side perched on the crest of a steep slope, cut by the railway in the foreground. The dark lines of substantial ditches descend the slope from either angle of the fort to cut off approach along this side. About 500 m south-east of these forts are crop-marks which suggest the additional presence of a fortlet and the small penannular ditch of a signal-station; these have not yet been tested by excavation.

Other photographs, taken in 1972, have revealed what appear to be the double ditches of another large fort, later reduced in size, on the low-lying flood-plain that just enters the foreground of this

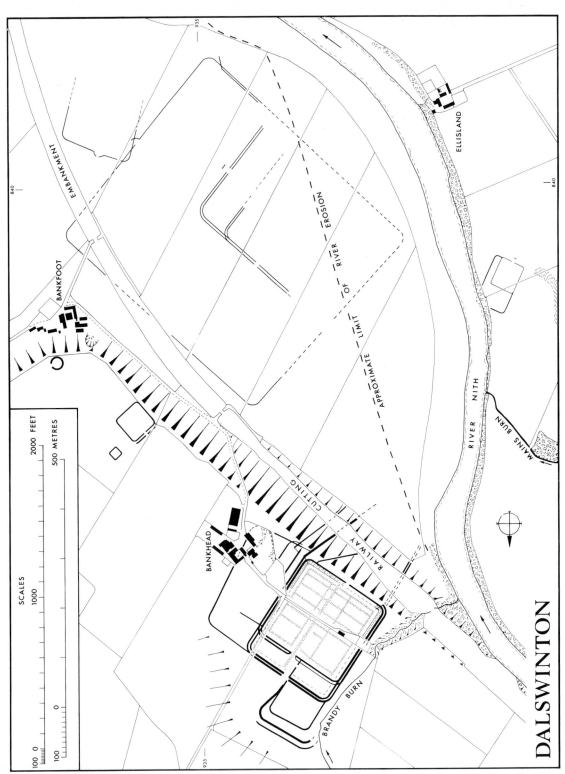

Fig. 14 Dalswinton: general plan.

75 Glenlochar; Roman fort, looking E. MR 67: July 1953.

view. In the same area there are also two Flavian marching-camps, one of them as large as 25 ha (62 acres). As such a position, liable to flood in winter, is less suitable for permanent occupation than the other site high above the valley floor, it may be assumed that these lower forts were held only briefly before transfer of the garrison to the better position. If so, we gain valuable insight into the rapidly changing situation of Agricola's campaigns, calling for frequent redeployment of troops and consequent new construction.

References

J.K. StJoseph, *J.R.S.* XLI (1951), 58–9 with Pl. VI, 1 (oblique view from W). I.A. Richmond and J.K. StJoseph, *Trans. Dumfriesshire and Galloway N.H. and Antiq. Soc.* (3rd series) XXXIV (1957), 9–21, excavation report with plan and Pl. I (oblique view from S). J.K. StJoseph, *Glasgow Arch. Journ.* IV (1976), 7–11 with overall plan and Pl. I (this view); *J.R.S.* LVII (1977), 132 (overall plan).

76 Glenlochar, Dumfries and Galloway; Roman fort, looking E. NX 735645. DV 68: July 1949.

GLENLOCHAR, Dumfries and Galloway (75–6)

The fort lies 3.5 km north of Castle Douglas on the east bank of the river Dee, at one of its few easy crossing-points. In normal years little can be seen (75) save a few irregularities in the ground formerly thought to mark the site of a medieval religious house. In years of drought, however, as in 1949, the plan of a large Roman fort (3.36 ha, 8.3 acres) appears with exceptional clarity (76). It is surrounded by three ditches (along two sides by four), between the outer pair of which, at the south-east angle, can be seen a line of dark marks suggesting holes for some kind of defensive obstacle. Other photographs show the system continuing along the north side. Within the rampart the street system shows as parch-marks and demonstrates that the fort faced west towards the river. In the *retentura*, beyond the site of the Headquarters Building, are plots which probably contained six barracks, divided by the *via decumana*, along the middle of which a dark line indicates a

127

77 Camelon, Central Region (Stirlingshire); Roman fort, looking SW. NS 863810. CNB 14: August 1980.

drain or pipeline. In the *praetentura*, this side of the *via principalis*, there is space for twelve further barracks: the total accommodation suggests that a *cohors milliaria equitata* was in garrison, at least in the Antonine period.

At the top left, the triple ditches of an annexe are seen joining the ditches of the fort. A little beyond the fort can be seen a fine dark line which curves away to pass under a modern lane: this marks the course of a ditch forming two sides and a rounded corner of a large marching-camp. It is one of three camps of larger than legionary size, which, together with several smaller ones on the land east of the fort, point to the continuing military importance of Glenlochar as a base or staging-point for campaigns (15 and Fig. 3).

Excavation in 1952 showed that the crop-marks are of three successive forts on the same site, all with timber-framed buildings. These forts are respectively of the late first century and the first and second Antonine periods of the second century. In the second Antonine period (*c.* A.D. 160) the rampart was widened and now overrides

one of the original ditches, which was carefully packed with turves. Ceramic evidence and the presence of early pits suggest that Glenlochar was first occupied by Agricola, but the actual remains of his fort have not yet been located. Excavation also revealed several interesting structural details; for example, that the turf for the rampart-facing had had to be fetched from the flood-plain of the river, the site itself being too well-drained for the growth of useful turf. The core of the rampart was of fine dark earth, not found naturally on the site. It was considered to be the residue of sieving the subsoil for the gravel which was required in large amounts for the streets; even the berm between the rampart and inner ditch had been gravelled and doubtless had to be kept raked. Further supplies of gravel could have been obtained from quarry-pits now seen as dark marks outside the east and south faces of the fort.

In the annexe, near the river-bank, other photographs reveal a large timber-framed courtyard building which can be recognised as a *mansio* or official rest-house of the posting service.

128

References

J.K. StJoseph, *J.R.S.* XLI (1951), 60 with Pl. VII (similar oblique); *J.R.S.* LV (1965), 79–80. M.V. Taylor, *J.R.S.* XLIII (1953), 107–9 with plan and section. Excavation report: I.A. Richmond and J.K. StJoseph, *Trans. Dumfries-shire and Galloway N.H. and Antiq. Soc.* (3rd series) XXX (1953), 1–16 with plan, sections and Pl. I (different oblique view). R.G. Collingwood and I.A. Richmond, *The Archaeology of Roman Britain* (2nd ed., London, 1969), Pl. IIA (oblique view of marching camp). S.S. Frere, *Britannia, A History of Roman Britain* (London, 1967), Pl. 15A (similar view).

CAMELON, Central Region (77)

Camelon lies 1.1 km north of the Antonine Wall beside the Roman road leading northwards to Stirling and the basin of the Tay. This road crosses the river Carron, a small tributary of the Forth, about 1 km beyond Camelon, and the position of the fort, so distant from the crossing, suggests that its primary concern may have been with the protection of a nearby harbour rather than with the protection of a bridge. Such a harbour would greatly facilitate the arrival of supplies for the eastern half of the Antonine Wall.

The fort has a splendid command of the low-lying carse land eastwards to Grangemouth and the shore of the Forth, nearly 7 km away. The river is now tidal only as far upstream as the Carron ironworks but, before the construction of a weir there at the end of the eighteenth century, no doubt tides reached further west. However, the Carron in its lower reaches has only a very slight gradient, flowing sluggishly towards the sea. Moreover, the nearest point on the river is as much as 0.5 km distant from Camelon. In the foreground of the photograph, the land at the foot of the scarp is now at *c*. 9 m above Ordnance Datum, and slopes gradually to the river. The geographical changes that must be shown to have taken place before a harbour here can be postulated, though not inconsiderable, are by no means impossible. Roy, indeed, marks an old course of the river within 150 to 200 m of the east side of the fort. Much depends upon the extent to which sea-level at the head of the Firth of Forth has changed since Roman times, and the effect of any such change (which is unlikely to have exceeded 1 to 3 m) upon the regime of the Carron. The theory of a harbour, first put forward by T.W.T. Tatton-Brown, has undoubted attractions, for it would explain the large size and the position of the fort and would account for the large annexes. To the arguments adduced by Tatton-Brown may be added the fact that the Antonine fort faced east as if its principal concern lay in that direction rather than to the north, the direction followed by the Roman road.

The second-century fort, visible in the photograph, occupies a level terrace of sand and gravel less than 18 m above sea-level. In Flavian times a fort had been built marginally further south, but its site and that of a large Antonine annexe which succeeded it have during the present century been covered with factories (top left). A second large annexe was attached to the north side of the Antonine fort (right), but has been to a great extent destroyed by recent quarrying.

Excavations in 1899–1900, prompted by the imminent construction of factories south of the railway, were in the event mainly confined to the Antonine fort to the north. There the fort's ditches enclose 3.12 ha (7.72 acres), and the whole circuit can be traced in the photograph except for the south corner, which is cut off by the railway. The buildings in the central range together with the barracks and stables in the *praetentura* (foreground) had foundations of stone, but those in the *retentura* were of half-timbered construction which the early excavators were unable to trace with the techniques then available. The garrison, to judge by the size of the barracks, may have been a *cohors milliaria* rather than a cavalry *ala*.

The level tongue of land extending from the fort to a point near Lochlands farm 1 km to the north-west, near where the Roman road crossed the Carron, was of considerable strategic importance as the jumping-off point for Roman campaigns further north. This is emphasised by the presence of no less than nine marching-camps. They vary in size and in date, but the northernmost two at least are of the Flavian period, to judge by the plans of their gates.

References

W. Roy, *Military Antiquities* (London, 1793), Pl. XXIX. D. Christison *et al., Proc. Soc. Ant. Scotland* XXXV (1900–1), 329–417 (excavations). R.C.A.H.M. (Scotland), *Stirling-shire* I (Edinburgh, 1963), 107–12 (with plan). D.J. Breeze *et al., Britannia* VII (1976), 73–95 (burials). T. Tatton-Brown, *Britannia* XI (1980), 340–3 (harbour). J.K. StJoseph, *J.R.S.* XLI (1951), 62 with Pl. VIII, 1 (steep oblique view looking W).

DALGINROSS, Tayside (78)

The fort at Dalginross is one of a series north of the Forth–Clyde line built at the openings of the major glens which afford the easiest routes for large forces entering or leaving the Scottish Highlands. The series is of Flavian date and was probably designed as part of Agricola's strategy in the last years of his governorship, when his lines of communication to the far north were stretched and consequently liable to attack from the rear.

78 Dalginross, Tayside (Perthshire); Roman fort and marching-camp, vertical photograph, N at top right. NN 773210. K17-AS 12: July 1977. Scale 1:4200.

None of this series of 'front-line' forts was re-occupied in the second century, Antonine garrisons being placed only along the road to the Tay.

The fort is situated where the river Earn emerges from the Highland front. The exact position, 1 km south of Comrie, lies on the edge of a gravel terrace above the bank of a tributary, the Water of Ruchill, seen at the left of the plate. Periodic

shifts in the course of this stream since Roman times have eroded about a third of the fort, whose double ditches can be seen just below a belt of dark trees at top centre. The site has long been under the plough, but the line of the defences can still be traced on the ground. The fort has an area of 2.43 ha (6 acres).

Outside the fort the broad single ditch and

accompanying rampart of an outer enclosure can be clearly traced. This enclosure used to be taken as part of a larger fort, an identification that would indicate two periods of military occupation at Dalginross in contrast to the single period attested at all the other forts in this series. The wide somewhat irregular curve of the south-east corner and the much sharper curve at the east corner, now obscured by buildings, together with the lack of parallelism between the north and south sides are, however, uncharacteristic of a fort's defences. Moreover, excavation in 1961, before the building of a bungalow near the east corner, failed to reveal any buildings. The enclosure is best interpreted as an outer defensive perimeter for the fort. Such an arrangement is rare but not unique (see Greensforge, **55**). Within the enclosure are several large pits, which are perhaps quarries for the gravel used in constructing the streets of the fort. Of the fort itself, the positions of two of the gates and part of the *intervallum* road are visible. On the original photograph the construction trenches of some of the timber buildings can be seen, some of which are too faint to appear on the reproduction (**78**); it does, however, pick out the overall darker tone of the interior of the fort compared with the area immediately outside.

Immediately south of the fort and on the same flat gravel terrace is a marching-camp of some 9.3 ha (23 acres). The narrow dark line of the ditch defining three of the four sides is clearly visible, as are three of the gates. Their position shows that the camp faced south-west; the gates at each end of the *via principalis* are unusually near to the south-west front. Each gate has an outward-curving ditch marking an external *clavicula*, while from the other side of the gateway-opening a straight spur of ditch extends outwards at an angle towards the *clavicula*. This combination defines a rare kind of camp entrance which has been called the 'Stracathro type', after the camp at the site of that name. The type is known only in Scotland, where all examples are of Flavian date. However, the camps which exhibit it vary considerably in size; they do not, therefore, represent the movements of a single force, but are likely nevertheless to indicate the handiwork either of troops from an individual legion or at any rate of troops directed by a single commander, whose ingenuity was responsible for the device.

All known examples of the Stracathro type of gateway have been flattened by the plough; but in the eighteenth century, when General Roy was carrying out his surveys of Roman sites, the land at Dalginross was still unploughed and the Roman earthworks were visible in relief. Roy's plan (see Fig. 15) shows that formerly there was in addition

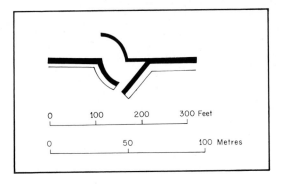

Fig. 15 Dalginross, marching-camp: plan of 'Stracathro-type' gateway, after General Roy. The interior of the camp is to the top of the plan.

an internal *clavicula*, unaccompanied by a ditch (and therefore now untraceable). The plan also confirms that at each gate the rampart turned outwards, accompanying the two external ditches defining the entrance. The combination of all these elements created a gateway very difficult for an enemy to penetrate.

In the middle of the camp some regular lines of rubbish pits can be seen running from the north-east side of the *via principalis*; they recall the more extensive examples at Inchtuthil (**21**) and perhaps indicate that the camp had a more prolonged occupation than usual. Dalginross lies *c.* 13 km as the crow flies from the 30-acre camps at Ardoch and Strageath, and 20 km from that at Dunblane. The conjecture may be made that Dalginross and one of these camps were held by the forces involved in A.D. 83 in the near-defeat of the Ninth Legion and its timely rescue by Agricola after a night's march.

References

W. Roy, *Military Antiquities* (London, 1793), Pl. XI. O.G.S. Crawford, *The Topography of Roman Scotland* (Cambridge, 1949), 41–5 with (inaccurate) plan of fort. J.K. StJoseph, *J.R.S.* XLI (1951), 64; LV (1965), 81; LIX (1969), 109, 113. Excavation (by A.S. Robertson); *J.R.S.* LII (1962), 162; *Proc. Soc. Ant. Scotland* XCVII (1963–4), 196–8.

ARDOCH, Tayside (79)

The Roman turf-and-timber fort of Ardoch is remarkable for the well-preserved state of its defences; this fort and Whitley Castle (**70**) are two of the best surviving examples in the Roman Empire. In the photograph, long shadows cast by low evening sunlight have emphasised both the earthworks and the uneven surface of the gravel moraine on which the site has been placed. The

79 Ardoch, Tayside (Perthshire); Roman fort, looking NW. NN 839099. BKW 37: October 1972.

gully of the river Knaik, a tributary of the Allan Water, protects the west side. This association with the Allan Water has suggested identification of the fort with *Alauna*, a place-name recorded by Ptolemy.

Here, as at Strageath (**80**), excavation has shown that three successive forts lie superimposed, and the complicated proliferation of ditches is in large part the result of this fact. The prominent rectangular fort belongs to the Antonine II period of the second century. Its predecessor, the Antonine I fort, had evidently housed a garrison of larger size; for this fort although of the same east–west width as its successor had had a greater length, extending further to the north (right). The north-east angle and north side of the Antonine I fort can be seen a short distance to the right of those of the later fort, having been chopped off by two ditches accompanying the new north rampart. The area of the Antonine I fort was 3.15 ha (7.8 acres); the Antonine II fort was reduced to 2.31 ha (5.75 acres), a size still large enough to house a milliary cohort of infantry. The earlier Antonine fort therefore probably contained a mixed force

of both cavalry and infantry. The defences of the original first-century (Flavian) fort cannot be identified with confidence; but since excavation showed that its buildings extended right up to the existing east and north ramparts (foreground), the Flavian rampart must have been further forward and its core must be represented by one of the banks dividing the later ditches. There is a first-century tombstone from Ardoch recording a soldier of *cohors I Hispanorum*; it seems probable that the Flavian fort was large enough to accommodate another regiment in addition to the Spaniards who were only 500 strong at that date.

The defences of the fort owe their remarkable preservation to the fact that they have never been levelled for agriculture. A number of other Roman forts in Scotland were in like state when General Roy made his survey in the mid-eighteenth century. The interior is, however, crossed by low ridges of nineteenth-century ploughing. Near the centre of the fort the site of a medieval chapel can be seen within a rectangular enclosure formed by a low earth bank. North of the fort lies a large annexe defended by a substantial bank and ditch,

132

80 Strageath, Tayside (Perthshire); **Roman fort**, vertical photograph, N at top. NN 898181. V-BC 57: July 1962. Scale 1:2500.

part of which can be seen on the near side of the modern A 822 road; its defences turn east in the belt of trees on the right of the photograph where they are cut by the defences of the largest of the several marching-camps which lie adjacent to the fort. The area in the right foreground, covered by a belt of fir trees and its dense black shadow, was chosen for yet another Roman fortified enclosure defended by double ditches, visible in other photographs, and by a massive turf rampart. The area is about 1.75 ha (4.3 acres). Since the larger fort itself shows the three periods of occupation normal in this part of Scotland, the smaller enclosure may be thought to represent either a separate stores depot or else a short-lived earlier occupation. An outpost fort might have been established at Ardoch between 81 and 83 in front of the temporary *limes* then held on the Forth–Clyde line. Alternatively the post may have been

held merely while the not inconsiderable work of levelling the hummocky moraine on the main site was in progress. This site occupies a somewhat better position but one which may not have been readily usable.

The Roman road running north-east to Strageath passes between the two forts on the far side of a field wall.

References

W. Roy, *Military Antiquities* (1793) Pls. x, xxx. D. Christison *et al., Proc. Soc. Ant. Scotland* XXXII (1898), 399–476 (excavation report). O.G.S. Crawford, *Topography of Roman Scotland* (Cambridge, 1949), 30–39 (with plans). J.K. St Joseph, *J.R.S.* XLVIII (1958), Pl. XII, 1 (oblique view from N); *Britannia* I (1970), 163–78 (the marching-camps); *Glasgow Arch. Journ.* IV (1976), Pl. 4 (this view) and overall plan. S.S. Frere, *Britannia, A History of Roman Britain* (London, 1967), Pl. 13 B (oblique view from SE). A.L.F. Rivet and C. Smith, *The Place-Names of Roman Britain* (London, 1979), 245.

STRAGEATH, Tayside (80)

The fort at Strageath lies 10 km north-east of Ardoch (79) on the Roman road leading from Stirling towards the crossing of the Tay at the fort of Bertha near Perth. The precise site is a knoll of glacial sand overlooking the crossing of the river Earn (off top of picture). The substantial ramparts of the fort are still visible on the surface despite having been under plough for several centuries (as General Roy's plan makes clear). Normally little else is visible, but in a summer drought the street and ditch systems of the fort and of its annexes show with unusual clarity when under a cereal crop. In this photograph the area occupied by the annexes (bottom third of photograph) carries a root crop, unresponsive to differences in the soil.

The Roman road coming from the south-west can just be seen as a faint parch-mark in the root crop, where it divides; the branch to the left bypasses the fort and makes for the river-crossing. The other branch traverses an annexe to enter the *porta praetoria* of the fort at a slight change of angle.

The fort itself is almost square, with its north-east angle invisible in a light-toned grass field. The complicated ditch system (marked by dark lines) is caused by repeated refortification, for excavation in progress since 1973 has shown that three successive forts occupy the site, and not all the ditches are contemporary. On the near side of the fort, the *porta principalis sinistra* seems at one stage to have been protected by an outlying *titulum*. The defences of the annexe, not seen in this photograph, are of matching complication. Finds show that the original fort was established here by Agricola, possibly in 81 or 83. This was soon evacuated, perhaps in 86 or 87; but the site was reoccupied on two occasions during the second century, in the first and second Antonine periods. Although the army of Severus advanced along the road in 208–9 the fort was not then re-established, but two very large marching-camps (25.5 and 52.6 ha), which are attributed to these campaigns, have been identified across the Earn at Innerpeffray.

The fine striations crossing the field are the sowing-lines of a cereal crop, but against this background the light-toned line of the *via principalis* can be seen running across the fort with the area of the *principia* on its right-hand side facing the *via praetoria*. The *principia* is outlined by thin parch-lines representing metalled paths; no stone buildings existed in any period. The *via sagularis* runs round the perimeter within the rampart and the *via decumana* extends from the back of the *principia* to the *porta decumana* (right) leading to the river. The approach to this gate was at some stage blocked by two wide ditches forming outlying elements of the defences.

The fort was only 1.7 ha (4.2 acres) in extent, but nevertheless in all three periods it housed a succession of very powerful garrisons, some members of which in the first century may have been outposted to the watch-towers along the Gask ridge beyond the Earn.

References

A. Gordon, *Itinerarium Septentrionale* (London, 1726), 42, Pl. 7 (plan). W. Roy, *Military Antiquities* (London, 1793), Pl XXXII (plan). O.G.S. Crawford, *Topography of Roman Scotland* (Cambridge, 1949), 40–1 with Pl. V (oblique view from E). *J.R.S.* XLVIII (1958), Pl. XII, 2 (oblique view from S); J.K. StJoseph, *Glasgow Arch. Journ.* IV (1976), 19–22 with plan of crop-marks and Pl. 6 (oblique view from N). For excavations, see *Roman Britain* reports annually in *Britannia* from Vol. V (1974).

8

SMALL MILITARY EARTHWORKS: FORTLETS, SIGNAL-TOWERS AND PRACTICE CAMPS

Fortlets

Roman forts, as we have already seen, varied very considerably in size: the term 'fortlet', as the diminutive of 'fort', should indicate something smaller even than a small fort. Precision in the use of terms is always desirable; accordingly the distinction between a (small) fort and a fortlet has been defined by the absence of an administrative headquarters building (*principia*) from the latter. A military site, however small, which was occupied by an independent unit with its own administration, is a fort; the garrison of a fortlet lacked its own administrative apparatus, because the troops comprised a detachment from a unit whose headquarters was elsewhere.

This definition admittedly suffers a disadvantage in that it can properly be applied only after the facts have been revealed by excavation; in practice, however, there is a large group of sites which are too small to be suspected of possessing *principia*, and which on analogy with such excavated examples as Martinhoe or Barburgh Mill, or the Milecastles of Hadrian's Wall, can safely be classified as fortlets. Ambiguity remains only within a range of slightly larger sites, of some 0.6–1 ha (1.5–2.5 acres), which might fall into either class; these include some of the 'forts' on the Antonine Wall.

Fortlets are one of the categories of site for which the Roman term was *burgus*. The second-century fortlet at Barburgh Mill, Dumfriesshire, had an overall area of 0.12 ha (0.3 acre) and was garrisoned by a single century with its centurion; Martinhoe, Devon, of Neronian date, is slightly smaller (0.09 ha, 0.22 acre) but had a garrison of approximately the same size. In upper Germany the late first-century fortlet at Kemel was only slightly smaller (0.07 ha, 0.18 acre), but seems to have had a garrison half the size; the Trajanic fortlet at Degerfeld had an area of 0.11 ha (0.27 acre) with almost a century in garrison.

The most systematic use of fortlets is on Hadrian's Wall, where one was placed at every mile along the frontier, and on the Antonine Wall in its first state, where a very similar distribution has been found. On Hadrian's Wall, the Milecastles seem rarely to have held more than 30 men and often perhaps as few as 8. The deduction can be made that these fortlets were occupied by troops concerned with patrolling the Wall and manning the turrets. The type of troops assigned these duties on the frontier is not recorded: they could have been auxiliaries detached from nearby forts, but perhaps more probably they belonged to formations of lower status known as *numeri* (p. 000).

Elsewhere in the North and in Wales fortlets are found along the roads, often in places where the intervals between forts is exceptionally great (83); but in Antonine Scotland their distribution represents a deliberate economising in the use of auxiliary units. A garrison of 30–80 men was easily able to exercise police functions, patrolling the road and maintaining surveillance of the native population; but widespread use of such small forces, often out of reach of immediate support, suggests confidence in the strength of the *pax Romana*.

Signal-towers

The smallest permanent works of all are those which enclose nothing but a tower used for observation and signalling. These also could be termed *burgi* by the Romans. The majority of towers were of wood; but in the second and later centuries some were built in stone: an example has recently been found on Holyhead Mountain, where it presumably served a purpose connected with sea-borne traffic. Scenes on the columns of Trajan and of Marcus Aurelius prove that signalling was one of the purposes of towers; obviously look-out was another. Unfortunately English lacks an embracing descriptive term; in this book 'signal-tower' and 'watch-tower' are used indiscriminately, without implying exclusive definition.

Such towers, normally surrounded by a small earthwork and ditch and possessing a single entrance-causeway (cf. Fig. 14), were used in a variety of ways. Some stand in isolated positions such as that on Eildon Hill North (8), which surveys a huge area invisible from the fort of Newstead below. Likewise serving as the 'eye' of a nearby fort is the tower at the entrance to the Sma' Glen in Perthshire; there is no view into the Glen from the fort at Fendoch itself because a ridge of moraine hides the valley floor, while a bend in the valley causes the upper slopes soon to pass out of sight. Other towers are members of a series; examples are found on the Gask Ridge or in the Stainmore Pass. At first sight they suggest a long-distance signalling system, perhaps connecting Inchtuthil with the southern part of its legionary command, or linking Hadrian's Wall with York. Yet, despite many years of aerial search, essential components of these supposed extended systems are missing over long sectors. Alternative explanations make better sense. In Scotland, the fortlet of Kaims Castle (NN 861129) enjoys a spectacular and commanding outlook north-eastwards towards Strathmore, a view which the fort at Ardoch lacks. The three signal-towers lying between these two sites divide the distance into four equal intervals each of 1000 yards (924 m). All three towers are surrounded by two ditches, unlike those on the Gask Ridge which possess but one ditch. At present only one tower (Westerton, NN 873146) is known between Kaims Castle and Strageath; this has a single ditch. If contact was intended between Kaims Castle and Strageath at least one more tower must remain to be found between Westerton and Strageath. Beyond Strageath lies the Gask Ridge, on which eleven towers are known, each (like Westerton) with a single surrounding ditch. These facts suggest that the Ardoch–Kaims Castle system was distinct from that further north-east, and that it was originally constructed for the security of Ardoch; but that later the line of towers was extended to Strageath and along the Gask Ridge. The completed series would serve a good local purpose as a cordon protecting Fife from infiltration by the Caledonians (p. 58). The Stainmore towers can also be seen in a local context, as an additional safeguard in the late first century, when the road was functioning as a patrolled cordon against large-scale movement on the high moors. Recent attempts to recognise an extension of the Stainmore system northwards into the Eden valley are unconvincing.

Roman signalling was relatively rudimentary. On Trajan's Column towers are accompanied by log-beacons and by straw-stacks; the former would give a light by night, while the straw, suitably dampened, would give a smoke-signal by day. Some towers are shown with a flaming torch projecting from an upper-storey window, and these could perhaps be used to semaphore. Vegetius (*Epitoma rei militaris* III 5), however, describes a somewhat more sophisticated semaphore system: towers, he says, can be provided with wooden arms, and messages can be transmitted by raising or lowering them.

The troops at any particular tower must have

been few in number; they were doubtless outposted from a neighbouring fort. Excavation in 1969 at Shielhill North near Ardoch found pieces of burnt daub associated with the tower, which suggests that the ground floor was enclosed as accommodation. The ground floor was certainly thus used in the turrets of Hadrian's Wall.

In the second half of the fourth century a system of rather more substantial towers, enclosed in strong walled fortlets, was built along the Yorkshire coast (47); as far as possible they were placed on high cliffs, and were evidently used in conjunction with naval vessels watching for Pictish sea-raiders from the North.

Practice camps

In the late first and second centuries, when the Roman army was at the height of its power and efficiency, there is evidence that at least some units received field-training in earthwork construction. The speedy erection of a defensible camp might be crucial on campaign, while the ability to use turf might often be required for new forts as well as camps. In the vicinity of Vetera (Xanten) in Lower Germany aerial photographs have revealed the existence of over sixty small camps; many are insufficiently large to represent the movements of troops. At Bootham Stray, 2.5 km north of York, two small camps survive from an original group of seven or eight; these lie on waterlogged ground although drier sites are available close by, and may also therefore be classified

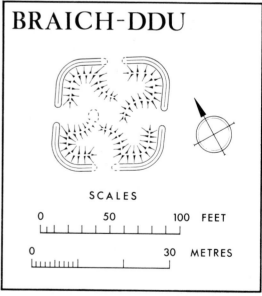

Fig. 16 Braich-Ddu near Tomen-y-Mur: plan of practice camp.

81 Old Burrow, Countisbury, Devon; Roman fortlet, looking WNW. SS 788494. AW 72: June 1948.

as practice camps. Similar groups of small camps exist near Hadrian's Wall (30). The group of military earthworks at Cawthorn (62) has been associated with the training of legionaries from York, but here it was full-scale forts which were being built.

More certainly identifiable as practice works are some groups of earthworks in Wales, for they are so small as to be useless for any other conceivable purpose (87). To build a rampart 2–3 m high in turf calls for skill and practice if subsequent collapse is to be avoided; but greater skill is needed for the turning of rounded angles and of *claviculae*, both of which were built to regular radii. It was upon these components that attention was concentrated; many of the earthworks are of the smallest possible size consistent with four rounded corners and one or two *claviculae*, but some have *titula* as well. The pure essence of the exercise is seen in the plan of Braich-Ddu (Fig. 16), a practice camp near Tomen-y-Mur, where the four *claviculae* meet in the middle and there is no room for anything else.

Several groups have been discovered; the best-known, perhaps comprising as many as eighteen camps, is found on Llandrindod Common (Powys). Most can be associated with a fort, but lie at a distance of some 2–3 km; evidently the combination of a healthy march with other field-exercises was considered advantageous.

Construction of practice camps may have been a comparatively short-lived form of military exercise, for examples are by no means plentiful. The large proportion with *claviculae* should fall within the period *c.* 70–130, and it may not be extravagant to suggest that this form of training was introduced on orders issued during Hadrian's visit to Britain. However that may be, there is evidence for his interest in field-training (*I. L. S.* 2487, 9133–5, his *allocutio* to the troops in Africa). After his death the new campaign in Scotland will have diverted energies into other channels.

References

Fortlets: R.G. Collingwood and I.A. Richmond, *The Archaeology of Roman Britain* (2nd ed., London, 1969), 68–9. V.E. Nash-Williams, *The Roman Frontier in Wales* (2nd ed. by M.G. Jarrett, Cardiff, 1969), 130–44. Barburgh Mill: D. Breeze, *Britannia* v (1974), 130–62. Martinhoe: A. Fox and W. Ravenhill, *Proc. Devon Arch. Soc.* XXIV (1966).

Signal-towers: Collingwood and Richmond, *op. cit.*, 60–6. Gask Ridge: A.S. Robertson in *Trans. Perthshire Soc. of Nat. Science* (special issue 1973), 14–29. Westerton: *Britannia* XII (1981), 319. Stainmore Pass: I.A. Richmond in

82 Stoke Hill, Devon; Roman signal-station or fortlet, looking E. SX 924953. MH 57: July 1953.

W.F. Grimes (ed.), *Aspects of Archaeology in Britain and Beyond* (London, 1951), 293–302.

Practice camps: R.W. Davies, *Arch. Camb.* CXVII (1968), 103–20. V.E. Nash-Williams, *op. cit.*, 126–30, and for Llandrindod Common, *idem*, 1st ed. (Cardiff, 1954) Pl. XXIV. G.D.B. Jones and W.A.C. Knowles, *Bull. Board of Celtic Studies* XVIII (1958–60), 397–402. J.K. StJoseph, *J.R.S.* LIX (1969), 126–7. J. Bennett in W.S. Hanson and L.J.F. Keppie (eds.), *Roman Frontier Studies* 1979 (B.A.R. Int. Series 71 (1), Oxford, 1980), 151–72.

OLD BURROW, Countisbury, Devon (81)

This fortlet and that at Martinhoe, which is slightly less well preserved, both stand on high cliffs on the north coast of Devon, and are both of an unusual type only matched in England at Stoke Hill, Exeter (82). Old Burrow consists of two concentric elements: (1) an outer enclosure 90 m (295 ft) across, somewhat curved in plan and having an entrance through its defending bank and ditch near the south-west corner (on the left of the photograph); (2) an inner rectangular area measuring 26.5 by 28.3 m (87 by 93 ft) defended by a turf-revetted rampart and two ditches, with entrance on the north-east side on the opposite face to the outer entrance. Martinhoe has the same arrangement, which compels an attacker to run the gauntlet of missiles hurled from the whole length of the north-west side and the north corner before arriving at the inner gate. At Martinhoe the fortlet contained two timber-framed barrack-like structures suggesting occupation by a *centuria*; at Old Burrow only the east half of the interior was examined and here only random post-holes appeared, together with a small cook-house. Thus Old Burrow was garrisoned either by a smaller force (on the assumption that one barrack remains to be found), or by troops camping out either in tents or in temporary structures. The difference appears to correspond with a difference in date of occupation. Old Burrow yielded material thought to be of Claudian date (A.D. 43–54)

138

whereas Martinhoe was occupied in the reign of Nero (54–68) and possibly even into the 70s.

Old Burrow stands on a cliff 332 m high with a superb view of the Bristol Channel and the South Wales coast. Martinhoe lies 90 m lower but with equally good outlook, and clearly the purpose of both was to observe the Channel for Silurian raiders and to give warning to the Roman navy. Ten kilometres to the east of Old Burrow, partly in sight, lies Porlock Bay, which may have afforded sufficient shelter for a small naval station. No connecting links for signalling southwards, for instance to Exeter, are known, so that the purpose of the posts seems to be purely tactical and local.

References

J.P. Bushe-Fox, *J.R.S.* XXII (1932), Pl. XIX (plan). *J.R.S.* LIV (1964), 171. A. Fox and W. Ravenhill, *Antiquity* XXXIX (1965), 253–8 (interim report); *Proc. Devon Archaeological Exploration Soc.* XXIV (1966), 1–39 (excavation report including Pl. VI, oblique view).

STOKE HILL, Devon (82)

The slight earthwork that marks this site occupies a summit 158 m (520 ft) high, 3 km NNE of the centre of Exeter. A subrectangular enclosure, *c.* 119 m square embracing 1.28 ha (3.16 acres), is formed by a ditch with a matching rampart showing in light tone on the photograph. Near the centre is a smaller enclosure, 34 m square with an entrance on the east; the entrance through the outer enclosure is not visible, and probably lay on the south side, where it is obscured by modern features. Excavation yielded only a coin of Carausius (286–93) and a third-century potsherd, both unstratified; but the character of the earthwork so closely resembles the mid-first-century fortlets of Old Burrow (81) and Martinhoe on the north coast of Devon that Stoke Hill is best accepted as of comparable date. It commands extensive views not only up the valleys of the rivers Exe and Creedy to north-west and north-east as well as southwards to the estuary of the Exe, but also over much other hilly country to the north-east and south-east and (less effectively) to the west. The reuse of the summit for a station of the Royal Observer Corps during the Second World War (82) emphasises the tactical value of the position.

Excavation failed to reveal traces of any substantial tower, but the position is such that only a low tower not requiring deep post-holes would be necessary, if one were needed at all. The earthwork presumably formed a link in the communications system of Legion II Augusta which lay at Exeter from the 50s to the 70s of the first century. Alternatively a date in the late third century would suggest use in connection with naval defence against the Saxon and Irish pirates of that period.

References

J. Fox, *Antiquity* XXVII (1953), 239–40 with Pl. VII (vertical). J.K. StJoseph, *J.R.S.* XLIII (1953), 97; *J.R.S.* XLV (1955), 88 with Pl. XXI, 2 (oblique). M.V. Taylor, *J.R.S.* XLVII (1957), 222. Excavation report: A. Fox and W. Ravenhill, *Trans. Devonshire Association* XCI (1959), 71–82 with Fig. 9 (oblique).

PEN-Y-CROGBREN, Powys (83)

Like many Roman roads in Wales, the road between the forts of Caersws and Pennal prefers to climb to the high plateau instead of pursuing a tortuous course through steep and narrow valleys. In the photograph, taken when the ground was under a light covering of snow, the road is seen following an easy route along a ridge between the headwaters of the Afon Twymyn, seen on the left, and the Clywedog. In the foreground on the summit of the ridge, at a height of 466 m, is seen the small fortlet of Pen-y-Crogbren, lying about half-way between the forts of Caersws and Pennal, *c.* 18.5 km from each. The fortlet is a rectangular earthwork measuring 23.5 by 20.2 m and thus covering 0.05 ha (0.12 acre). Excavation has shown that the rampart was of turf, 3.05 m wide and still standing 1 m high; there was no ditch since rock lies close to the surface. The corners are unusually sharp, a structural detail which may reflect the poor quality of the available turf. The single entrance-causeway can be seen facing the road; it was found to be defended by a gate-structure of four posts probably carrying a tower. The interior had been stripped of turf and metalled, and although no buildings were traced in the sector excavated much charred wood lay on the gravel. Finds suggested a date in the second quarter of the second century for the fortlet's construction.

Small intermediate stations of very similar character but varying size occur elsewhere in Wales, for instance at Brithdir, Erglodd, Hirfynydd and Pen-min-Cae; they allowed a wider spacing of cohort forts than might otherwise have proved necessary and thus permitted economies in manpower. A secondary advantage would be the provision of shelter for travellers on these often remote and exposed routes.

References

J.K. StJoseph, *J.R.S.* LI (1961), 129. M.V. Taylor, *ibid.* 157–8 with Pl. XIII, 1 (view of section through turf rampart). V.E. Nash-Williams, *The Roman Frontier in Wales* (2nd ed. by M.G. Jarrett, Cardiff, 1969), 142–4 (plan).

83 Pen-y-Crogbren, Powys (Montgomeryshire); Roman road and fortlet looking E. SN 856935. CII 33: February 1979.

DERE STREET, CHEW GREEN, Northumberland (84–5)

The photograph gives a striking impression of the course of Dere Street northwards across the Cheviots. The road makes a steep, well-engineered zig-zag descent of the 122 m north-facing slope of Harden Edge (below the camera) to cross the River Coquet; it then climbs to the opposite slope, passing to right of the Roman earthworks, and sweeping round the east side of Brownhart Law. There, about 1 km beyond the earthworks, a signal-station was discovered by aerial reconnaissance in 1945, to the left of the road and near the head of the first deeply entrenched side-valley. The position affords extensive views to the north-west, so that in clear weather contact could quickly be established with the fort at Newstead 33 km away, by means of the signal-towers on Rubers Law and Eildon North Hill.

The Roman works at Chew Green are well-preserved and indicate long or frequent use. They were numbered by Richmond. The earliest (I) is a large marching-camp (7.6 ha), with internal *claviculae*. The south and west sides are nearest the camera; the south-east corner and part of the east side have been destroyed by later works, but beyond these the north-east angle and north side may clearly be distinguished (85). They are cut by the rampart and ditch of a second marching-camp (III) whose south side approaches the north defences of a large well-defined rectangular enclosure (left foreground). This second camp runs northward beside Dere Street and encloses 5.7 ha. Five of its six gates are protected by *titula* but the south gate lacks one, apparently because of proximity to the enclosure, which must have been already in existence. This enclosure (IV) of 2.61 ha (6.46 acres), well placed on a spur of the hill (85), has a prominent rampart and large rock-

140

84 Dere Street and the Roman military earthworks at Chew Green, Northumberland; looking N. NT 7808. F 90: July 1945.

cut ditch; the four gates have internal *claviculae* and two appear to possess *titula* as well.[1] Excavation in 1936 revealed metalled streets and pits in the interior, and the conclusion was then reached that this was the construction camp for the visible fortlet (V) which lies to the east beside Dere Street. It seems more probable, however, that the substantial defences and internal features of IV indicate a permanent fort. The fortlet (V) is 0.43

1. But the supposed *titulum* at the north gate of IV is more probably part of an upcast mound outside the ditch of III.

ha (1.06 acres) in area and on its south side has two adjoining annexes. It is of Antonine date and has been found to overlie a somewhat smaller Flavian fortlet (II), invisible on the surface. Thus, if the original fortlet (II) is of Agricolan date, Chew Green IV might represent a late Flavian fort, in turn succeeded by an Antonine fortlet. In addition to the routine duty of guarding the road, the garrison at Chew Green was well placed to assist baggage-trains negotiating these steep hills and to control the head of the Coquet valley, seen in the foreground.

141

85 The Roman military earthworks at Chew Green; looking NNW. BAJ 12: January 1970.

References

W. Roy, *Military Antiquities*, Pl. XXII (plan). I.A. Richmond, 'The Romans in Redesdale', *Northumberland County History* XV (1940), 70, 75–6 with plans and oblique views from S and W; *Arch. Aeliana* (4th series) XIV (1937), 129–50 (excavation report). Brownhart Law: J.K. StJoseph, *Proc. Soc. Ant. Scotland* LXXXIII (1951), 170–74 with Pl. XXXIV (steep oblique view).

DURISDEER, Dumfries and Galloway (86)

The Roman road up Nithsdale from the direction of Dumfries extends as far as Durisdeer, where it turns north-eastwards to run for 15 km through the Lowther hills towards Crawford in Clydesdale, near which it rejoins the more direct Annandale road from Carlisle to the north (see 10). From Durisdeer to the watershed between the two main rivers is barely 4 km, and thence to Clydesdale the straight and open valley of the Potrail Water carries the road at an easy gradient. From Nithsdale to the watershed there is a choice of two routes; the northern, taken by the modern A 702 road through the Dalveen Pass, is reached by way of the Carron Water, flowing in a valley that has been deepened and widened by glacial erosion. A steep 65 m climb at the head of the valley above Upper Dalveen leads to the watershed at 335 m. The climb can only be avoided, as it is by the A 702 road, by terracing a course at a more gentle gradient into the rocky valley-side, a considerable task even with the use of blasting powder. The southern and more direct route, followed by the Roman road and by the medieval 'Well Path', lies along the Kirk Burn, involving indeed a greater climb (to 400 m) but at a lesser gradient, and with less abrupt changes of slope. However, the Kirk Burn flows in a much narrower valley, and a narrow pass of this kind was disliked and as far as possible avoided by Roman military engineers. Here there was virtually no choice, and the road

86 Durisdeer, Dumfries and Galloway; Roman fortlet, looking W. NS 903049. UW 68: May 1957.

was therefore guarded by a fortlet, set in the very throat of the pass and sited with great skill on a natural knoll between two streams. To north-west and south-east the view is restricted by steep hillsides, but the fortlet has a good command of the road itself up and down the valley. The remoteness of the site has ensured that the earthworks are magnificently preserved. The single gate faces uphill and is protected, unusually, by a *titulum*. In the photograph the Roman road appears in the left distance between two rows of quarry-pits, and continues past the near side of the fortlet.

That it was judged important to place the fortlet within the pass, rather than on easier ground outside the entrance near Durisdeer village, is evident from the results of excavation in 1938, which showed that considerable effort had been expended on levelling the summit of the knoll and on cutting a ditch through the living rock.

The fortlet has an area of 0.19 ha (0.47 acre), measuring 52 by 36.6 m overall; but because of the use of much rock rubble in its construction the rampart was exceptionally wide (9.1 m), so that a space of only 0.06 ha (0.14 acre) was available inside. Unfortunately very little is known about the internal buildings. Excavation revealed a line of post-holes, evidence for a structure in timber. The garrison was probably a century of infantry, perhaps outposted from Crawford. The date of the fortlet is known to be Antonine, probably Antonine I (c. A.D. 142–54); the site is 18 km (11.25 miles) from the Antonine I fortlet at Barburgh Mill and 20 km (12.5 miles) from the fort at Crawford. The road itself was probably constructed in Flavian times to connect the fort of Dalswinton (74) with Crawford, but whether in the first century there were any intermediate posts in this 42.5 km (27 mile) stretch of road is unknown.

143

87 Gelligaer Common (Fforest Gwladys), Mid-Glamorgan; Roman practice camps, looking SSE. ST 138992. AWZ 69: February 1969.

References

J. Clarke in S.N. Miller (ed.), *The Roman Occupation of South-Western Scotland* (Glasgow, 1952), 124–6. D. Breeze, *Britannia* V (1974), 139–54 *passim* (excavation of Barburgh Mill). I.D. Margary, *Roman Roads in Britain* II (London, 1957), 195–6 (Road 77).

GELLIGAER COMMON, Mid Glamorgan (87)

There are seven practice camps in the hills about 2 km north of the fort at Gelligaer; they consist of three groups of two with a seventh standing alone some distance away. The photograph shows the most easterly pair under a light cover of snow. That on the right is the better preserved; it measures *c.* 23.7 by 20.7 m (78 by 68 ft) and has two gates, one of them protected by an internal *clavicula* with a radius of 6.7 m (22 ft). The other camp, which is *c.* 30.5 m (100 ft) square, is less well preserved; its eastern side runs down to the small pylon and its western (right) side, though not visible on this particular photograph, can be traced on others and on the ground. Both the east and west sides appear to have gates with internal *claviculae* built to a plan which is the mirror image of the usual arrangement, and the photograph suggests that there is a third gate with a normal *clavicula* on the north (near) side.

References

V.E. Nash-Williams, *The Roman Frontier in Wales* (2nd ed. by M.G. Jarrett, Cardiff, 1969), 128–9. R.C.A.H.M. (Wales), *Glamorgan* I, Pt 2 (Cardiff, 1976), 103, Nos. 749, 750, with Fig. 57 (plan) and Pl. 14b (oblique view looking S). *J.R.S.* XXXIV (1944), 76 (discovery by A. Fox). J.K. StJoseph, *J.R.S.* LI (1961), 126. R.W. Davies, *Arch. Camb.* CXVII (1968), 103–18 (general account).

PART THREE

URBAN SITES

9

CITIES AND TOWNS

Towns and history go hand in hand. Few towns ever arose in fully developed form; understanding of their growth comes with historical analysis. An aerial photograph of a Romano-British town, as of any other, inevitably shows elements of differing date; in particular the defences, which often so neatly define the site, are rarely an early feature and have to be placed in their proper context. But whereas an informed observer in a medieval and modern town can deduce something of its history from a study of its plan and inspection of its architecture, detailed information on the development of a Roman town is normally obtainable only after excavation.

The presence of defences is important, not only because of their historical implications but also because, for want of other definite criteria, it has been conventionally used as a distinguishing characteristic. In point of size there is little to differentiate a small walled 'town' in Roman Britain from a village; it is the existence of defences which has been taken to distinguish 'small towns' from other forms of nucleated settlement. The distinction is certainly sometimes artificial in terms of size and perhaps may turn out to have little significance in terms of function.

Study of their plans suggests that the towns of Roman Britain fall into two classes, those with regular grids of streets and those without. The former class comprises administrative centres, in the establishment of which Roman organisation and Roman prestige were involved to greater or lesser degree, and where in the early days financial subvention and some practical assistance may have been provided by the government to ensure a proper standard. The difficulty to be overcome was that of creating a number of such places at much the same time in a province where nothing of the sort had been seen before and where resources were limited. The nearest source of technical aid were the legions of the province, with their skilled surveyors, architects and craftsmen. It was in the government's interest to encourage urbanisation since Roman civilisation was based on the town, and the processes of administration and education could most easily function through them.

Settlements of this first class can properly be described as cities, for they possessed the apparatus of local self-government and controlled their surrounding regions. The majority were provided to serve as the capitals of the various tribal *civitates*; but the class also contains places of higher rank – the three *coloniae* of Roman veteran legionaries (Colchester, Gloucester, Lincoln) and any Latin *municipia* that may have been created. Veteran colonies were deliberate implantations of military settlers who in the first century were often of Italian origin; the sites chosen for colonies in Britain were former legionary fortresses from which the garrison had moved on and where the land in consequence was already imperial property. The charter of a *municipium*, by contrast, was normally awarded to existing native cities whose Romanization and political importance were held to deserve it. In Britain only Verulamium seems certainly to have been a *municipium* in the first century, but by its closing decades London may have received promotion to this status. Other cities also possibly achieved the grade later on, but sure evidence is lacking. Veteran colonies ceased to be created after the time of Hadrian, but grants of the rank of *colonia* still continued to be made on occasion to important existing cities; York for example had gained the title by 237.

The second class of town, lacking a street grid, shares one characteristic with the first; towns of both classes very often had their origin in the settlements which had sprung up outside early forts for merchants and camp-followers. When the garrison moved on, the civil settlement, if it had had time to send down roots, remained; there seems to have come a moment when military land was made over to the civil authorities, after which the settlement sometimes expanded over the site of the fort. It would have been at this stage that the street grids of towns intended to serve as administrative centres were laid out, as can be shown to have happened at Cirencester. But in the second class of town little planning seems to have occurred. These places expanded in ribbon development along their roads; any subsidiary streets were mere lanes leading in any direction necessary. Such haphazard growth can be detected

147

in the photographs of Kenchester, Irchester or Chesterton (103, 104, 105).

Although this kind of 'military' origin can be identified in some towns of other provinces, it seems to be especially characteristic of towns in Britain. The reason perhaps lies in the relatively backward character of pre-Roman Britain, where few large nucleated settlements yet existed at places suitable for subsequent urban development. Where they did exist, they were very apt to have a supervisory garrison implanted, as seems to have happened at Canterbury and Verulamium, not to mention Colchester. But in general the new Roman strategic roads, and the forts which were placed at intervals along them, imposed a fresh pattern on southern Britain to which secondary urban development found it convenient to conform. In Roman Britain the 'central place' pattern, by which some modern geographers seek to explain the distribution of towns and markets, is very largely a creation of military strategy rather than of free economic forces. This is not to deny that such centres as Chesterton or Irchester owed their later prosperity to the workings of trade and industry.

With few exceptions the towns of Roman Britain possessed defences. The development of these can be seen to have been a complicated process. In the first and early second centuries it is probable that only cities of the highest ranks – *coloniae* and *municipia* – were entitled to defences from the outset. By the time of Claudius, indeed, automatic provision of defensive walls round such cities was no longer considered essential. At Cologne a wall was built for the new *colonia*; but at the contemporary *colonia* at Colchester the earthen rampart of the preceding fortress was actually taken down without replacement; the disastrous results of this action were experienced in 61. The lessons of that year were not forgotten. Verulamium had already been provided with a bank and ditch; in the later first century the newly founded *coloniae* at Gloucester and Lincoln retained the old legionary defences and soon refaced the ramparts in stone. Other urban defences pre-dating the late second century, such as the wall of Colchester itself and the second earthwork circuit at Verulamium, can be explained on grounds of status; those that cannot, as at Silchester and Winchester, probably owed their existence to their location within the client kingdom of Cogidubnus, where royal prestige was the inspiration.

It was only later that urban defences became almost universal. The majority of the cities and towns of Britain were encircled with a bank and ditch in the late second century. This is such an unusual phenomenon in the Roman Empire, unparalleled for instance in Gaul or Germany, that some special cause and single occasion should be sought; for if the defences do not relate to a single programme, they are difficult to explain. Some at least of the cities were by then rich and ambitious enough to have built walls of stone had the choice been theirs and time no object. The advantage of building earthworks lies in the speed with which large bodies of unskilled labour can erect them; stone walls take longer to build and are more costly. On the evidence of the latest dates yielded by excavation the earthwork programme should be placed in the final twenty years of the second century; and it should relate to a threat or crisis. The events leading up to the crisis of 196 still provide the best context, when the governor Albinus was planning to strip Britain of most of its troops in order to fight for the imperial throne. In that case the earthworks would be precautionary. It would appear that the embargo on town defences other than at chartered cities was lifted; and once lifted could not be reimposed. Thus the developments of the third century followed without difficulty.

In the third century walls were added to the front of existing ramparts, as at Silchester (88), for this was the best way to maintain their defensive capacity; old earthworks tend to grow vegetation and to suffer erosion. Yet the fact that the defences *were* thus renewed rather than left to obsolescence shows that further dangers threatened; this deduction is confirmed by the building of walls during the third century even round towns which had not received earthworks earlier. The province was entering the period of German raiding from across the North Sea.

It is a curious and noteworthy fact that when, as at London or Chesterton, walls were put up where no previous bank had existed, they were nevertheless reinforced with a bank of earth behind. In part this may have been done to dispose of the spoil from the ditches in a tidy manner, and to provide better access to the wall-top. But there was another advantage: such a wall did not require the thickness of a free-standing wall and so could be built faster and more cheaply. In general, free-standing walls (3–4 m thick) were built only round new late Roman coastal forts such as Richborough or Portchester (44, 45).

Normally, as was natural, the new wall followed the course of the older earthwork where one existed; but sometimes a different line was taken. At Caistor by Norwich the later circuit is of reduced size on the south (94); at Mildenhall, Wiltshire (102), where the wall was not built until the fourth century, a larger area was enclosed. Sometimes the building of defences involved alterations to the road systems, either locally at the gates (as at the south gate of Chesterton) or more generally, as at Mildenhall, where the absence of a gate for the old road along the Kennet valley in the direction of Silchester suggests that the route was disused or more probably diverted.

The final phase in urban defences is often marked by the addition of external towers (as at Caerwent, Chichester and Chesterton, **93, 92, 105**) in the middle of the fourth century. These may take various forms, rectangular or **U**-shaped, but their purpose was certainly the support of arrow-firing catapults with range and flanking power sufficient to keep an enemy from the wall. Their provision usually necessitated modification of the existing ditch system; often a new wide ditch was dug. Thus strengthened, town walls frequently remained serviceable (with necessary repairs) until late in the Middle Ages.

Many walled areas, especially of towns in the second class, are small, and some are as little as 2 ha. Even the *civitas* capitals and other cities in the first class rarely exceed 52 ha (130 acres), and the largest of all, London, had a walled area of 133.5 ha (330 acres). Not being original features of the towns, the defences often exclude parts of the settlement which thereafter became suburbs; nevertheless, the fortified cores of the cities are rarely so small as those of Roman Gaul which were walled only after extensive barbarian destruction.

There are, however, a few large – even very extensive – settlements where no signs of defences have yet been found. In the absence of excavation and of informative aerial photographs, the character of such places remains largely uncertain. Some may have grown up round religious centres, as at Frilford in Oxfordshire or Wycomb in Gloucestershire (**126**), and reached exceptional prosperity as market centres; but it is hard to see why they remained undefended. In general, priority was no doubt given to places possessing facilities of whatever sort which were of importance to the government.

The 'small towns' of the second class had few identifiable public buildings save temples, and sometimes a market hall and *mansio* (or *praetorium*) of the public posting system (as at Kenchester and Chesterton, **103, 106**). Probably storage facilities for reserves of food should also be expected but have not yet been positively identified.

The cities were better provided. The principal public building was the *forum* and *basilica*: a civic centre, containing the local senate-house, the shrine of the city goddess, the hall of justice, the record-office and other organs of the local administration. Rooms or buildings for guilds of traders

and religious associations, such as the guild of *dendrophori* recently attested at Verulamium, were also provided. On the Continent varying types of *forum* are found, all deriving from prototypes in Italy. In north-west Europe one of the most popular was the so-called 'double *forum*', which had a separate religious precinct; in Britain this occurs only at Verulamium. British *fora* vary considerably in size, but architecturally they normally resemble the compact headquarters building of a fortress. This fact reflects the relative poverty of the cities in their early years when these centres were being designed, and possibly also illustrates the type of technical aid given by the army, whose staff would be the nearest source of expertise.

Classical temples are rare in British towns. The most numerous class of temple both in town and country was the Romano-Celtic, which can appear in both rectangular and polygonal form, as at Silchester or Weycock Hill (**91, 138**). These buildings were not intended for congregational worship but for individual devotion; theatres were, however, sometimes provided for large-scale assembly at times of festival, as at Gosbeck's Farm near Colchester (**137**) or at Verulamium. No doubt urban theatres (which have been found also at Canterbury, Cirencester and Colchester in addition to one at Brough on Humber known only from an inscription) were also used for public entertainment; but whether classical plays were performed is doubtful. Many theatres in the north-west provinces belong to a type which, like the temples, is described as Romano-Celtic; the plans and fittings show that these buildings were a compromise between the classical theatre and amphitheatre, in which the stage is often very small. This and the absence of a proper back wall to the stage (*scaenae frons*) may suggest that any performances produced there were of a less sophisticated character.

Some cities had full-sized amphitheatres. Two are illustrated, from Cirencester and Dorchester (**95, 96**). In both, the seating was carried on an earthen bank lacking masonry substructures (apart from an arena wall at Cirencester). A third amphitheatre, adjacent to the legionary fortress at Caerleon, is also illustrated (**24**). Legionary amphitheatres often had arenas that occupied a proportionately larger part of the total area than urban examples; the reason is presumed to be that they were used for military exercises as well as for gladiatorial entertainment.

Other public buildings include market halls and the large inns or *praetoria* associated with the posting system. An example of the latter at Silchester is illustrated (**91**). Local authorities had a duty to provide remounts and accommodation for the public service on selected routes.

Many towns have yielded evidence, in the form of wooden water mains and large sewers, that they possessed a supply of running water; the presence of public baths is a further indication, for the great quantities of water used in these establishments could hardly have been provided by wells or water-carts. It was normal practice to build one or more aqueducts which tapped a convenient source such as a spring or stream, at a sufficiently elevated level to enable the water to flow under gravity to a high point on the edge of the town. There it entered a large tank whence it was distributed by pipe. Sewers are a necessary accompaniment since the water flowed continuously. One of these tanks (*castellum aquae*) is known at Lincoln together with its aqueduct; but at the majority of towns the aqueducts themselves have not yet been located. One that supplied Dorchester is illustrated (**97**).

In all these towns, as well as in the *vici* mentioned below, the normal commercial building was a long but narrow structure set end-on to the street. Examples can be recognised in photographs of Silchester, Chesterton and Old Carlisle (**89, 106, 68**). The front part of the building could be used as a shop, the rear as a dwelling and workshop area; very often craftsmen made on the premises the goods which they sold, whether these were metal goods or items of food or clothing.

Although all towns below the rank of *municipium* ranked legally as *vici*, the word *vicus* is often today associated especially with the civilian settlements which grew up in the neighbourhood of forts. In the north, where forts were garrisoned over very long periods, large *vici* developed; examples are illustrated at Chesterholm, Old Carlisle and Piercebridge. They naturally had a much stronger military association than the similar settlements in southern Britain, whose connections with the army were early severed by the advance of units to fresh positions. A large component of the population consisted of retired military personnel, as well as the usual merchants, craftsmen and shopkeepers.

Town life was quick to develop in Britain. Some settlements were already in prosperous existence before 60, but the majority were established between 70 and 140. Despite the occasional conflagration to which half-timbered cities were particularly liable, the second century was an age of great prosperity, which continued into the third. The view used to be expressed that the economic crisis and inflation of the later third century exerted a catastrophic effect on urban prosperity. Since the war, however, excavation has revealed little support for this theory, and it can be shown that many towns remained prosperous throughout the fourth century also. At some of them, however, a change can be detected in or after the late second century; the early almost feverish activity of traders and manufacturers lost its momentum and gave place to a quieter and more sleepy maturity, in which much space in the larger towns was taken over by the luxurious houses of the wealthy, which were often set in extensive grounds. The period of boom had given way to smaller-scale market-town activity.

In recent years some evidence has been recovered suggesting that urban life continued well into the fifth century. The sites of many Romano-British cities were so well chosen in relation to roads, sea-routes, navigable rivers and surrounding agricultural regions that they are still represented by important modern successors. Sometimes actual continuity of occupation can be established; but elsewhere there may have been longer or shorter periods of total or semi-desertion before the advantages of position and of the defensive walls reasserted their influence. A few Roman cities such as Caistor by Norwich, Silchester, Verulamium or Wroxeter are today empty fields, for varying reasons never having been reoccupied in post-Roman times. It is these sites which afford both the aerial photographer and the excavator his best opportunities.

Industry played a significant role in the prosperity of towns; but being normally organised on a small and even domestic scale it has left few remains which can be distinguished from the air. The manufacture of bricks and tiles and the quarrying of building-stone must clearly have been important; this aspect of industry is illustrated in **95**, which shows some of the limestone quarries at Cirencester. The great pottery industry of the Nene Valley is represented by the photograph of Normangate Field (**107**). Pottery-manufacturing sites in general offer few distinguishing characteristics to the aerial photographer, and the remains of the mining industries of Roman Britain have been altered or destroyed by subsequent working of the same deposits.

References

S.S. Frere, *Britannia, a History of Roman Britain* (3rd ed., London, 1978), Ch. 12. S.S. Frere, *Verulamium Excavations* II (London, 1982). J.S. Wacher, *The Towns of Roman Britain* (London, 1975). P. Marsden, *Roman London* (London, 1980).

88 Silchester (*Calleva Atrebatum*), Hampshire; general view of Roman city, looking E. SU 639625. CL 14: June 1949.

SILCHESTER (*CALLEVA ATREBATUM*), Hampshire (88–91)

General view of Roman city (88)

Silchester, the *civitas* capital (administrative centre) of the British Atrebates, today lies almost entirely in arable fields which respond well to aerial photography. The city was extensively excavated by the Society of Antiquaries between 1890 and 1909, and in consequence a great deal of the plan is established, although much still remains to be learnt of the chronology of its buildings and of the history of the settlement. The techniques of that time enabled the excavators to trace the plans of stone buildings satisfactorily, but many timber-framed structures probably remain to be found, both beneath the stone buildings and also occupying areas of the town-plan now blank. Aerial photographs have also recorded stone buildings not found in the Antiquaries' excavations.

The city overlies a pre-Roman Belgic settlement occupying the east end of a gravel plateau, almost 90 m above sea-level, which is surrounded by streams and valleys on all sides save the west. In the early Roman period the settlement is thought to have formed part of Cogidubnus's client kingdom, and to this time belong two successive lines of earthwork fortification. The earlier encloses an area smaller than that defended by the third-century town wall (marked on the photograph by the belt of trees surrounding the two central fields); its buried ditch, invisible on the photograph, lies for the most part beneath the later walled city, but emerges from beneath the wall in the left foreground. The second line, the so-called 'Outer Earthwork', succeeded the first at least on the west side, but runs outside the picture, below the camera. At one time the earthwork was believed to have surrounded the entire site on a line some distance in front of the stone walls, enclosing 95 ha (235 acres); but much of this hypothetical circuit has been disproved, and it now appears that these defences were built only on the west side to bar approach across the level plateau.

The town wall itself was added to the front of a late second-century rampart of gravel. Although this excluded some outlying parts of the settlement it enclosed 40 ha (100 acres) of the city's core. Walled areas of this or slightly larger size seem to be normal in Romano-British *civitas* capitals,

151

89 Silchester; an area of the W part of the Roman city, looking NE. YN 82: June 1959.

which are also characterised both by rectangular street grids, well exemplified here, and by public buildings, some of which are illustrated on succeeding plates.

There are five principal gates. The street grid is based on the *cardo maximus* connecting the north and south gates and the *decumanus maximus* joining the east gate (below the farm in the background) to the west gate (at the angle of the wall in the centre foreground). From the north gate ran a road to the Thames crossing at Dorchester (Oxon.) and from the south gate a road to Winchester with a branch to Chichester. The road from the east gate led to London and from the west gate to Cirencester and Gloucester. From a second gate on the west side (in the centre of the right-hand sector of wall in the foreground) a road led to Badbury Rings (5) and Exeter. At the centre of the town lay the *forum* in the large *insula* interrupting the median east–west street.

Silchester is one of four or five Romano-British cities where occupation completely ceased in the sub-Roman period. More normally the wise original choice of site and the advantages of communication provided by the Roman road system ensured continuity of settlement or later reoccupation, so that the majority of Romano-British cities still remain important urban centres (see Chichester, **92**). Silchester suffered the disadvantage of lying some 13 km from the Thames, an important artery of commerce, and it is Reading on that river which in modern times has assumed the administrative and commercial roles which Silchester was intended to fulfil.

References

G.C. Boon, *Silchester: the Roman town of Calleva* (Newton Abbot, 1974) with bibliography. *Idem, Archaeologia* CII (1969), 1–82 with various aerial photographs. Outer Earthwork: *Britannia* X (1979), 331.

90 **Silchester**; the *forum*, looking S. SU 639625. YN 65: June 1959.

Western part of the Roman city (89)

The parch-marks of the street grid of *Calleva* have been well known since at least the sixteenth century when they were noted by Leland and Camden. This photograph just catches the tree-clad city bank in the bottom left-hand corner near where the west gate gives passage to the *decumanus maximus*: this is the broad street running from the corner to the middle of the top margin. The dark line down the centre of the street indicates either a sewer or a water-pipe trench and similar lines may be distinguished in other streets. Visible in the foreground from left to right are parts of Insulae XI, XIII and XV; across the centre are Insulae X, XIV and XVI, and at the top IX, II and III. The area is crossed, top left, by a modern farm road, and the *forum* (90) lies beyond Insulae II and III outside the area of the photograph. Crop-marks show that most of the streets were lined with buildings. The left (north) side of the *decumanus maximus* was bordered by long narrow strip-buildings (shops and workshops) which do not show clearly; in the near right-hand corner of Insula XIV can be seen the plan of a large courtyard house (XIV, 1), many of whose rooms show as white patches indicating the presence of solid floors. Excavation showed that many had floors of red-tile *tesserae* but in the east wing were four rooms with mosaics and others with the same plain tessellation. The photograph shows several features which do not appear on the excavators' plans: for instance, a building in the north-west corner of Insula III, indications of two rows of column-bases in Insula XIII, Block IV (the rectangular structure in the north-east corner of the *insula*), and others in the building immediately across the street in Insula XIV. Clearly there is plenty of scope for further excavation.

References

W.H.St John Hope and G.E. Fox, *Archaeologia* LV (1896) (excavation of Insulae XIII and XIV). G.C. Boon, *Silchester: the Roman Town of Calleva* (Newton Abbot, 1974), *passim*.

The forum (90)

In the foreground, running from left to right above an oblique modern farm track, is seen the *decumanus maximus*; a dark line down its centre denotes a drain or water-pipe trench. The parch-

91 Silchester; site of inn in Insula VIII, looking W. YN 57: June 1960.

marks of other streets parallel and at right angles are also visible. The *insula* in the upper centre of the photograph is occupied by the *forum* and *basilica*, the civic centre of the city. The main entrance is in the centre of the left-hand (east) side, and is approached by a street running from the neighbourhood of the east gate. Round a large rectangular gravelled piazza are three ranges of rooms; the fourth (west) side was occupied by the great *basilica*, on the right-hand side of which can be made out a row of chambers comprising civic offices, the *curia* (senate-room) and municipal shrine, extending back to the *cardo maximus* (north-south street). The apse which housed the *tribunal* at the south end of the *basilica* is visible; the corresponding apse at the north end was early replaced by three rectangular rooms and is not seen on the photograph. The building as a whole measures *c.* 84.5 m north–south by 95.5 m east–west, thus covering 0.8 ha (almost 2 acres). This is small when compared with the *fora* of e.g. Veru-lamium (1.9 ha) or London (2.9 ha); but when considered in relation to the size of the city it well illustrates the emphasis laid on imposing public buildings during the development phase of

154

Romano-British cities. The Silchester *forum* was built in the first quarter of the second century, and in plan resembles the Headquarters Building (*principia*) of a legionary fortress; but there is evidence that during the fourth century whatever floor the *basilica* had possessed had been removed and that the hall had been given over to workshops used by iron- and bronze-smiths. It seems clear that considerable changes affecting social and political organisation had occurred around 300.

References

G.E. Fox and W.H. StJohn Hope, *Archaeologia* LIII (1893), excavation report. G.C. Boon, *Silchester, the Roman Town of Calleva* (Newton Abbot, 1974), 108–20 with Pl. 8 (vertical view). *Britannia* IX (1978), 464–5; *ibid.* XII (1981), 362; *ibid.* XIII, XIV (forthcoming).

Site of inn in Insula VIII (91)

The largest building at Silchester after the *forum* is that which lies close to the south gate, and which has been interpreted as a public inn with official functions. The building comprised three wings surrounding a courtyard. Each wing, about 60 m long, had a central range of rooms with a corridor on both sides. The rooms in each wing were grouped to form two or three distinct sets, as if to provide private accommodation for important visitors. A separate bath-building stood at a little distance.

The photograph shows how close the building lies to the city wall which runs beneath the trees on the left. The south gate is beyond the top of the picture. The continuous light line crossing the centre of the picture over the near ends of the two wings is an agricultural mark. The building lies in a double *insula* (VIII) and is approached by a street (centre right, above the agricultural line) which leads to the main entrance. Although the inn may not have been built before the third century there is no sign that this street once continued southwards beneath the later courtyard. Instead, an oblique lane leads past the north wing towards the foreground, where it gave access to an outer yard and to the bath-building, which stood on the same axis as the south wing and partly overlay the original first-century defensive ditch; neither feature is visible in the photograph. The west wing contained the largest set of rooms, several of which were heated by hypocausts. This may have provided the accommodation for the governor when he came on circuit, a suggestion reinforced by the addition of what looks like an apsed audience-chamber towards the south end of the west wing. Part of the arc of the apse shows as a parch-mark.

The public posting system of the Roman Empire was based upon road-stations of various grades and functions. A *mansio* was an inn at which official travellers and others holding warrants could obtain accommodation and changes of mount. Other buildings named *praetoria* may have been rather larger and may sometimes have housed permanent officials. Since all these buildings had to be maintained at local expense there is no reason to doubt that private travellers who could afford it were also made welcome as far as there was room for them. That outsiders could have access at least to the bath-building is implicit in the independent access to it.

The street along the north (right) edge of the *insula* has a central drain or water-main trench. Near the top right-hand corner of the photograph is the sixteen-sided temple which stood in a large walled precinct occupying the south half of Insula VII.

References

J.K.StJoseph, *J.R.S.* LV (1965), Pl. XIII, 1 (this view).
G.C. Boon, *Silchester: the Roman Town of Calleva* (Newton Abbot, 1974), 138–44.

CHICHESTER (*NOVIOMAGUS REGNENSIUM*), Sussex (92)

Chichester was the *civitas* capital (administrative centre) of the Regnenses. This people did not constitute a tribe in the pre-Roman period, when the region had formed part of the kingdom of the Atrebates; but they seem to have been organised by the Roman government into an artificial *civitas* on the death of King Cogidubnus, one of whose palaces has been identified at Fishbourne, 2 km west of Chichester. The name Regnenses is taken to indicate the people of the (former) kingdom, distinguishing this southern half of the Atrebates from the new and more restricted *civitas Atrebatum* centred on Silchester. This explanation still carries conviction despite recent attempts to evoke in the Chichester region a tribe of the Regini, otherwise unattested.

The defences of the city followed the development normal in Roman Britain. An earthern rampart thrown up in the late second century was strengthened with a wall in the third century; in the fourth century external towers were added, probably to carry arrow-firing or stone-throwing catapults. At Chichester the defences enclose 40 ha (100 acres). In the foreground, south of the Cathedral and Bishop's Palace, is seen the south-west wall together with some external towers: both wall and towers were very largely rebuilt in the medieval period. From the south-west corner the wall then curves round to the site of the north gate at the top of the picture and a little further on turns south round the grass expanse of Priory Park.

The town plan is based on the rectangular intersection of the *cardo maximus* and *decumanus maximus*. The latter is seen crossing the city just behind the Cathedral towards the site of the east gate near the top right-hand margin. Beyond the gate the line of Stane Street bends sharply north-east to take up an alignment for London, and a short distance along it lay a large cemetery. Outside the walls, beyond the picture to south-east of the east gate, an amphitheatre has been identified.

The street system can be assigned to the late first century; before this date there had been some civilian building, but certainly for some years after 43 much of the future city had been occupied by a military base and supply centre associated with Legion II Augusta. There is also growing evidence that a native settlement had sprung up nearby in the late Augustan period, although its precise location is still unknown.

In the fifth century civilised life was drastically reduced, if it did not entirely disappear. Signs of

92 Chichester (*Noviomagus Regnensium*), **Sussex; site of Roman city**, looking NE. SU 861948. CL 77: June 1949.

Saxon occupation within the walls are few until the eighth or ninth centuries, and it was not until the Norman Conquest that the bishop's see was transferred from a rural estate at Selsey to the present site within the city. From this time the city revived, and presents a good example of a Roman centre still in full occupation.

References

J.S. Wacher, *The Towns of Roman Britain* (London, 1974), 239–55. Alec Down, *Chichester Excavations* III (Chichester, 1978).

CAERWENT (*VENTA SILURUM*), Gwent (93)

In the late second century, when most cities in Roman Britain first received defences, the area enclosed was often 40–50 ha. Caerwent, the capital of the Silures of South Wales, was much smaller, for here the walled area is only 17.8 ha. The *civitas* was not wealthy, consisting, as it did, very largely of mountainous terrain; only the coastal plain was readily accessible to Romanization and there the legionary fortress of Caerleon and its *canabae*, only 13 km further west, must have attracted away much of the prosperity which

would otherwise have accrued to Caerwent. Nevertheless the place had all the trappings of a city – *forum*, temples, public baths, street grid and a large inn (*mansio* or *praetorium*).

Caerwent lies on the Roman road from Gloucester to Caerleon; this road that ran straight through the city is still the most prominent feature of the photograph although the modern village is now bypassed to the north. It is possible that in the late first century an auxiliary fort lay here and that this attracted the original nucleus of civilian settlers; but if so the defences have not yet been located. In the late second century earthwork defences were erected which a century later were reinforced by a stone wall. The rectangle formed by the defences is clearly distinguishable; fine stretches of Roman wall survive along the south (left) and north sides. In the middle of the fourth century external towers were added; some of these can be seen along the south wall.

Today the site has lost its commercial and administrative importance to Newport and Cardiff and the settlement has shrunk. In Roman times the main street each side of the *forum* was packed with strip-buildings of the commercial sort, and elsewhere within the walls stood substantial private

156

93 Caerwent (*Venta Silurum*), Gwent; Roman city, looking NW. ST 469906. AN 59: June 1949.

houses, many of which were excavated in an extensive programme of work carried out between 1899 and 1908.

References

Excavations: T. Ashby *et al., Archaeologia* LVII–LXII. Defences: V.E. Nash Williams, *Archaeologia* LXXX (1930), 229–88. V.E. Nash-Williams, *Bull. Board of Celtic Studies* XV (1953), 159–67. J.S. Wacher, *Towns of Roman Britain* (London, 1974), 375–89 with plan.

CAISTOR BY NORWICH (*VENTA ICENORUM*), Norfolk (94)

This small walled *civitas* capital lies on the east bank of the river Tas (foreground), 5 km south of Norwich. In contrast to villages and small towns, *civitas* capitals in Roman Britain had planned street grids. Caistor is one of the smallest of these capitals, enclosing 14 ha (35 acres) within the walls, which surround the large left-hand field on three sides. It was here that vertical aerial photographs taken by the Royal Air Force during a drought in July 1928 showed for the first time how much of the plan of a buried Romano-British city could be recorded from the air.

The city wall is seen to be later than the street grid, which it overlies on the south (right) side, excluding an east–west street; two north–south streets are cut by the accompanying ditch. Outlying streets also exist beyond the defences on the north side of the city (invisible in this photograph). The main east–west street was provided with a central drain, now showing as a thin dark line, as was the central north–south street. The *forum* occupied much of the large *insula* east of the central north–south street. The public baths lay in the foreground, to right of this same street, near the site of the west gate.

The most north-easterly *insula* within the walls is bisected diagonally by a street whose line is taken up by the modern road beyond the defences. This pattern suggests that the first nucleus of the street grid was expanded to north and east from an original corner where the oblique road meets the grid. Another indication of irregularity here is provided by a narrow east–west street bisecting the northern *insulae*. On the south side of the city,

157

94 Caistor by Norwich (*Venta Icenorum*), **Norfolk**; looking E. TG 230035. ABL 61: June 1960.

although traces of buildings are visible on the south side of the most southerly street, it is probable that settlement in this area was sufficiently thin, when the wall came to be erected, to warrant exclusion.

Towards the right-hand side of the photograph there are traces of twin ditches, which appear to have bounded the city on the south side before the wall was built round a more restricted area; the rest of this possible early circuit is at present undiscovered.

The well-known early Anglo-Saxon cemetery lies *c.* 300 m beyond the medieval church.

The causeway which crosses the broad ditch outside the south gate is not original, as the photograph confirms; the presence of three light patches elsewhere in the ditch suggests incomplete excavation at these points.

References

R.E.M. Wheeler, *Antiquity* III (1929), 182–5 with Pl. I (vertical view). J.K. St Joseph, *J.R.S.* LI (1961), 132 with Pl. X, 1 (new vertical); *idem* in J.S. Wacher (ed.), *The Civitas Capitals of Roman Britain* (Leicester, 1966), Pl. III (the same vertical). S.S. Frere, *Britannia* II (1971), 1–26 with Pl. I (1929 vertical). S.S. Frere, *Britannia, A History of Roman Britain* (London, 1967), Pl. 18A; (1978), Pl. 8A (this view). J.S. Wacher, *The Towns of Roman Britain* (London, 1975), 227–38 with Pl. 42 (this view).

CIRENCESTER (*CORINIUM DOBUNNORUM*), Gloucestershire (95)

The amphitheatre of *Corinium* lies outside the Roman city some 200 m south-west of the west or Bath gate, on an area of rough ground. It was approached by a metalled road which skirted the structure to the north. The amphitheatre consists of a vast oval bank, over 41 m thick and 8.2 m high, through which two entrances, one at each end of the long axis, lead to an arena with diameters of 48.5 and 41 m. The seating was found to be carried on a series of small terraces cut into the bank and revetted by low drystone walls, and it has been calculated that there was accommodation for 8000–9000 people.

The rough ground, known as 'The Querns' (95), has been extensively quarried for limestone. A large hollow occupying the left foreground has been shown to be a quarry-pit of Roman date later

95 Cirencester (*Corinium Dobunnorum*), Gloucestershire; Roman urban amphitheatre and quarries, looking SW. SP 020013. AIL 12: February 1964.

used for burials; here an extensive inhumation cemetery, with closely packed graves, developed in the late Roman period, mainly for the urban poor. Further signs of quarrying were encountered beneath the amphitheatre itself, which probably made use of a hollow thus created; we may assume that a great deal of the material composing the seating-banks was waste rubble from these quarries, which are evidence of a large-scale industry. Stone buildings within the city were already in existence by the late first century, and these quarries were a source of building-material conveniently close.

Excavation has established that the seating-banks were erected after the beginning of the second century and were at first lined with timber and drystone masonry; in the late second century mortared stone walls replaced the early revetments and the north entrance passage at least (the only one to be examined) was vaulted to extend the seating capacity. Later still the vaults were removed,

and large timbers once more used to line the passage. At some late or post-Roman period the entrance was drastically narrowed and a door fitted, while within the arena a substantial timber building was erected. Excavation was on too limited a scale to define the date or function of these changes, but it is tempting to suppose that the amphitheatre had become a stronghold.

References

J.S. Wacher, *Antiq. Journ.* XLIII (1963), 23–6; XLIV (1964), 17–18. A.D. McWhirr, *Antiq. Journ.* XLVII (1967), 185–8; LVIII (1978), 64–72. J.S. Wacher, *The Towns of Roman Britain* (London, 1975), 299; *idem, Cirencester Roman Amphitheatre* (Department of the Environment Official Guide, London, 1981).

MAUMBURY RINGS, DORCHESTER, Dorset (96)

Maumbury Rings lies 500 m SSW of Roman Dorchester (*Durnovaria*) beside the Roman road

159

96 Dorchester (*Durnovaria*), Dorset; Maumbury Rings, Roman amphitheatre, looking SW. SY 691899. LR 76: May 1953.

running towards Weymouth. The overall axes of the earthwork measure 105 m (345 ft) and 99 m (325 ft) respectively, and the arena is 66 m (216 ft) long by 49.5 m (162 ft) wide. Excavation by H. St George Gray between 1908 and 1913 showed that in origin the earthwork had been a Neolithic henge-monument but that about the middle of the first century A.D. very considerable modifications were undertaken to convert it into an amphitheatre. This date is inconveniently early for an amenity associated with the nearby Roman city, and it is probable that the work is military and to be connected with a fort or fortress of the conquest period as yet unlocated. At this stage the surface inside was lowered by 3 m to create an arena, which was spread with sand and surrounded by a timber palisade; and three small chambers (*carcares*) were cut in the edge of the bank, one opposite the original (north-east) entrance, and the other two at each end of the short axis. Subsequently modifications had been made, notably in the construction of a second entrance at

the south-west end opposite the first, probably in connection with use of the amphitheatre by the rising town. Before the middle of the second century the amphitheatre had become disused and a cemetery developed at the main north-east entrance. At the end of the third century there seems to have been some reconditioning of the monument, but details are scanty. Thereafter the earthwork was deserted until the Civil War, when in 1642–3 it was converted by the Parliamentarians for use as an artillery fort to defend the southern approach to Dorchester. The chief visible features of this phase are the ramp running up over the south entrance, and two similar ramps rising round the inner faces of the two sides.

References

R.C.H.M., *Dorset* II Pt 3 (London, 1970), 589–92. R. Bradley, *Archaeologia* CV (1976), 1–97. S.S. Frere, *Britannia, A History of Roman Britain* (London, 1967), Pl. 19A; (2nd ed., 1974), Pl. 9A (oblique view).

97 Dorchester, Dorset; Roman aqueduct near Poundbury hill fort, looking W. SY 682911. AAT 13: May 1960.

DORCHESTER, Dorset, Roman aqueduct (97)

The hill fort of Poundbury, enclosing 5.46 ha (13.5 acres), lies at a height of 90 m on chalk, 1 km WNW of Dorchester. Excavation of the defences in 1939 showed two periods of construction, the first in an early phase of the Iron Age, the second in the first century B.C. The photograph shows two ramparts on the west side, and the slighter defences on the north side which runs along the crest of a steep slope above the flood-plain of the river Frome.

An earthwork marking the course of the aqueduct of Roman *Durnovaria* approaches the north-west corner of the hill fort from the top right-hand edge of the photograph. Water was probably diverted from the river Frome at Notton Mill, *c.* 10 km upstream, and was led along the south side of the valley on a skilfully surveyed course in an open channel, which falls 7.62 m (25 ft) in a distance of 18.5 km (11.5 miles), a gradient of 1 in 2400, or 0.04%. The channel was normally *c.* 0.75–1.0 m deep and 1.5 m wide at the bottom, and was capable of discharging *c.* 58 865 cubic metres of water a day. In the stretch covered by the aqueduct eight side-valleys enter the main valley from the south, but the channel maintains its even gradient by appropriate deviations.

It is noteworthy that, with the exception of the example at Lincoln, no aqueduct in Britain is known with masonry substructures. In this country a supply of water at an adequate height is usually available at no great distance from towns and forts, so that the need did not arise for long aqueducts which might involve considerable engineering work in crossing valleys. Remains of aqueducts are known at the gold-working site at Dolaucothi in South Wales, at some forts such as Bowes in Yorkshire, Lanchester in County Durham and Great Chesters in Northumberland, and even at a few villas. In towns there must have been a special need for constant water supply, in particular for the public baths; at a number of towns large sewers provide good evidence that such a supply existed, and at some sites the discovery of water-pipes in lead or wood points to the same conclusion. Few towns, however, have as yet yielded traces of the aqueducts themselves. At Wroxeter an open channel very similar to the present example is known, although it is only *c.* 1 km in length; while at Lincoln the water was brought in a large pipe set in concrete. On arrival at the upper end of a town the water entered a large tank (*castellum aquae*), from which it was distributed by pipes under gravity pressure to bath-buildings and fountains. Rarely was the water laid on to private dwellings; in Britain only at Wroxeter has a system of this kind been found.

References

R.C.H.M., *Dorset* II Pt 3 (London, 1970), 487–9 (Pound-bury); 586–8 with map (aqueduct). Dolaucothi: G.D.B. Jones, *Bull. Board of Celtic Studies* XIX (1960), 71ff. Bowes: R. Tomlin, *Yorks. Arch. Journ.* XLV (1973), 181–4. Lincoln: F.H. Thompson, *Arch. Journ.* CXI (1954), 106–28; J.S. Wacher, *Towns of Roman Britain* (London, 1975), 126–32. Wroxeter: J.P. Bushe-Fox, *Excavations on the Site of the Roman Town at Wroxeter* III (Oxford, 1916), 13 with Pls. VI, VII; Wacher, *op. cit.* 368–9 with Pl. 73. G. Webster and D. Hollingsworth, *Trans. Shropshire Arch. Soc.* LVI Pt 2 (1959), 153–7.

WROXETER (*VIROCONIUM CORNOVIORUM*), Shropshire (98–100)

The centre of the city

Legion XIV Gemina established a fortress at Wroxeter shortly before 60; probably even earlier

an auxiliary fort had been placed on the bank of the Severn about 1 km to the south of this. Wroxeter was an important crossing-point of the river and occupies a strategic position of great significance facing the approaches into northern Central Wales. After 67, when Legion XIV left Britain, the fortress was occupied by Legion XX Valeria Victrix and was not given up by the army until shortly before 90 when Chester became the base of the legion after its return from Scotland.

Had the number of legions in Britain continued at four, Wroxeter might have become a *colonia* with a settlement of veterans established there, for there was being developed a policy of matching the number of legions in a province with an equal number of *coloniae*, from which a flow of recruits with the Roman citizenship, brought up in military families, would be assured. However, after the reduction to three, when Legion II Adiutrix was transferred to the Continent in *c.* 87, need for a fourth *colonia* lapsed, and instead Wroxeter became the capital of the *civitas* of the Cornovii. During thirty years of military occupation a civil settlement must have grown up in the vicinity of the fortress; its population became the nucleus of the new city, whose public buildings were established on the site of the fortress where the defences were now demolished.

The early years of the city are still to a large extent archaeologically obscure, except that the foundations of an extensive bath-building (*thermae*) were laid; but in the reign of Hadrian a new programme of public buildings was inaugurated. Work on the unfinished *thermae* was discontinued and a *forum* was laid out over the site, occupying a large part of the *insula* to south of a farm (98). The *forum* carried an inscription set up in 129–30. Soon afterwards a new and substantial bath-building was constructed in the next *insula* to the east; a large fragment of one of its walls still stands 6.7 m high and the rest has been excavated and consolidated for public inspection. The building is noteworthy for its large exercise hall (*basilica*). The same *insula* contained a pedestrian market precinct (*macellum*) and a large public latrine. Later in the second century the city was encircled by a rampart and ditch; these cross the photograph from left to right, passing below the most distant fork in the modern system of lanes (cf. 100). During the third century this circuit was found to be too small, and a much larger circuit of some 75 ha (180 acres) was then enclosed by a town wall with accompanying bank and ditch. However, the original street grid was not continued over the extended area which seems to have been served by few streets, and those haphazardly laid out.

By the end of the third century the *basilica* in the

98 Wroxeter (*Viroconium Cornoviorum*), Shropshire; vertical photograph of the centre of the city, NNE at top. SJ 5608. RC8-BC 15: July 1975. Scale 1:3500.

forum had been demolished, and perhaps not much later the baths *basilica* was allowed to become derelict. Recent excavations have shown, however, that several large timber-framed buildings were set up within its shell. These changes point to a considerable reorganisation of city life at Wroxeter in the fourth century and later, but the full implications must await the excavation of some of the large town-houses visible from the air.

The photograph was taken during the drought of 1975 and shows in remarkable detail the street plan and buildings in the centre of the city. The parch-marks indicating the position and plan of the *forum* lie to west (left) of a modern lane running from top to bottom across the photograph: farther to the north-west large town-houses are visible. On the opposite, right-hand side of the lane can be seen the rectangle of the *macellum* and the baths beyond it, including a round-ended swimming-bath (*natatio*).

The western defences of the first-century fortress are known to underlie the north–south lane, but no traces of this military period are visible except the double ditches of an annexe seen to left of the farm. This lies in an area north-west of the *forum*

99 Wroxeter; Insulae I, IV and XV, looking SE. BTV 3: July 1975.

which is described in the next section (99), while the area north-east of the baths is discussed with reference to 100; but the overall relationships, and in particular the line of the second-century defences with the regular grid of streets within it, are best appreciated on the vertical photograph.

References

For recent plans of Wroxeter see J.S. Wacher, *Towns of Roman Britain* (London, 1975), 361; G. Webster and D. Charlesworth, *Viroconium, Wroxeter Roman City* (Department of the Environment Official Guide, London, 1973); A. Baker, *Trans. Shropshire Arch. Soc.* LVIII Pt 3 (1967–8), Fig. 39 facing p. 200 (all except the last failing to plan the *forum*). *Insula* numbers are as follows: Insula 1 contains the modern farm with 2 and 3 to the right (3 containing the walled precinct). Insula 4 contains the forum and 5 the baths with 6 and 7 to right. Insulae 8–11

run below these. Insula 15 lies left of the forum and 16 north of 2. For a different vertical photograph, J.K. St Joseph, *J.R.S.* LXVII (1977), 156–7 with Pl. XV, 2.

Insulae I, IV and XV (99)

To the right of a modern farm are seen the pale crop-marks which indicate the walls of the *forum* and *basilica* (excavated in 1923–7). From near the left-hand end of the farm two parallel dark lines extend down the photograph to curve round a right angle to the south, disappearing below a later town-house. These represent a pair of early military ditches and are now thought to mark part of the defences of an annexe to the early legionary fortress which underlies the centre of Wroxeter. This annexe probably served as a stores enclosure attached to the fortress. Excavation has shown

100 Wroxeter; Insulae II and XVI, looking N. EB 87: July 1949.

that the western defences of the fortress itself lie below the modern lane beyond the farm.

To left of the ditches is a broad street bounding the north side of Insula I; near the centre of the photograph it approaches the light-toned line of a much narrower street running obliquely. Parallel with this, and some 12 m away, is a broad dark line as of a wide ditch. This ditch is thought to mark

the earthwork defences on the north side of the city in the second century, before expansion led to the construction of a new defensive line much further north. Another part of this early circuit is seen in 100.

The centre of Wroxeter has a regular grid of streets, of which the part surrounding the *forum* and neighbouring *insulae* is clearly seen in the

165

photograph. The north–south street bounding the near side of the *insula* of the *forum* changes alignment just inside these old defences – an indication of secondary extension. The new area taken in by the enlarged circuit of defences contains few known streets and no sign of a regular street grid. The part of it showing in the photograph (light-toned area, left) reveals no stone buildings, but some alignments of post-holes and a number of large, regularly disposed rectangular and circular pits are visible. These suggest that the foundations of timber-framed buildings unresponsive to aerial photography may well exist in the vicinity.

A little to the right of centre is seen a winged corridor building over 50 m long, with a walled court or garden on its far side into which a long porch and other rooms extend. It is approached from the direction of the *forum* by its own street, beside which stood a substantial courtyard house. Smaller buildings faced the street running south from this, and in the distance, beyond (to right of) the *forum* are faint traces of a tightly packed row of strip-buildings fronting the street which underlies the modern lane. Part of this development was excavated in 1912–14.

References

J.K. StJoseph, *J.R.S.* XLIII (1953), 88; XLV (1955), 88 with Pl. XIX (different view). A. Baker in *Trans. Shropshire Arch. Soc.* LVIII Pt 3 (1967–8), 197–219. J.S. Wacher, *The Towns of Roman Britain* 358–74 with Pl. on p. 369 (different view). J.P. Bushe-Fox, *Excavations on the Site of the Roman Town at Wroxeter, Shropshire in 1912, 1913, 1914* (Oxford, 1913, 1914, 1916). D. Atkinson, *Report on Excavations at Wroxeter 1923–27* (Oxford, 1942) (*forum* excavations).

Insulae II and XVI (100)

The effect of drought on a sandy subsoil has revealed Roman town buildings with great clarity. The street along the eastern edge of Insulae II and XVI runs from top to bottom of the photograph and shows traces of a central sewer; two streets defining Insula XVI run westwards. At the north-east corner of this *Insula* another broad, light-toned crop-mark emerges from beneath the east–west street and curves southwards towards the fork in the modern lane; there are indications of a ditch on its near side. This feature, another part of which is seen in 99, is not yet properly understood. In essence it seems to represent an earthwork defence delimiting the second-century city before its expansion northwards to the line of the later city wall; but interpretation is complicated by the presence of the city's aqueduct on much the same line further east and by the apparent use of the

flattened rampart as the basis for a street (see description of 99).

In the foreground is seen a courtyard house with two other substantial houses adjacent, all three fronting the north–south street; west of these lies an even larger house with ranges round at least three sides of a rectangular courtyard. The dark lines marking the walls suggest that their masonry has been robbed; but several rooms, particularly in the left-hand house, appear in very light tone. This must indicate that solid floors, presumably in tessellation, mosaic or *opus signinum*, survive not far below the surface, stunting the growth of the crop. A fainter range of similar rooms runs up the courtyard of the building, and this suggests the presence of an earlier building at a lower level, perhaps in half-timber but with equally solid floors, which has been replaced during redevelopment.

In the foreground, to right of the north–south street, lies part of a very large rectangular walled enclosure which contains few known buildings apart from a granary or stores building. Beyond the enclosure, in the corner of the next *insula*, parts of two more large courtyard houses are visible, and further details can be seen in 98 near its right margin. A large room on the far right-hand corner of the nearer house seems to have been equipped with a channelled hypocaust. Insula XVI (upper centre) contains smaller buildings, some of them lying well away from the streets; a few show rather faintly as if belonging to a comparatively early period and buried to a greater depth.

The photograph illustrates the types of houses which wealthy Cornovian families occupied in the *civitas* capital. These large houses tend to be grouped near the administrative and commercial centre of the city. Few examples of the strip-house type used by traders and small-scale manufacturers appear in these *insulae*, but they are attested elsewhere.

References

J.K. StJoseph, *J.R.S.* XLIII (1953), 88 with Pl. XI, 2; LXVII (1977), Pl. XV, 2 (vertical). J.K. StJoseph in J.S. Wacher (ed.), *The Civitas Capitals of Roman Britain* (Leicester, 1966), 22 with Pl. I (this view). A. Baker in *Trans. Shropshire Arch. Soc.* LVIII Pt 3 (1967–8), 197–219.

MILDENHALL (*CUNETIO*), Wiltshire (101–2)

The small town of *Cunetio* lies 2.5 km east of Marlborough on the south bank of the river Kennet where a Roman road from Cirencester to Winchester crossed one from Silchester to Bath. Finds of early coins, brooches and samian have led to the suggestion that a conquest-period fort

101 Mildenhall (*Cunetio*), Wiltshire; small Roman town, looking E. SU 216695. BTT 11: July 1975.

lay here. This is very probable, but, if so, its defences now lie too deeply buried to be seen as crop-marks. The photographs reveal two successive defensive circuits round a civilian settlement.

The earlier of these consists of a bank and two ditches enclosing an almost rectangular area of about 6 ha (15 acres); this is much too large for an auxiliary fort; moreover, the ground rises outside the south defences, so any fort in this position would be overlooked at no great distance. There can be little doubt that it is an example of the programme of earthwork defence undertaken by the towns of Britain in the late second century. The normal later history of such defences was for the banks to be faced with walls during the third century and for external towers to be added in the middle of the fourth.

At *Cunetio* the masonry phase was later than normal and took a different line. A wall 3.15 m thick standing on massive foundations ran outside the old ditches on the south side but inside them on the east; on the west side it ran as much as 80 m outside the earlier lines, turning north on the near side of the lane in the foreground (101). The wall has been dated by excavation to the fourth century, and its towers, which project 5 m, have been found to be of one build with the wall. There were six towers along the south side (three at 36 m intervals each side of a gate), and the series continued on the other sides.

The photographs illustrate the contrasting conditions encountered in repeated reconnaissance. Both photographs have virtually the same viewpoint. In 101 the dark band of the early ditch

167

102 Mildenhall; looking E. AW 26: June 1948.

system shows clearly, as do the parch-marks of streets. Crossing the photograph from top to bottom in a straight line runs the road from Silchester. This lies obliquely to the defences and no doubt is earlier than the settlement. Near the centre of the photograph the road is joined from the north (left) by the Cirencester road, which crosses it and then bends west and south to leave the earthwork by a causeway across the ditches on its way to Winchester. At the other gate-positions causeways are indistinct; but the second, less regular, east–west street running towards the foreground appears definitely to be cut by the ditch system. 101 also shows some substantial masonry buildings along this street, and on other photographs more such buildings appear both inside the defended area and outside to the south.

102 gives a clearer impression of the early ditch system and of the fourth-century wall beyond it to the right. Along the wall three of the rectangular tower-bases are clearly visible in the distance. On their nearer side is the emplacement of a large gateway projecting both forwards and backwards from the wall; the Winchester road had evidently been realigned, for the earlier causeway lies some 35 m further west. The course of the wall on the east side of the town (top) clearly cuts across the Silchester road with no sign of a gateway through it, but at latest by the fourth century this road seems to have bypassed the town to the south.

The unusual relationship of the successive defences at *Cunetio* is noteworthy, but difficult to explain. We should probably assume that the earthwork had become so flattened and the

103 Kenchester (*Magnae*), Hereford and Worcester; walled town. Vertical photograph, N to left. SO 441427. K17-AI 172: July 1975. Scale 1:3100.

ditches so levelled by the passage of time that they were considered neither a useful contribution nor an impediment to the new line chosen for the wall. This would accord with the practice elsewhere in the fourth century of building massive free-standing curtain-walls without earthen ramparts.

References

J.K. St Joseph, *J.R.S.* XLIII (1953), 90 with Pl. XIII, 2 (oblique view looking WSW). Excavations: F.K. Annable, *Wilts. Arch. Mag.* LVI (1955), 191–2; LVII (1959), 233–5; LXI (1966), 9–30. D.R. Wilson in W. Rodwell and T. Rowley (eds.), *The Small Towns of Roman Britain* (B.A.R. 15, Oxford, 1975), 12 with Pls. VIIIA, VIIIB (obliques looking N and W).

KENCHESTER (*MAGNAE*), Hereford and Worcester (103)

The defended area (*c.* 9 ha) of this small walled settlement lies almost entirely within the large field to west of (below) a modern farm. A long reach of the south-east wall is visible as a straight light line (centre right), and the ditch system appears as a broad dark band along the two adjoining north (left) sectors.

The main Roman road bisects the settlement from east to west on its way into Wales towards Clyro and Brecon. Two other Roman roads join it outside the east gate. The first, followed by the straight modern lane, leads to Wroxeter; the other, indicated by a somewhat discontinuous white band, leads south for 300 m before making a sharp turn westwards to head in the direction of Abergavenny.

As at the comparable though somewhat larger town of Chesterton, the internal street plan is entirely irregular, and the layout of the town wall suggests that it was designed to enclose as much as possible of a linear roadside settlement. At Kenchester the short length of wall marking the east side lies just clear of the lower margin of the farm buildings, and the roadside settlement evidently extended east of this outside the defended area. Excavation would be necessary to determine whether the extra-mural area was developed later, or whether it was already in existence and was arbitrarily excluded. The resemblance to the pattern of the settlement within the walled area suggests that it was broadly contemporary, and that the position of the east gate was chosen in order to exclude the crossroads and any requirement to provide three gates instead of one.

Defences in the form of a rampart and ditch were erected here towards the end of the second century; later a stone wall was added to strengthen the bank, and later still external towers were provided.

The main street carries a centrally placed drain showing as a dark line; excavation in 1924–5 showed that it was *c.* 1 m wide and about half as deep: stone culverts also flanked the road on each side. The drain is absent in the excluded part of the settlement. Ribbon development occurs along each side of the street with properties containing so-called strip-buildings separated by short lengths of lane set roughly perpendicular to the street. One of these lanes on the south side extends further than the others and then turns south-east to serve other buildings, including one of the two large town houses visible on the photograph. Both these houses lie behind the main frontages

where more space is available, and neither conforms to any planned layout.

References

J.K. StJoseph, *J.R.S.* XLIII (1953), 92 with Pl. XIV, 1 (oblique); LXVII (1977), 157 with Pl. XVIII (this vertical view). D.R. Wilson in W. Rodwell and T. Rowley (eds.), *The Small Towns of Roman Britain* (B.A.R. No. 15, Oxford, 1975), 10 with Pls. IVa, b (obliques) and further bibliography. R.C.H.M., *Herefordshire* II (London, 1932), 93–5 with plan.

IRCHESTER, Northamptonshire (104)

Irchester is the site of a small Roman walled town on the south bank of the river Nene, 17 km ENE of Northampton; it lies on a Roman road following the valley from Whilton Lodge (*Bannaventa*) to Chesterton (*Durobrivae*). Excavation south of the town has shown extensive traces of Iron Age settlement, which continued to thrive throughout the first century A.D., spreading both east and west of the later walled circuit. During the second half of the second century, as at other such settlements, earthwork defences were erected round the nucleus of what was probably at that time a fairly diffuse inhabited area, and later still the front of the rampart was cut back to receive a wall of stone.

The wall on the south side is seen as a parch-mark at the bottom of the photograph, just to the north of the white lane; on the other three sides it is concealed by the hedges surrounding the field. The area inside the circuit is just over 8 ha, but considerable extra-mural settlement continued, at least on the east and south sides, until the late fourth century.

Within, the most prominent features are the parch-marks of a very irregular street system. The main north–south street enters at the site of the south gate (bottom), and there are known to be small gates also near the centres of the east and west sides, though not, apparently, on the north; but the striking feature is the absence of through roads on either axis and of a rectilinear street grid. It is clear that no road crossed the Nene to the north directly from the town, nor did the east–west road along the valley cross the walled area. Presumably it passed outside to the south. The manner in which the side streets tend to radiate out to the corners of the walled area suggests that the majority were laid down after the defences had been created. Near the north-west (top left) corner of the town, however, one of the streets can be seen to be cut by a small subrectangular enclosure. The street pattern is characteristic of a village rather than a planned

104 Irchester, Northamptonshire; Roman walled town, looking N. SP 917667. BCJ 84: June 1970.

settlement, and this lack of regularly planned streets is one of the features which differentiates the 'small towns' of Roman Britain from its cities.

Neither the east nor the west side of the defences is laid out in an exactly straight line; each makes a slight bend at the points where photographs show a broad dark band running from the east gate straight across the town. This dark band, which is overlain by the north–south street, is suggestive of an early ditch system, such as might have defended the south side of a conquest-period fort lying below the north half of

the later town. If there were such a fort, the indications are that it was very large, c. 4 ha (10 acres) in area. An early fort is certainly more probable than that the ditch system demarcated an original nucleus of the civil town, for it was at the south edge of the later defended area that the excavations of 1962–3 revealed the primary bank, later cut back for a wall. For a small settlement of this sort to have had two phases of earthwork defence, each enclosing such disparate areas, would be very unusual.

The photograph shows that the north–south

105 Chesterton (*Durobrivae*), **Cambridgeshire; Roman walled town.** Vertical photograph, N at top right. TL 122908. K17-U 167: June 1970. Scale 1:4500.

street was closely built up with long narrow strip-buildings of the type normal in such settlements. A square Romano-Celtic temple is visible just north of the first branch street to the right, about one-third of the way to the east gate, and in the left foreground, south of the nearest east–west street an octagonal building which may be a second temple has been recorded. In contrast to both Kenchester and Chesterton (**103, 105**) no really large buildings seem to be present at Irchester.

In 1853 the inscribed tombstone of Anicius Saturninus, *strator* to the governor (i.e. the official in charge of the governor's mounts) was found reused as the lid of a later grave-cist in the south-east quarter of the town. The secondary grave was probably very late, since burials in inhabited spots were forbidden by law; the death of this officer while presumably still serving has been taken to suggest the presence of stud farms in the Irchester district.

References

J.K. St Joseph, in J.S. Wacher (ed.), *The Civitas Capitals of Roman Britain* (Leicester, 1966), 26–7 with Pl. V (more distant oblique from S). Defences and extra-mural settlement to S: D.N. Hall, N. Nickerson and J.K. Knight, *Arch. Journ.* CXXIV (1967), 65–128. D.R. Wilson in W. Rodwell and T. Rowley (eds.), *The Small Towns of Roman Britain* (B.A.R. 15, Oxford, 1975), 11 with Pl. VIB (this view). R.C.H.M., *County of Northampton* II (1979), 91–6 with plan and Pl. 3A (similar oblique view). Inscription: *R.I.B.* 233.

CHESTERTON (*DUROBRIVAE*), Cambridgeshire (105–6)

The site of *Durobrivae*, the 'fortified place by the bridge' lies beside the river Nene, 5 km west of Peterborough, in the parish of Chesterton, although often wrongly attributed to Water Newton. With a walled area of 17.8 ha (44 acres) it is the largest of the so-called 'small towns' of Roman Britain. The town plan, clearly visible on 105, shows essential differences from that of a *civitas* capital with a planned grid of streets. At *Durobrivae*, the walled area is the same size as that at Caerwent and larger than that at Caistor by Norwich (94). However, the most prominent feature of 105 is the straight course of Ermine Street, the main Roman road from London to Lincoln, which maintains the same alignment for 16 km. Until damaged by ploughing in recent years the road ran on a high *agger* across the town, and from it, as at Kenchester (103), small lanes lead off in various directions as convenience dictates. The plan suggests that the full extent of this development was not reached before the defences were erected in the late second or early third century. Nevertheless, the walls were clearly intended to enclose as much as possible of the nucleus of a settlement centred in the northern half of the walled area, and to embrace much of the roadside development extending south-east of this. The flood-plain of the Nene, which includes the three low-lying meadows on the right-hand side of 105, and that of a tributary, the Billing Brook (the light-toned field in the photograph), determined the limits to north-east and north-west of the area that was walled.

A *mortarium* stamp of a local potter (*Cunoarus Vico Duro [brivis]*) attests the status of the settlement as a *vicus*; it has been suggested that in the late empire the town may have been promoted to the rank of *civitas* capital, but the evidence for this is very inconclusive. The place began, no doubt, as a civil settlement outside the first-century fort which guarded the bridge over the Nene (the fort lies across the Billing Brook, beyond the top margin of 105). Subsequent prosperity, however, was owed in part to the position within a rich agricultural area and in part to the situation on both a main road and a navigable river; but special importance also accrued from its role as the centre of the important Nene Valley pottery industry. From the middle of the second century the manufacture of high-grade colour-coated vessels captured an enormous market.

The late second- or early third-century town-wall does not seem to have been preceded, as so often elsewhere, by an earthwork defence. The wall has three gates. The north gate is obscured by a hedge. At the other two, the wall can be seen to be staggered to allow the gatehouses to stand obliquely or even at right angles to the circuit, so that any attackers would be immediately overlooked from the wall as they approached the gates. In 105 there is a hint, confirmed by later photographs, of the presence of external rectangular towers along the south-west front: they were probably additions of the fourth century.

The north gate led via the Nene bridge, 0.7 km distant, to a large industrial suburb now in Castor parish (Normangate Field, 107); but many pottery kilns and other workshops also lay west of the town. The south-west gate gave access to a road leading to Irchester: this road can be seen diverging from beneath a modern farm track at a point where it crosses a suburban street at right angles. Along the further course of the road are faint marks of buildings, some of which are perhaps mausolea. The street at right angles also passes through an area of cemeteries on its way to the Billing Brook, and in the other direction probably connected with Ermine Street outside the south gate, where several extra-mural buildings were excavated in 1957 before the modern dual carriageway of the A 1 road was constructed.

Within the walls, both sides of Ermine Street are lined with buildings, principally strip-houses end-on to the road, and many more appear along the minor lanes. In 106 a considerable number of these buildings are visible, as well as traces of two larger structures. Near the bottom right-hand corner is a large courtyard building, perhaps *c.* 60 by 45 m overall. Its main rectangle is partly obscured by the dark band of ploughing across the middle of the photograph; on its north-east side a wing connects with the Ermine Street frontage. A noteworthy fact is that the building is aligned neither to the main road, nor to the other nearby streets. This building was perhaps a *praetorium*

173

106 **Chesterton**; oblique view, looking N. AOK 91: June 1966.

or *mansio* of the posting system. In the next *insula* to the north, and not visible on the photograph, lies a second large rectangular building, aligned with the south-west side of Ermine Street. This might be a market building, but the presence of what look like three temples behind it may perhaps suggest alternatively a religious function.

In 1975 a hoard of silver vessels and other objects was discovered by use of a metal-detector somewhere in the south part of the town; many of the pieces carried inscriptions showing a Christian context. The date of the hoard falls in the first half of the fourth century. The discovery is of unusual importance, both for its evidence of wealth and cosmopolitan contacts and also because this is the earliest collection of Christian silverware so far known from anywhere in the Roman world. Whether the hoard indicates the existence of a church within the town is a question that can be decided only by excavation, for the silver could conceivably have been brought from elsewhere and buried during some crisis. The answer to the question is of some importance to our view of the character of late Roman *Durobrivae*.

References

E.T. Artis, *The Durobrivae of Antoninus* (London, 1828), Pl. XXIII (plan). J.K. StJoseph, *J.R.S.* XLIII (1953), 91; XLVIII (1958), 98 with Pl. XIV (oblique view from S); LI (1961), 132. *Idem* in J.S. Wacher (ed.), *The Civitas Capitals of Roman Britain* (Leicester, 1966), 25–6 with Pl. IV (oblique view looking W). D.R. Wilson in W. Rodwell and T. Rowley (eds.), *Small Towns of Roman Britain* (B.A.R. 15, Oxford, 1975), 9–10 with Pl. I (our **105**), II (a) and (b) (oblique views looking NE and E), III (a) (oblique view of extra-mural area looking W). For plan of town incorporating all features revealed by aerial

107 Castor, Cambridgeshire; Normangate Field, Roman industrial area, looking SW. TL 117978. ZF 83: June 1959.

photography see D. Mackreth, *Durobrivae* No. 7 (1979), 19–21. Silver treasure: *Britannia* VII (1976), 333, 385–6, and K.S. Painter, *The Water Newton Early Christian Silver* (British Museum, 1977). Status (argument from milestone): C.E. Stevens, *English Historical Review* LII (1937), 199; A.L.F. Rivet, *Town and Country in Roman Britain* (London, 1958, 1964), 135; W. Rodwell, *Britannia* VI (1975), 96.

NORMANGATE FIELD, CASTOR, Cambridgeshire (107)

Normangate Field lies on the north bank of the river Nene, 2.4 km north-west of *Durobrivae* on the opposite side of the river. Ermine Street crossed the river here and on the north bank a number of roads diverged. The two principal branches were King Street, which took a more direct route to Lincoln along the fen edge, and the so-called 'Fen Causeway' which ran east across the fens to Norfolk. In addition to these, several local roads and lanes served the area. During the second century an industrial suburb of *Durobrivae* began to develop here, eventually covering some 28 ha (69 acres). The main industry was the production of Nene Valley or Castor colour-coated pottery, but manufacture of iron goods was also carried on. The pottery industry was extremely successful, being fortunate to start the manufacture of fine table wares at a time when the Samian industry of Gaul was beginning to decline, and no doubt the local products were able to undercut on transport costs. Markets were won in many parts of Britain, and production expanded over several km up and down the river

175

108 Thorpe (*Ad Pontem*), Nottinghamshire; Roman fortlet, small town and possible supply base. Remains in **Wharf Close** looking N. SK 760504. BYL 12: June 1976.

valley; here also some prosperous villas are known to have existed.

The earliest potters, from the early to middle part of the second century, produced only for a local market and may have had their workshops within the town, firing their grey-ware products by the bonfire method on the open ground across the river. Colour-coated wares, however, required proper kilns, and during the later second century the area began to fill up with workshops and other buildings including shrines and mausolea. As early as 1828 E.T. Artis, who pioneered the study of Roman archaeology of this area, published drawings and plans of kilns.

Ermine Street crosses the top of the photograph coming from the river on the left. From the bridgehead a second road runs towards the centre of the photograph, where it turns north-east towards the Fen Causeway. At the bend a ditched drove-way branches off, aiming at the huge villa

now under Castor Church 1 km to the north-east. On the line of the hedge which crosses this drove-way in the foreground runs a third metalled road not clearly visible but connecting the Fen Causeway with the Ermine Street–King Street junction away to the right. A fourth street runs westwards from near the bend in the road at the centre of Normangate Field.

In the foreground at least three ring ditches can be seen; they probably represent Bronze Age barrows. One partly underlies the drove-way, but beyond it another is respected by adjacent Roman enclosures and may still have been visible as a tumulus in Roman times. Elsewhere a number of irregular dark areas, sometimes showing characteristic rectangular extensions, clearly represent filled-in clay pits of the pottery industry; some smaller marks may indicate the sites of kilns.

The features in the foreground have never been examined, but a large area towards the top right-

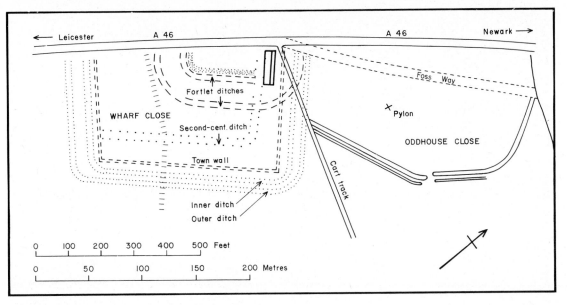

Fig. 17 Thorpe, plan of enclosures (after J. S. Wacher).

hand corner has been excavated. This work re-vealed two circular shrines, an aisled barn and (adjacent to Ermine Street) a large aisled workshop and kilns.

References

E.T. Artis, *The Durobrivae of Antoninus* (London, 1828). J.K. St Joseph, *J.R.S.* LI (1961), 132 with Pl. XI, 1 (this view). R.C.H.M., *Peterborough New Town* (London, 1969), 23 with plan and Pl. 3A (oblique view looking NE). G. Dannell, *Durobrivae* II (1974), 7–9.

THORPE (*AD PONTEM*), Nottinghamshire (108–9)

Wharf Close

The site at Thorpe lies 5 km south-west of Newark, on the Foss Way beside the river Trent, which just enters the left-hand margin of the photograph. The Roman name suggests a bridge over the Trent here, but no road leading to a crossing is known on either bank, although the second-century defended settlement had a gate on the riverward side.

The line of the Foss Way coincides with that of the modern A 46 road as far as the north-east side of the settlement. There other photographs show (109) the Roman road diverging eastwards across the top right-hand field (Oddhouse Close), to left of a pylon. This sector of the Roman road is thought to be a late first-century rectification, involving a realignment of the original road.

The photograph (108) shows defences in the field known as Wharf Close belonging to at least three phases.

(1) Just above a tree beside the modern road the rounded corners and part of the north-east alignment of two parallel widely spaced ditches appear. These belong to a first-century fortlet which is thought to measure *c.* 78 m north–south over the rampart. To judge by the configuration of the surface, the fortlet might have been *c.* 0.5 ha (1.4 acres) in size and would thus be a small road-post garrisoned only by a detachment. The contemporary Roman road is unlikely to have passed through it, but probably ran past the north-west side. A section cut across the defences in 1963 showed that ditches had been recut and that the rampart overlay two phases of Iron Age timber buildings.

(2) During the second century, civilian occupation developed on the site of the fortlet and was provided with earthwork defences. The broad dark band of a ditch *c.* 6 m wide cuts across the fortlet's ditches near the north end of the field and then turns south-west. The broad ditch does not reappear towards the south-west end of the field, and so probably turned north-west and is now masked by the defences of phase 3. If so, the defended area measured *c.* 150 m north–south and rather less east–west, with a possible area of 1.5 ha. It may have been at this stage or slightly earlier that the Foss Way was realigned, and now ran parallel with, and just inside, the north-west defences. Excavations in 1952 revealed post-holes of a timber gateway near the south end of the north-west side.

109 Thorpe; remains in Oddhouse Close, looking NE. VK 46: July 1957.

(3) In the late third or the fourth century a larger enclosure was defended by a stone wall 2.6 m wide with sharp rectangular corners and by two ditches which were later transformed into a single wide one. The north-east, south-east and south-west sides of the enclosure are visible in the field; the north-west side lies just beyond the modern road, defining a space of *c.* 170 m by 128 m, or *c.* 2.1 ha.

To this phase belong the foundations of a stone building in the northern corner of the field, which can be seen as a narrow line in light tone defining a rectangle and overlying the broad ditch of phase 2. This is a strip-building, end-on to the Roman road, *c.* 30 m long by *c.* 6 m wide, with a passage or long narrow room on the north side. The general position of other roadside buildings is represented by light parch-marks, and an east–west street follows an irregular course from just south of the outer ditch of the fortlet to a gate in the south-east wall of the latest enclosure. The street seems to have had a central drain now showing as a dark line. If this road continued beyond the defences it might perhaps have been aiming at Ancaster.

110 Catterick Bridge, North Yorkshire; Roman *vicus* (*Cataractonium*), looking N. SE 225991. DQ 80: July 1949.

Oddhouse Close (109)

The interpretation of the remains at Thorpe is complicated by the presence in the next field to the north (Oddhouse Close) of an irregular polygonal or kite-shaped enclosure of *c.* 2 ha (109), which is traversed by the Roman road. Excavation in 1965 showed the surrounding ditch to be 4 m wide with a second, slighter ditch along the south-east side. The ditch had a turfy filling as if derived from a demolished military rampart, and late first-century pottery was found in the lower levels. These facts suggest that the enclosure may be contemporary with the fortlet, perhaps forming a supply depot defended by it. But there are other possibilities, and the relationship of the enclosure to the fortlet needs to be defined by excavation.

The Foss Way is thought to have been the backbone of a frontier zone for a short period during the 40s of the first century, but for long after that it will have retained a military importance. Nevertheless the known military sites along the line of the Foss are few in number. In later centuries even quite small settlements received defences. These might either have been part of a general security precaution, or have been designed to protect installations of the public posting service or of various other officials concerned with tax-gathering or with the collection of grain for the army. Unfortunately the photographs of Thorpe reveal no substantial stone buildings which might give a clue to the reason here.

References

J.K. St Joseph, *J.R.S.* XLIII (1953), 91; XLVIII (1958), 98 with Pl. XV, 1 (Oddhouse Close, oblique photograph from SW). D.R. Wilson, *J.R.S.* LI (1961), 177–8; LIV (1964), 159–60 (Fig. 12, plan of Wharf Close) with Pl. XIII, 1 (Wharf Close, oblique, from SW); LVI (1966), 203–4 (Fig. 10, plan of both fields). G. Webster, *Arch. Journ.* CXV (1958), 53 with Pl. IXA (oblique, both fields from E). J.S. Wacher (ed.), *The Civitas Capitals of Roman Britain* (1966), 28–9 (Fig. 1, general plan) with Pl. VI (oblique, Wharf Close from SW). W. Rodwell and T.

179

111 Piercebridge (*Magis*), **Durham**; Roman *vicus*, looking N. NZ 211157. GU 41: July 1951.

Rowley (eds.), *Small Towns of Roman Britain* (1975), 12 with Pl. VIIa (oblique, Oddhouse Close from S), Pl. VIIb (steep oblique view, Wharf Close from NE). *Trans. Thoroton Soc.* LXIX (1965), 19–39 (W gate).

CATTERICK BRIDGE, North Yorkshire (110)

The river Swale flows from left to right across the centre of the photograph, and the parch-mark of the main Roman road to the North, Leeming Lane, is visible on both sides of the river, which was here crossed on a bridge. The site was first occupied by a Flavian fort set on the high ground above the bridge, and now largely covered by Thornborough Farm seen at the left-hand margin. From the middle of the second century a civilian settlement (*vicus*) of timber-framed buildings developed below the fort on each side of the Roman road and was gradually rebuilt in stone. Probably about the middle of the third century the *vicus* was

surrounded by a wall enclosing 6.27 ha (15.5 acres). The circuit is defined by a narrow parch-mark running obliquely from near the farm towards the bottom of the photograph, and then parallel with the lower edge, before turning back at right angles towards the river. Inside the fortified area parch-marks of streets form a rough grid.

The photograph was taken before the construction of the Catterick bypass which today runs in a deep cutting slightly to the west of the line of the Roman road. Excavation in 1959 in advance of this work revealed buildings of various dates between the second and fifth centuries, including a large bath-house, a tannery and a substantial *mansio*, none of which appear on the photograph. Subsequent excavations on the north side of the river, in Brompton on Swale parish, have discovered a second fortified area originating in the middle of the second century at a time when

180

the fort at Thornborough Farm was disused. Only in the fourth century did civilian suburbs spread over the land north of the river.

References

J.R.S. L (1960), 217–18 with plan. *Britannia* IV (1973), 278–9 (Brompton on Swale, plan).

PIERCEBRIDGE, Durham (111)

The photograph shows the line of Dere Street on the north bank of the river Tees (bottom right). Here, in 'Tofts field', under corn when the photograph was taken, the irregular street system of a large civilian settlement (*vicus*) can be made out. The long street running west from Dere Street is aiming at the east gate of a late third-century fort which underlies the modern village to left of the photograph 150 m away. It is to be expected that such an important river-crossing was also guarded by a fort of an earlier period, but this has not been located. Traces of stone buildings, mainly of 'strip' type, can be seen along all the streets, and the settlement must have covered at least 4.4 ha (11 acres). Excavations in Tofts field have shown that here Dere Street was first metalled towards the end of the first century, and elsewhere in the field a late first-century oven was found underlying later buildings. The river has shifted northwards since Roman times, for in 1972 a substantial Roman masonry bridge abutment was unearthed 100 m south of the present course, and in the neighbourhood of the bridge further extensive traces of civilian settlement were found on the south side of the river.

References

J.K. StJoseph, *J.R.S.* XLV (1955), 82–3 with Pl. XVIII, 2 (this view). *Britannia* III (1972), 309 (Holme House; *ibid.* IV (1973), 280 (bridge abutment). *Britannia* V (1974), 413 (Tofts field); *ibid.* VI (1975), 234–5.

PART FOUR

THE COUNTRYSIDE

THE COUNTRYSIDE

New methods of investigation, by aerial photography and by field survey, have brought great changes in modern understanding of the rural economy of Roman and pre-Roman Britain. The immediate revolution in thought which followed the classic excavation of the Iron Age farmstead at Little Woodbury, and the gradual recovery thereafter of a more balanced view, are described below under Chisenbury Warren (122).

Britain was a Celtic province in which the less Romanized inhabitants continued to practise a traditional way of life which might be affected to varying degrees by new techniques, new tools, and new pressures introduced as a result of membership of the Roman Empire. The presence of a large army, which had to be fed, supplied and at least to some extent paid from British resources, was a powerful fresh factor in the economy, as also in different ways were the growing towns and new market centres connected by a network of new roads. New social groups acquired wealth; even the most conservative peasant settlements must have bowed to the pressure for greater production (p. 217).

The villa itself was of course a Roman introduction, but large rural farms had not been uncommon during the Iron Age; several of them can be shown to have put on a new guise as the influence of Romanization spread, and it is likely that others did too. Likewise there had existed large nucleated rural settlements in pre-Roman times; some of these continued to exist after the conquest and others were newly established. Undoubtedly, however, despite the survival of a peasant economy in many regions, the growth of wealth under Roman rule favoured the development of large estates based on the villa economy. Peasants in some areas may have been bewildered to find that their tenure of ancestral holdings based on tribal usage was becoming less secure, and that they had little alternative to becoming tenants of a great landlord. At the same time the pressure for greater corn production must have caused new land to be taken into cultivation, a process assisted by the inevitable clearance of woodland for building-materials and for fuel supply.

Agriculture in Roman Britain was perforce more intensive than in the Iron Age because of the need to feed the army, the new towns and the Roman administration. However, it was still very largely based on what is known as the Celtic field system – small rectangular fields whose lynchets survived extensively on the chalklands of southern Britain until swept away by the agricultural changes introduced during the Second World War. It is a matter of great regret that the Cambridge collection of aerial photographs began to be formed only after this extensive destruction. A few undamaged groups of Celtic fields still survive on the chalk downs; two are included here (123, 124). Another large group, apparently newly created in the Roman period, is illustrated at Grassington in Yorkshire (134). The small size of the fields was conditioned by the use of a simple and rather primitive plough.

Aerial photographs have shown that similar small fields were widespread also on gravel river-terraces and other low ground including the Fenland, where most of the surface remains have long since been destroyed by medieval and subsequent ploughing. Indeed, these discoveries, when considered together with the results of much recent field-walking and ground survey, have caused a dramatic revision of estimates for the population of Roman Britain. A total of 1.5 million was considered reasonable in 1930; a recent assessment (P. Salway, *Roman Britain*, Oxford, 1981) is three to four times that figure.

The continued use of the Celtic system of small fields, despite the improved agricultural methods and tools introduced in the Roman period, is perhaps not surprising in areas where it had long existed and where field-banks (lynchets) had become so substantial as to defy reform. But the appearance of similar patterns of small fields round sites first occupied in the Roman period, for instance in the Fenland, must indicate both poverty of material equipment and the strength of the ancient social system controlling the practice of peasant agriculture. One of the few changes which can sometimes be recognised is towards a more regular pattern of fields in areas probably newly enclosed during Roman times (123). Elsewhere, however, in the Midlands, particularly in the region between Nottingham and Doncaster, huge areas of rather larger fields, regularly laid out, have been recognised from the air in recent years; these testify to a planned agricultural expansion seemingly undertaken in the second or third century (28). To what extent these enclosures were pastoral is still uncertain; but in so far as any were arable they suggest a response to the capabilities of more powerful ploughs.

In northern England pastoralism had always played a prominent role. Recent discoveries have shown that arable farming was far more widespread even in pre-Roman times than was formerly suspected, and have also pointed to a great expansion in both types of activity during Roman times. The farms themselves, however, remained of native type; an example at Ewe Close is illustrated (135).

The great majority of villas are found south of the Pennines. They represented a fully Roman way of life and their greater resources enabled their owners to practise a more developed type of agriculture. Nevertheless, evidence for the cultivation of larger fields is curiously lacking; at many villas the cultivation of fields of the 'Celtic' type is thought to have continued. All the more interesting are the remains of the field system near Arbury Banks, Hertfordshire (113–14), which appear to surround a villa at Ashwell. These fields are of very different character and support the view that at some villas at least the changes which might be expected were introduced. Further evidence is provided by the strip-fields noted at Chignall St James (117).

10

VILLAS

The term 'villa' was used in Roman times to denote a house in the countryside, normally forming the centre of a farm or estate. Modern archaeologists have experienced some difficulty in arriving at a definition which satisfactorily embraces both the essential characteristics laid down in ancient sources and the observed remains; for while the status of a large rural establishment in masonry is rarely in doubt, it is clear that in Roman Britain not all farmsteads were sufficiently Romanized to qualify for inclusion. A villa must express, however humbly, its links with Roman architecture. To exclude a house merely on the ground that it was built of timber would be perverse, for (particularly in the east of the country) quite extensive and well-appointed buildings are known in this material. Questions of size, shape and function need to be considered. One definition recently offered is as follows: 'Villa in Latin means farm; but a farm which is integrated in the social and economic organisation of the Roman world' (A.L.F. Rivet, *The Roman Villa in Britain*, London, 1969, 77).

However, even function may in practice confuse the issue; for while, strictly speaking, a villa must be a house devoted either to civilised country leisure or to the pursuit of agriculture, it would be pedantic in archaeological terms to exclude from the class a large country house which may turn out to have belonged, for instance, to a wealthy potter in the region round Chesterton (105); we must take a wide view of country activities.

Even in pre-Roman times British farming was by no means a subsistence agriculture. Surpluses were accumulated which could support a warlike aristocracy and a fair amount of trade; towards the end of the period agricultural products were exported to the Continent. The villa system was founded on these beginnings. Growth of large estates in single ownership facilitated agricultural planning; new crops were introduced. Use of the improved, heavier plough enabled fresh areas to be cultivated; introduction of the scythe facilitated the feeding of livestock over the winter months; corn-drying ovens improved the treatment of the harvest. Farmers in some parts of the province probably specialised in the production of wool and of meat. There is a close observable relationship between towns and the distribution of villas; both were intimately tied up in a marketing network. Undoubtedly it was the villa system which enabled the province to support a greatly increased population and to continue the export of corn to the Continent.

Numerous though villas are in the southern half of Britain – the total is over 750 – the pattern of their distribution is in marked contrast with the density revealed in northern France by the aerial reconnaissance of R. Agache. There special measures seem to have been taken in the first century, possibly in connection with the commissariat of the Roman armies on the Rhine, to judge by the abrupt changes in land use.

Although the economic aspects of the villa are of great importance, and at small villas may be the sole claim to interest, it should not be forgotten that the larger villas were the homes of wealthy and educated families. The sculpture, mosaics and remains of wall-paintings which such houses produce can greatly illuminate the cultural life of Roman Britain. One such villa, at Chedworth, where much of the site is available for inspection by the modern visitor, is shown on 119.

To the study of villas, as to that of other classes of site, aerial photography makes several contributions. It has revealed hitherto undiscovered examples, and can record the topographical setting of a villa; it can reveal the pattern of outbuildings, surrounding enclosures, and sometimes even field systems with a clarity which only the results of extensive excavation would otherwise provide; and under favourable conditions it can illustrate the plan of the house in considerable detail, even suggesting the presence of tessellated or mosaic floors. What it cannot do, except in the broadest outline and by the use of analogy, is to illuminate the history of the site shown on the photographs.

Nevertheless suggestive information can sometimes be obtained. At Little Milton (112) photographs show the villa overlying earlier enclosures which may belong either to an Iron Age or to an earlier Roman predecessor in timber. At Cromwell (121) and at Allington Hill (115) a timber building is actually visible and may well be earlier than the

112 Little Milton, Oxfordshire; Roman villa at Ditchend Barn, looking E. SP 624003. CU 61: June 1949.

masonry villa. The photograph of Cromwell also illustrates the great complexity of ditched enclosures which can be expected at any long-inhabited agricultural site. That an Iron Age farm lay nearby is suggested by a 'pit-alignment'; this belongs to a somewhat enigmatic class of boundary-marker which consists of a line of close-set pits, often *c.* 2 m across and 1 m deep, in which excavation has revealed no sign of upright posts. The villa at Lockington (**120**) lies close to a more clearly defined pre-Roman settlement and, like that at Ashwell (**113**), evidently farmed the same lands. How the transition of tenure was effected is a question difficult to decide; probably even excavation could not resolve it.

References

S. Applebaum in H.P.R. Finberg (ed.), *The Agrarian History of England and Wales* I Pt 2 (Cambridge, 1972), 19–250. A.R. Birley, *Life in Roman Britain* (London, 1964), Chs. 6–7. R.G. Collingwood and I.A. Richmond, *The Archaeology of Roman Britain* (2nd ed., London, 1969), Ch. 7. S.S. Frere, *Britannia, A History of Roman Britain* (3rd ed., 1978), Ch. 13. A.L.F. Rivet, *Town and Country in Roman Britain* (London, 1958). A.L.F. Rivet (ed.), *The Roman Villa in Britain* (London, 1969). I.A. Richmond in P. Salway (ed.), *Roman Archaeology and Art, Essays and Studies by Sir Ian Richmond* (London, 1969), 135–49. P. Salway, *Roman Britain* (Oxford, 1981), Chs. 19–20. M. Todd (ed.), *Studies in the Romano-British Villa* (London, 1978). J.S. Wacher, *Roman Britain* (London, 1978), Ch. 4. Villas in northern France: R. Agache and B. Bréart, *Atlas d'Archéologie aerienne de Picardie* (Amiens, 1975); R. Agache, *La Somme Pré-Romaine et Romaine* (Amiens, 1978).

LITTLE MILTON, Oxfordshire (**112**)

A small corridor-villa, *c.* 25 m long, of simple plan is seen to lie within one of a number of rectangular ditched enclosures. At least three different phases in the plan of these enclosures may be distinguished and some of the ditches have evidently been recut. The villa overlies a ditch which seems to be associated with a curvilinear enclosure belonging to the earliest phase. The house, which had a range of six rooms, two of them small and one narrow, is flanked by a corridor on the east side. Faint indications suggest the possibility that the corridor was later subdivided into rooms. A small four-roomed building, aligned to the villa, lies about 6 m away to the south. It was perhaps joined to the main building by a shed or other

113 Ashwell (Claybush Hill), Hertfordshire; possible Roman villa site and fields, looking SE. TL 265384. BZE 13: July 1976.

temporary structure. Other photographs show a walled enclosure or farmyard about 40 m square, extending westwards from the villa.

The house is typical of one of the classes of small Romano-British villas, termed by Richmond 'the cottage house'; these sometimes prospered sufficiently to be eventually enlarged and to become the nucleus of a grander plan, as happened at Bignor; but here the house remained compact. The narrow room may possibly have housed a staircase, since the building is hardly long enough to require a through-passage.

The system of ditched enclosures exists only in the vicinity of the villa; it probably represents not arable fields but orchards, vegetable gardens or dairy-paddocks. Smaller closes occupy parts of some of the larger ones and may be later subdivisions. Dark marks that appear within the main enclosures may be pits, either contemporary with the villa, or earlier and possibly associated with a pre-existing Roman timber building or even with an Iron Age farm.

Comparatively few of these modest villas have been excavated to modern standards. Excavation, if ever to be undertaken at Little Milton, should not be long delayed. Development of the modern

189

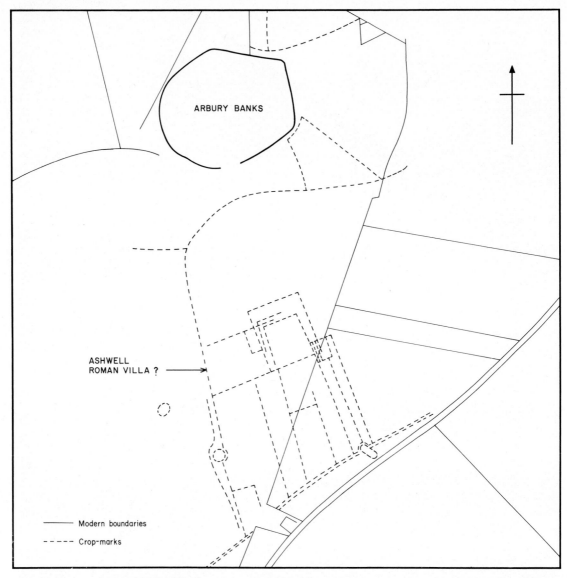

Fig. 18 Interpretative sketch of field system at Ashwell. The top of photograph 113 faces the bottom of this plan.

farm has caused the farmyard and its buildings to reach half as near again to the site as they did in 1949 when the photograph was taken.

References

J.K. St Joseph, *J.R.S.* XL (1950), Pl. VI, 2; XLIII (1953), 94. D.R. Wilson, *Britannia* V (1974), 253–4, 257. Collingwood and Richmond, *The Archaeology of Roman Britain* (1969), 135–6, Fig. 46c.

ASHWELL (CLAYBUSH HILL), Hertfordshire (113)

In the left foreground on a southward slope of chalk lies a rectangular enclosure of 150 by 115 m (1.7 ha) demarcated by a broad well-cut ditch with a wide entrance on the far side; within are two further rectangular lines of ditch, not necessarily contemporary with the outer one. Where the broad ditch is overlain by an existing hedgerow, this ditch is seen to cut across a smaller square enclosure defined by two ditches, at least on the south-west and north-west sides. Surrounding the main enclosure, and for the most part contemporary with it, a number of ditched fields may be clearly distinguished. One field boundary, parallel to the bottom of the photograph, seems to be earlier, and at the top left corner is a small oval enclosure not contemporary with the main ditch. These features suggest that the site under-

114 Arbury Banks, Hertfordshire; Iron Age defended settlement, looking N. TL 262387. OM 51: June 1964.

went slow development over several periods. No buildings are visible but the main enclosure probably surrounded a timber-framed farmstead.

Fields distinct from the normal Celtic type (124) and field systems definitely associated with villas are extremely rare in Roman Britain. Here the fields are long and comparatively narrow, suggesting use of a more effective plough than the Celtic *ard*. They average *c.* 216 by multiples of *c.* 13 m. In the background they adjoin a road or drove-way marked by parallel ditches which are interrupted by the oval enclosure. Near the right-hand top corner one of the field boundaries runs up to, and then partly surrounds, a circular mark probably indicating a Bronze Age barrow; similar relationships have been noted in Celtic field systems, and probably imply continuing respect for the dead. Some 400 m north-west of the enclosure lies Arbury Banks (114), a defended Iron Age settlement where aerial photographs

have revealed pits and house sites in remarkable detail. It is tempting to speculate that the Iron Age estate was succeeded in Roman times by a villa on a neighbouring slope. Outlying boundaries of the field system can be seen (Fig. 18) to swing round the defences of Arbury Banks in a manner suggesting that this earthwork may have been incorporated in the Romano-British farm.

Reference

J.K. St Joseph, *J.R.S.* LXVII (1977), 160 with Pl. XVII, 2 (panorama in the reverse direction showing relationship with Arbury Banks).

ARBURY BANKS, Hertfordshire (114)

The site lies 1.2 km south-west of Ashwell at a height of *c.* 90 m above sea-level and is a partially bivallate fortification of *c.* 5 ha, within which a number of domestic enclosures, numerous storage

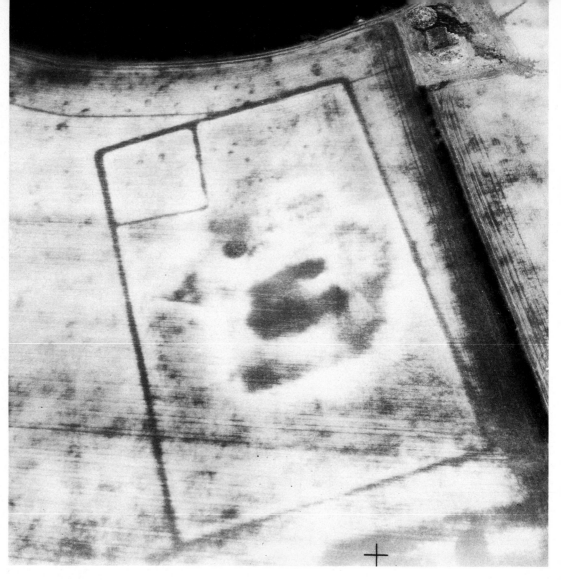

115 Allington Hill, Bottisham, Cambridgeshire; Roman villa enclosure, looking SE. TL 577588. AIM 8: April 1964.

pits and a probable Bronze Age barrow can be seen as crop-marks.

The circle in the foreground defined by a broad ditch but lacking a causeway is probably a barrow, for the regular circumference and the width of ditch distinguish it from any of the other enclosures. To its left, the large post-holes of a rectangular building partly overlaid by a small ditched enclosure can be seen; from nearby, a roadway seems to run across the site to an entrance through the defences towards the top of the photograph. There is an opposite entrance in the south-west side of the circuit. In the distance a large rectangular enclosure surrounds a circular house, and other enclosures both penannular and subrectangular can also be distinguished. The distribution of storage pits is by no means haphazard; they occur in lines and in groups in some

areas, while others are devoid of them. What may be the principal building lies beyond the middle of the earthwork; now only a vaguely circular dark area can be distinguished, as if there had been a long history of reconstruction.

Sites of this kind, whether defended or not, were common in the Iron Age of lowland Britain, but in the Roman period although peasant sites often present an irregular plan, surrounding earthworks were not provided and existing ones tended to be abandoned. There are old records of coins and a few Romano-British potsherds and other objects having been found here, so that it is likely that occupation may not entirely have ceased in the Romano-British period. But Arbury Banks lies close to a possible villa at Ashwell (previous section) whose field system (113) came up to the outer ditch of the settlement, and this suggests

192

116 Lidgate, Suffolk; Roman villa, looking N. TL 731570. BFE 55: April 1971.

that the significance of the site as a tenurial centre had been transferred.

References

V.C.H. *Hertfordshire* IV (1914), 148. R.C.H.M., *Hertfordshire* (London, 1911), 38. J.K. StJoseph, *J.R.S.* XLV (1955), 89.

ALLINGTON HILL, BOTTISHAM,
Cambridgeshire (115)

The photograph reveals an elongated enclosure of 1.2 ha, with sharp angles. The dark soil filling ditches strongly contrasts with the bare chalky soil of the field around. The site lies on a west-facing slope at an altitude of 36 m above sea-level, just north-west of the curving edge of a wood. The centre of this main enclosure shows an area of darker soil which probably represents the robbing of a masonry villa; it has yielded sherds of third- and fourth-century pottery. Beyond this dark patch can be seen two groups of large post-holes arranged in parallel rows. The further group, comprising six post-holes in each row, clearly represents an aisled building some 25 m long, while the nearer one, less clearly marked, appears to be similar. These large timber buildings may antedate the (inferred) masonry villa, or they may be outbuildings associated with it. In the east corner is a subsidiary enclosure, possibly for stock. At the nearer end of the large enclosure, and close to the boundary ditch, are faint indications of some circular houses, presumably for farm workers.

References

J.K. StJoseph, *J.R.S.* XLV (1955), 89; LV (1965), 88–9. D.R. Wilson, *Britannia* V (1974), 256 with Pl. XXIVB (this view). R.C.H.M., *North-East Cambridgeshire* (London, 1972), 12–13 with Fig. 22 (plan). V.C.H. *Cambridgeshire* VII (1978), 46 with Pl. IVA (this view).

LIDGATE, Suffolk (116)

This Roman villa lies some 11 km south-east of Newmarket, on a slope facing south-west. The parch-marks seen in the photograph occurred in a crop of winter wheat affected by a long dry spell in the spring; and they give an exceptionally clear picture of the villa's arrangements. The main block has a length of *c.* 51.8 m (170 ft) and had wings projecting forwards *c.* 10 m at each end. Close inspection shows that the building is of at least two periods of construction. In the second, the back wall of the main range seems to have been rebuilt a little nearer the camera, and new ranges of small rooms added along the outside of each wing and along the back of the house. The addition at the back may originally have been built as a passage, and later subdivided. An oblique wall approaches the east wing and may underlie its enlargement; this perhaps represents an early range of outbuildings. The villa appears to have an enclosed courtyard in front, for a wall prolongs the line of the eastern face of the building and then turns westward towards the nearer end of a large barn. The latter measures *c.* 24.5 m long by 8.25 m wide (80 by 27 ft) and has six buttresses on each long side. It seems probable that other outbuildings lay along the eastern boundary wall where they have been obscured by a modern field-division. If so, the villa bears some resemblance to a class of large villas well known in northern France and Switzerland. At the top of the photograph are indications of a wide boundary ditch, which runs obliquely to the modern field-edge and may well be contemporary with the villa.

Despite the size of the house, there is little indication of mosaic floors; the larger areas of parching seem rather to indicate the collapse of stone walls around the edges of rooms. If this is indeed so, the absence of mosaic floors is a characteristic shared with many other villas in the south-east of the province; those most richly provided with luxurious fittings tend to be concentrated towards the south-west. Nevertheless a villa of this size must have been the centre of an important agricultural estate.

References

J.K. StJoseph, *Antiquity* XLV (1971), 224–5 with Pl. XXXV (this view); *J.R.S.* LXIII (1973), 345. D.R. Wilson, *Britannia* V (1974), 258.

CHIGNALL ST JAMES, Essex (117)

The courtyard building shown with exceptional clarity in this photograph lies 6 km north-west of Chelmsford and faces south-west over the valley of the small river Can, a tributary of the Chelmer.

The overall measurements are *c.* 57 m south-east–north-west by 46 m; at a short distance (*c.* 11 m) beyond the north-west wing the corner of a second building is defined by parch-marks, but the photograph gives no indication that this is a detached bath-building, as has been suggested.

The house presents unusual features which distinguish it from the majority of Romano-British courtyard villas. Despite its size and although the building clearly represents a single period of construction, there is no indication of hypocausts or of mosaic floors. The main north-east wing (right) is composed of a range of seven rooms of roughly equal size (only one of which is subdivided), together with one through-passage linking the internal and external corridors. The other two wings, however, exhibit a regular division into single large rooms divided from the next by passages, an arrangement which recalls the guest-rooms found in *mansiones* or in the palace at Fishbourne. In this respect the building bears a resemblance to the planning of the villa at Vicques in Switzerland, as has been pointed out by J.T. Smith; he regards such subdivisions as one of the characteristics of his 'unit-system' villas, thought to indicate joint occupancy or ownership by separate (although probably related) family groups.

Undoubtedly many villas do show evidence of co-proprietorship or joint occupation by more than one family, whether these were equal inheritors of the estate or the households of grown-up sons. The plan at Chignall St James, however, does not fit easily into such a classification. There is no sign of division in the main wing between two halves linked by a large central shared dining-room or hall; the distinction lies between the main wing and the two side wings and, despite lack of luxury (as already noted), might be better explained as the country retreat of an administrator or city notable and his guests: the villa is within 45 km of London. Apart from the enigmatic traces to the north-west, outbuildings in the vicinity of the villa, such as would be expected at a working farm, are notably missing; excavations in 1978–9, however, did reveal evidence of agricultural activities slightly further away. These began in the first century B.C. and continued to the end of the Roman period. They included a system of strip-fields *c.* 5 m wide and 100 m long at least twenty-three in number and extending over more than 0.8 ha.

References

Britannia VIII (1977), 405–7 with plan (Fig. 23); IX (1978), 449; X (1979), 308; XI (1980), 376; XII (1981), 348 (field-

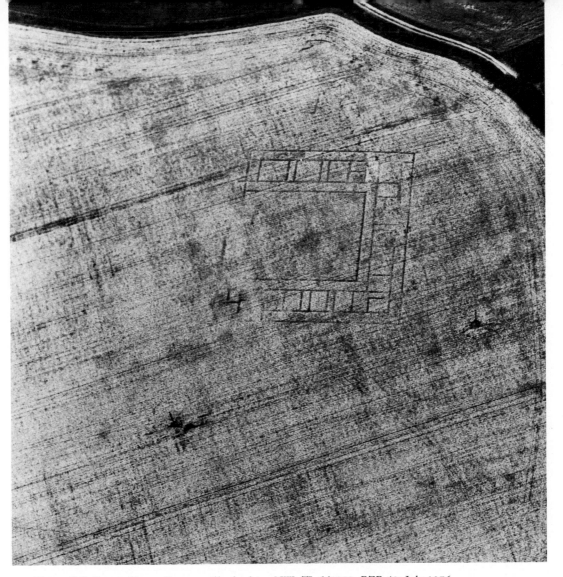

117 **Chignall St James, Essex; Roman villa**, looking NW. TL 662108. BZB 49: July 1976.

system). J.T. Smith in M. Todd (ed.), *Studies in the Romano-British Villa* (Leicester, 1978), 168. For Vicques see F. Staehelin, *Die Schweiz in Römischer Zeit* (3rd ed., Basel, 1948), 392, Abb. 80 (plan).

ISLIP, Oxfordshire (118)

A large winged corridor-villa lies at the north end of a walled courtyard crossed obliquely by a hedgerow, part of which has been uprooted. The main range, *c.* 44 m long overall, consists of eleven rather long narrow rooms; in the centre an apse projects to the back. A circular building stood *c.* 20 m forward of the north-west (nearer) wing, and there is a suggestion that a second, larger, circular building lay in front of the other wing, though at a greater distance. The ground here falls to the north, so that the villa faced up the slope. The walled courtyard is laid out obliquely within a much larger walled enclosure, about 260

Villas standing axially at the back of an oblong by 210 m in size, that is some six times its area. walled court form a type known from examples in northern France, Germany and Switzerland but few have been recognised hitherto in Britain. One such is the well-known villa at Ditchley, also in Oxfordshire, and another is illustrated at Lidgate in Suffolk (116). The design shows some concern for architectural appearance, here emphasised by the long balanced facade.

A very unusual feature of the Islip villa is its obliquely arranged outer walled enclosure, which is unlikely to be contemporary with the inner. The site lies only 1 km north-west of the well-known Romano-Celtic temple site at Woodeaton.

References

J.R.S. LIII (1963), Pl. X, 2 (by M.J. Aitken). D.R. Wilson, *Britannia* V (1974), 257 Pl. XXVB (this view).

118 Islip, Oxfordshire; Roman villa, looking SE. SP 532134. BCJ 18: June 1970.

CHEDWORTH, Gloucestershire (119)

Chedworth, 13 km south-east of Cheltenham, is one of the best known of the large villas so characteristic of the Cotswold region. Discovered in 1864, the villa was soon afterwards excavated; since 1924 it has been in the ownership of the National Trust. Cover-buildings have been erected over some of the rooms and most of the rest exposed or laid out in plan on the surface. Only the eastern extent of the south wing is still unknown. In the centre of the courtyard stands a nineteenth-century building which combines a custodian's house and a museum. The north wing (left) is 99 m in length and the west wing 68.5 m.

The villa lies 3.5 km north-west of the Foss Way at the head of a minor east-facing coombe whose steep sides are today heavily wooded and in consequence overshadow the site; no doubt in

Roman times the ground was more open. The north and west wings were constructed on platforms terraced into the hill-slopes, but the south wing stood at an altogether lower level on the valley floor. In post-Roman times erosion buried the remains of the west and north wings to some depth, and the extensive spoil from the excavation was used to create a terrace on which the custodian's house was built.

Occupation started before the middle of the second century, and even at that stage the establishment was large, consisting of three separate buildings grouped round the west end of the courtyard. Later, possibly in the early fourth century, the various buildings were connected by adding more rooms and a connecting portico, which was also carried across the front of the courtyard to divide a garden from what was probably the working area of the farm. It was at

196

119 Chedworth, Gloucestershire; Roman villa, looking E. SP 053135. GX 20: July 1951.

this stage that a series of fine mosaics was installed in the principal rooms. Later still the north wing was extended eastwards by at least four rooms.

An unusual feature is the apsed Nymphaeum and cistern in the north-west corner (left foreground), which captured the waters of a spring and distributed them to the baths and elsewhere. At first, perhaps, the shrine of a water-nymph, it seems later to have been adapted for Christian use, for the sacred chi-rho monogram was carved on three of its stones.

The photograph gives a good impression of the main building of a great Romano-British country house. However, the stables, barns and outhouses remain unknown. Building-debris scattered for 80 m eastwards down the valley is known from chance finds, and other subsidiary buildings once stood on terraces in the woods above the north and west wings.

References

R. Goodburn, *The Roman Villa, Chedworth* (National Trust, 1972). R.C.H.M., *County of Gloucester* I (London, 1976), *Iron Age and Romano-British Monuments in the Gloucestershire Cotswolds*, 24–8 with plan.

120 Lockington, Leicestershire; native site and Roman villa, looking E. SK 483294. BYL 47: June 1976.

LOCKINGTON, Leicestershire (120)

The site lies just above the flood-plain of the Trent, nearly a mile from the river and not far from its confluence with the Soar.

The photograph suggests one form in which continuity between a pre-Roman and a Roman farm may be recognised, although excavation is required to establish the details of the process. That this was more complex than a simple take-over of an Iron Age village by a Roman villa is suggested by surface finds from the former extending into the second century or later.

In the foreground the ditches of irregular drove-ways, fields, native closes and about twenty circular or penannular hut-circles are seen. Several of the smaller closes are at least partly double-ditched and probably represent late Iron Age farm enclosures round which ditches may have been recut from time to time as was proved to be the case at the classic site at Stanton Harcourt,

Oxon., excavated by W.F. Grimes (*Oxoniensia* VIII–IX (1943–4), 47 ff.). About eleven of these closes can be counted, and although some overlapping of ditches shows that not all features are contemporary, the fact that the majority of enclosures lie adjacent to drove-ways raises the question whether this is a nucleated settlement or village rather than a succession of single isolated farmsteads; the plan indeed suggests instead the gradual expansion of a family community. The main drove-way runs north–south bisecting the settlement and is flanked by two pit-alignments or fences of close-set posts, although these are not necessarily contemporary with each other.

At the top of the photograph, *c.* 150 m away from the native settlement, can be seen a corridor-villa with 'incipient' wings and extra rooms at the left and back which may be additions to the original house; the villa overlies another native close. The dark lines of the crop-mark suggest robbed walls. The building is *c.* 36–42 m long and

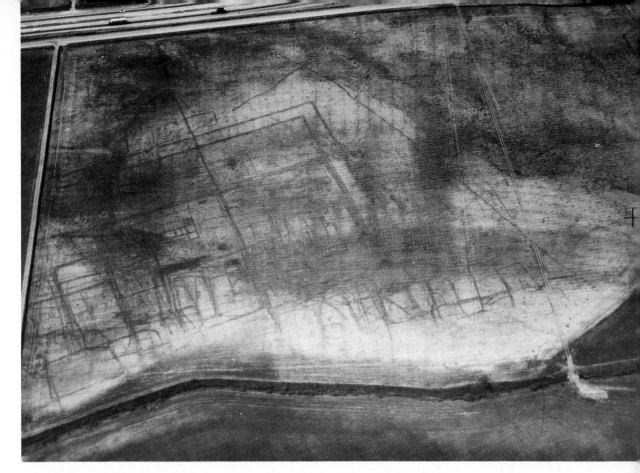

121 Cromwell, Nottinghamshire; Roman villa, looking W. SK 802625. BCE 69: June 1970.

lies within a large trapezoidal enclosure surrounded by straight walls or ditches, double on at least two sides; the regularity of this layout contrasts strongly with the lack of planning visible in the native part of the site. Nearby lie various farm buildings including two large aisled barns symmetrically disposed on either side of the front (east) of the main enclosure. Further buildings lie in or adjacent to a second enclosure to south of the first. Once again overlapping of features, especially in the yard south of the villa, points to growth and changes of organisation.

References

J.K. St Joseph, *J.R.S.* XLI (1961), 133–4; XLVIII (1968), 128; *Antiquity* XLII (1968), 46–7, Pl. XI (native site). D.R. Wilson, *Britannia* V (1974), 253, 257, Pl. XXIIA (villa). M. Todd, *The Coritani* (London, 1973), 98–9.

CROMWELL, Nottinghamshire (121)

The photograph shows an extensive group of overlapping crop-marks that have developed on a level gravel terrace of the river Trent, 9 km downstream of Newark. With sites of complicated plan such as this, the importance of studying all available photographs is evident. Features which are vague or indistinct on one photograph may be seen more clearly on another taken under different conditions or in a different year.

In the left centre a villa is seen; its length is perhaps 25 m overall. A corridor extends between wing rooms projecting on its east (near) side, behind which is a range of *c.* six rooms; further wing rooms project on the west side and other structures may have stood to the south, where the ground is disturbed. All walls show as dark lines, which suggests that their masonry has been robbed. On the west side of the house lies a small walled space as for a garden, within which can be seen two rows of post-holes perhaps of an earlier timber dwelling. A long dark rectangular patch on the near side of the villa may represent an ornamental water cistern.

The villa stands centrally within a rectangular enclosure, *c.* 200 m long by 150 m east–west, formed by two parallel ditches (or walls now robbed) *c.* 8 m apart. They extend a little way into the field on the left, as other photographs show, before turning east; the eastern side, facing the Trent, only some 250 m away at its nearest point, appears to be open. The enclosure is crossed by a long straight east–west ditch, extending beyond it and on the Roman alignment; this is possibly an earlier boundary ditch, perhaps associated with the timber house. Another ditch crosses at right angles just west of the villa. Within the enclosure and parallel to it are the fainter parallel lines of a smaller similar double-ditched enclosure which may be contemporary either with the timber house or with an early phase of its successor. In the north half of the larger enclosure there exist marks which may represent rectangular farm-buildings overlying the inner enclosure and set obliquely to it. All walls show as dark lines, which again suggests that their masonry has been robbed.

Outside the north sector of the large enclosure and running obliquely to it is a pit-alignment, from which a short sinuous ditch extends south-eastwards towards the middle of the west side of the enclosure. The relationship of these various features suggests that the pit-alignment preceded the villa. It may indeed have been associated with the small closes seen in the left foreground, for these closely resemble Iron Age settlement remains.

In the foreground the land slopes down to the flood-plain of the Trent; the ground at the top of the slope is criss-crossed by the ditches of numerous small enclosures. Many of these too are likely to have preceded the villa; but some, especially in the right-hand half of the photograph, are more regular and perhaps enclosed contemporary orchards or paddocks. Excavation should be able to reveal the type of husbandry practised here.

References

J.K. St Joseph, *J.R.S.* XLIII (1953), 94–5; LI (1961), 131 and Pl. XI, 3 (different view). D.R. Wilson, *Britannia* V (1974), 253, 257 with Pl. XXIII (this view). M. Todd, *The Coritani* (London, 1973), 78, 90, with Fig. 21 (*J.R.S.* view).

11

VILLAGES AND NATIVE AGRICULTURAL SITES

Villas represent only the more Romanized half of the farms of Roman Britain: a great deal of land continued to be worked from establishments of traditional native character showing few specifically Roman features in their plans or methods of construction. Not infrequently such farms appear in loose groupings, as at Landbeach (127), where the appearance of the site differs little from that of the presumed pre-Roman settlement at Lockington (120). Very similar scattered groups of homesteads are numerous in the Fenland (128, 132), a region newly made habitable in the Roman period.

In addition to these small farms, much more closely nucleated settlements are known which deserve the description of 'village', as at Kelmscott (125). Many sites of this sort exist in the Fenland (130), and others are known elsewhere; an example on the chalkland of Wiltshire is illustrated, at Chisenbury Warren (122). The agricultural associations of such sites are not in doubt. Some may have been inhabited by peasant freeholders; others, especially those in the Fens, are likely to be tenant-holdings. The drainage of the Fens was so large an enterprise that the hand of the government is justly suspected; the area may well have been taken over as an imperial domain (saltus).

Other villages grew up beside roads and doubtless played a more commercial role; others again may owe their existence to the attraction of a religious centre. Religion and the festivals associated with it played an important social and economic role in the Celtic world. A cult-centre attracted pilgrims and periodic crowds; it was thus also a focus for merchants and purveyors of services. Wycomb (126), where road and temple both appear, may serve as an example of these less agriculturally centred villages. In the north, a local variety of settlement is illustrated at Ewe Close (135), where the development of a family farmstead into a small village may be suspected.

In the Fenland both main roads (133) and drove-ways (132) attest communication and transport by land; but another important means of moving produce to its market was by water. The Car Dyke (128) is a Roman canal built along the Fen edge, where one of its functions was un-doubtedly to divert local flood-water into more distant escape-channels. A role in long-distance transport is still doubtful since there is uncertainty whether the canal was navigable from end to end. Nevertheless it could certainly have played a part in local movement of produce to the rivers and so to places of trans-shipment to sea-going craft.

Elsewhere large rivers such as the Thames must have had a similar role. The enormous oak baulks employed in the quays and riverside revetments of Roman London are far too long and heavy to have been brought there overland; in all probability they were floated downstream. The importance of river transport is also reflected in the location of military bases such as Carpow (2), Chester, Colchester, Gloucester, Longthorpe (26) and York (25).

Surface remains of ancient fields still survive occasionally in the form of lynchets. On a slope the downhill movement of soil caused by continual ploughing, aided by the forces of erosion, creates banks at the lower ends of fields ('positive lynchets'); at the same time scarps are gradually cut into the subsoil at the upper ends as the soil-cover is removed ('negative lynchets'). As fields rarely slope in only one direction, lynchets may also form along the sides of fields, and the process is often accelerated by the dumping of large stones cleared from the field itself. In course of time the combined negative and positive lynchets might attain a considerable height, sometimes up to 3 or 4 m, forming an obstacle to ploughing in later ages. Large areas of these fields therefore survived intact for study until the modern era of powerful machinery; even now their traces can sometimes be faintly discerned as soil marks.

On level ground lynchets do not form, but ancient fields on the flat were often surrounded by ditches. Although surface traces of the ditches have long since been obliterated, they can still be detected as crop-marks (133). In this way considerable areas of ancient cultivation have been mapped.

References

S. Applebaum in H.P.R. Finberg (ed.), *The Agrarian History of England and Wales* I Pt 2 (Cambridge, 1972), 7–

122 Chisenbury Warren, Enford, Wiltshire; Romano-British village, looking SW. SU 178537. AND 87: March 1966.

250. A.R. Birley, *Life in Roman Britain* (London, 1964), Chs. 6–7. H.C. Bowen in A.L.F. Rivet (ed.), *The Roman Villa in Britain* (London, 1969), Ch. 1. R.G. Collingwood and I.A. Richmond, *The Archaeology of Roman Britain* (2nd ed., London, 1969), Ch. 10. S.S. Frere, *Britannia, A History of Roman Britain* (3rd ed., London, 1978), Ch. 13. C.W. Phillips (ed.), *The Fenland in Roman Times* (London, 1970). I.A. Richmond in P. Salway (ed.), *Roman Archaeology and Art, Essays and Studies by Sir Ian Richmond* (London, 1969), 150–65. P. Salway, *Roman Britain* (Oxford, 1981), Chs. 19–20. C. Thomas, *Rural Settlement in Roman Britain* (C.B.A. Research Report No. 7, London, 1966). J.S. Wacher, *Roman Britain* (London, 1978), Ch. 4.

CHISENBURY WARREN, ENFORD, Wiltshire (122)

The pre-war conception of Celtic villages of Iron Age or Roman date on the chalk of southern England was exploded by the Little Woodbury excavations of 1938–9 which demonstrated that what had previously been taken as pit-dwellings were really storage pits. The conclusion that clusters of these pits could all belong, as at Little Woodbury itself, to 'isolated farmsteads' inevitably followed. Calculations of population were dramatically reduced, and for a while it became fashionable to think of rural society as based almost entirely upon isolated farmsteads. In recent decades the balance has been slowly redressed with the demonstration that, side by side with isolated farmsteads, nucleated agricultural settlements or 'villages' also existed in the countryside at large as well as in special areas such as the Fenland.

Chisenbury Warren is a good example of this newly recognised type of settlement. It lies at a height of 150 m on the chalk towards the north-east of Salisbury Plain, and is surrounded by a large area of Celtic fields of which one sizeable group is very regularly laid out. The site itself covers 5.9 ha (14.5 acres), and consists of a wide 'street' *c.* 635 m long with about eighty rectangular hollows on either margin though principally on the uphill side. These hollows, presumably for buildings, are mainly *c.* 12 m long, with a few extending to 18 m. At either end of the village street, where it branches out between the fields, triangular open areas have been left, although that at the north-east end has later been encroached upon by buildings. Such triangular 'village greens' appear to be a characteristic of this type of settlement. Whether the inhabitants were freeholders or were tenants of some large estate –

123 Totterdown (Fyfield Down), Fyfield, Wiltshire; field system, looking NE. SU 134715. AAU 84: May 1960.

possibly even an imperial estate – is a question which cannot easily be resolved. The apparent absence of villas from the region can be taken as an indication of peasant economy.

References

H.C. Bowen and P.J. Fowler in C. Thomas (ed.), *Rural Settlement in Roman Britain* (C.B.A. Research Report No. 7, London, 1966), 51–3 with Figs. 4 and 5 (plans). J.K. St Joseph, *J.R.S.* LIX (1969), 128.

TOTTERDOWN, FYFIELD, Wiltshire (123)

The chalk downland 230–40 m above sea-level on the north side of the Kennet valley, 6 km WNW of Marlborough, shows an extensive area of ancient cultivation. Towards the north, in the left background of the photograph, the field system is bounded by a trackway beyond which the ground has never been cultivated. As it runs north-eastwards the track forks, the outer branch continuing towards the corner of a wood, the other entering the cultivated area and soon turning a right angle bounded by field-banks (lynchets). Just right of the centre of the photograph the

track forks once more, one branch making for the wood and the other, not easily distinguishable, passing below some bushes and then expanding to end in an irregular 'green' just short of an area surrounded by the lynchets of fields but itself never cultivated. This area lies immediately above the clump of trees beside a standing building. Sarsen stones are still scattered about the surface. Either there was a settlement here, or the land was pasture left uncleared of stone. Elsewhere sarsens have been cleared from the cultivated fields and dumps of them are to be found in the field-banks.

The Celtic fields round the periphery of the photograph are of irregular shape and probably have their origin in the Iron Age: a settlement of that period is known beside the trackway in the background. In the centre of the photograph, however, lies an area of much more regular fields mainly about 30 m wide, laid out from the double-lynchet trackway and divided by a prominent straight NNW–SSE lynchet. Excavation has shown that these fields, to judge by the scatter of pottery (presumably brought out with the manure from the settlement's middens) in the plough-soil, were in use in the late first and early second century, but apparently no longer. It has been

203

124 Smacam Down, Cerne Abbas, Dorset; Celtic fields, looking WNW. SY 656994. AY 16: June 1948.

suggested that they represent a temporary expansion of cultivation into marginal land.

References

H.C. Bowen and P.J. Fowler, *Wilts. Arch. Mag.* LVIII (1961–3), 98–123 with Fig. 1 (map) and Pl. Ib (this view). *Idem*, in C. Thomas (ed.), *Rural Settlement in Roman Britain* (C.B.A. Research Report No. 7, London, 1966), 58–61 with Fig. 9 (plan of part of area) and Pl. XI (oblique view from W).

SMACAM DOWN, CERNE ABBAS, Dorset (124)

The site lies 2 km south-west of Cerne Abbas. Celtic fields of this type, which were a common feature of the chalk downlands of southern Britain until swept away by the agricultural developments brought about by the Second World War, may date from any period from the Bronze Age to late Roman times, but their maximum extent was undoubtedly reached in the Iron Age and Romano-British periods. The fields are normally small and tend to be square or rectangular. Until the development of effective ploughs towards the end of the Iron Age, cross-ploughing was needed to break the sods efficiently, and this practice would encourage the planning of square fields. It is sometimes possible to detect small plots where fields have been subdivided (perhaps because of the workings of rules of inheritance), and also larger units formed by overploughing former lynchets – possibly indicating the use of better ploughs. Both phenomena can be seen in the foreground of the photograph.

On the summit of the ridge (183 m, 600 ft) amongst some bushes lies a farming enclosure measuring *c.* 60 by 50 m in the centre of which is a hut-circle. About 50 m west of this is a Long Barrow of the Neolithic period.

References

J.K. StJoseph, *J.R.S.* XLIII (1953), Pl. XV (this view). R.C.H.M., *Dorset* I (London, 1952), 83–4 with Pl. 106a (this view).

125 Kelmscott, Oxfordshire; native agricultural settlement, looking NNW. SU 262993. ZR 10: July 1959.

KELMSCOTT, Oxfordshire (125)

The photograph shows a palimpsest of house sites and small agricultural enclosures, closely grouped together, and overrun by the parallel lines of more recent ridge-and-furrow cultivation. The settlement is situated on flat ground, part of a gravel terrace *c.* 700 m north of the upper Thames near Lechlade, at a height of *c.* 70 m above sea-level. It clearly represents a village rather than a succession of isolated farms. The fertile land of the upper Thames Valley is dotted with many such villages, but so complicated a plan as at Kelmscott is seldom seen. It is undated, but analogy with other sites such as Stanton Harcourt (*Oxoniensia* VII–IX, 1943–4) suggests that the line of circular or subrectangular ditched enclosures along the left border of the right-hand field began

life as domestic sites of the late Iron Age; that they enjoyed a long life is indicated by the evident signs of much recutting of their surrounding ditches. To left of the field boundary is a line of subrectangular closes approximately parallel to them; they may represent associated small pad-docks, or possibly even a replacement of the house sites, for some at least show faint indications of circular structures within. To left of these again, lie other rectangular and circular features of more than one period.

The area of settlement is bordered on either side by lengths of irregular ditch, themselves clearly recut time and again; but several smaller rectilinear ditches extend over the left-hand boundary ditch as far as ditches demarcating a straight length of trackway. This trackway turns left through a right angle at the top of the field

205

126 Wycomb, Andoversford (Whittington), Gloucestershire; Romano-British settlement, looking NE. SP 028201. ASM 31: July 1967.

and runs, as other photographs show, on a fairly straight course for almost 1 km towards Kelmscott, eventually to join another track at an oblique angle. In the foreground the trackway is seen to have turned a second right angle, skirting a broad curving ditch, and to be making for a fourth length of track which runs to the bottom of the picture. The neat regularity of this track and its associated enclosures suggests a Roman date.

References

J.K. St Joseph, *J.R.S.* LI (1961), 134 with Pl. XII, 1 (this view). D. Benson and D. Miles, *The Upper Thames Valley: An Archaeological Survey of the River Gravels* (Oxfordshire Archaeological Unit, Survey No. 2, Oxford, 1974), 31 (map, showing only part of site).

WYCOMB, ANDOVERSFORD, Gloucestershire (126)

The site, which lies in the Cotswolds, 8 km ESE of Cheltenham and 1 km from the Whittington villa, may be described as an unwalled roadside village of some size. There is plentiful evidence of Iron Age and earlier occupation, to which probably belong the ring ditches in the left background near the small river Coln, one of the head-waters of the Thames. Much digging took place in 1863–4 before construction of a railway embankment, now disused, which crosses the photograph from bottom left to top right. The digging revealed a stone building 12.5 m square, probably to be identified as a Romano-Celtic temple, and at least a dozen other stone structures, variously orientated,

127 Landbeach, Cambridgeshire; native agricultural site, looking E. TL 483646. BXZ 41: June 1976.

besides pitching for foundations, 'hypocausts' and floors; of some 1100 coins half came from the area of the temple. Beyond the railway a metalled road, *c.* 3 m wide, visible on the photograph, approaches from the north-east; the ground on either side appears to have been heavily built up, and indeed the buildings may have extended over a distance of some 500 m. The road seems to serve only the settlement, and the relationship of Wycomb to the wider Roman road system is not clear. The road forks beneath the embankment at a point where the temple stood, on a plot surrounded by streets, evidently forming the focus of the settlement. Short lengths of side streets branch from the main road to left and right, and these must indicate the presence of other buildings which cannot be identified on the photograph. Over the years, casual finds of both pottery and coins have been numerous, and they suggest that

the life of the village spanned the whole of the Roman period. The occupied area, to judge from the distribution of surface finds, is 530 m long and extends over at least 11 ha (27 acres).

References

J.K. St Joseph, *J.R.S.* LIX (1969), 128 with Pl. VI, 1 (this view). R.C.H.M., *County of Gloucester* I, (London, 1976), *Iron Age and Romano-British Monuments in the Gloucestershire Cotswolds*, 125–6 with plan and Pl. 48B (this view).

LANDBEACH, Cambridgeshire (127)

The site lies on low ground 7 km NNE of Cambridge, only *c.* 10 m above sea-level, on a gravel terrace about 2 km west of the river Cam; the Car Dyke passes *c.* 1 km to the east, and the Roman road which runs north from Cambridge towards Ely passes *c.* 1 km to the west. A ditched

128 Car Dyke, Willow Farm (Bullock's Haste), Cottenham, Cambridgeshire; Roman canal, looking SSW (before bulldozing). TL 465703. ANB 18: March 1966.

trackway approaching from the south-east (top right) traverses the crop-marks of a large agricultural site before losing itself on the edge of modern Landbeach in the foreground. The trackway has a straight layout suggesting a Romano-British date, and is evidently a comparatively early feature of this landscape, for in the background it is cut by four successive ditches outlining rectangular fields. In the centre of the picture lies a large irregular enclosure within which a subsidiary trackway leaves the main one in a NNE direction; not far west from the junction can be seen a small double-ditched close, the existence of which may be the reason for the double bend of the main track, designed apparently to avoid it. To northwest of this close lies a cluster of others; these seem to indicate a late extension of settlement in that direction, for what may be the line of the original ditch of the enclosure (elsewhere widened by recutting) is overridden by one of the cluster. Here there are at least five closes with adjoining paddocks: others can be seen attached to the inner side of the main enclosure ditch. Each probably represents a house site.

Lengths of other ditched trackways are visible to south (right) of the large enclosure as well as more fields or paddocks. Although the settlement has not been dated, it appears to be typical of agricultural sites of the second and third centuries on the Fenland margin. Both size and complexity indicate prosperous development; the visible crop-marks cover *c.* 22 ha, but vertical photographs, which reveal more crop-marks a little to the north, suggest that the area of this settlement was in fact much larger.

References

C.W. Phillips (ed.), *The Fenland in Roman Times* (London, 1970), 200. J.K. StJoseph, *J.R.S.* LXVII (1977), 160.

CAR DYKE, WILLOW FARM (BULLOCK'S HASTE), COTTENHAM, Cambridgeshire (128–9)

The Cambridgeshire stretch of the Car Dyke is a canal cut for 9 km across the low gravel promontory dividing the river Cam from an old course of the Ouse. Some 30 km downstream, measured along the western course of the Ouse, and 12 km southeast of Peterborough, the canal leaves the former course of the river and then runs continuously for 85 km along the Fen edge to the river Witham at Lincoln, crossing the Nene at Peterborough and the headwaters of several smaller rivers on the way.

The canal has usually been credited with a dual function. One was water management involving the control and diversion of flood-waters; the

208

129 Car Dyke; (after destruction of earthworks), looking SE. BXZ 4: June 1976.

other was to provide a continuous navigation link, enabling barges carrying meat or corn from the farmlands of Cambridgeshire and the Fens to be towed to Lincoln and thence via the Foss Dyke (another canal) to the river Trent. From there York is readily accessible by river; alternatively (after trans-shipment on the Humber) goods could reach the frontier regions of the Wall. In recent years, however, the capacity of the Car Dyke to carry barges has been thrown in doubt.

Dating evidence for the canal's construction is meagre; the Hadrianic period seems the likeliest possibility. It has long been known that much of the course is laid out in a series of straight sectors which may meet at sharp corners; one is visible in the photographs. Such sharp corners would impede the passage of all but the smallest barges (*J.R.S.*

LXVII (1977), 160). Another feature at first sight difficult to explain is the presence of causeways: two or three are visible here, and five others are known within a short distance. The close spacing of these causeways strongly suggests that they are secondary.

Excavation of a section across the Car Dyke in 1947, towards the left-hand edge of **128** and some 365 m south-east of the angle made by the canal, proved that the Dyke was flat-bottomed, some 2.7 m deep and 10.3 m wide at the top, with banks of gravel upcast on either side. The excavation encountered a made causeway at a point where a Roman drove way approached the canal; the causeway was formed of gravel derived from demolishing the banks, and it sealed 0.4 m of silt which scientific examination showed to have

130 March, Cambridgeshire; Fenland settlement (Flaggrass), before ploughing, looking N. TL 434985. ET 16: May 1950.

been laid by running water. Excavation of other causeways is desirable to discover whether any are original undug features which would prevent navigation; but even for flood control an unimpeded flow of water would be required. It seems likely that all or most of the causeways in the Cambridgeshire length of the Dyke must be secondary features dating (like the excavated example) from the beginning of the fourth century, or perhaps slightly earlier, when the necessity for maintaining the canal was no longer regarded as pressing, or when management had broken down.

A section across the Lincolnshire Car Dyke (*Britannia* X (1979),189) shows that it too was flat-bottomed, *c*. 13 m wide and some 4 m deep. Here, too, causeways for the passage of Roman roads have been noted, and two of them have been claimed to be of solid undug gravel. The observation, however, was made during excavation carried out for other purposes by machine, and the point has not been established with all the degree of proof which it deserves. A study of levels has shown that at least at the surface the height of the canal above sea-level varies; in one locality there was a fall of 6 m over a distance of 350 m. The level of the bed, however, rather than of the surface of the canal is what is crucial to the

question whether the Dyke was a continuous water course, and no information is available on this subject. Rises and falls are to be expected on canals, but investigation of the possibility of flash-locks is still totally lacking.

For the present, the possibility that the Car Dyke was used for long-distance haulage must be regarded as dubious though not disproved. It seems wise to conclude that the main purpose of the canal was for water control. The extensive low-lying system of fields and farms at Spalding Common (133) well illustrates the liability of such areas to flooding unless effort were made to divert the flood-water caused by heavy rainfall round the edge of the Fenland. But even if the Car Dyke turns out not to be navigable from end to end, there seems no reason why barges could not have used parts of it as a link between the rivers and collection centres for produce.

The photographs give a good impression of the damage done to archaeological monuments by modern agricultural improvements. **128**, a photograph taken shortly before the earthworks were bulldozed in 1966, shows the bed of the Car Dyke just above the farm, in places still holding water, while the light-toned line in the ploughed field marks its north-easterly bank. In the next field to

131 March; Fenland settlement, after ploughing. XR 56: March 1959.

the left are to be seen some closely spaced parallel ridges which represent lazy-bed cultivation; further examples occur on the other side of the canal. There, too, much of the course of a wandering drove-way is visible, in part already flattened by the plough. On either side of it are ditched enclosures, of which the smaller possibly indicate habitation-plots. Much pottery has been picked up on the surface.

On 129 the broadest gap in the dark tone of the Car Dyke represents not a causeway but the filling of a pond which straddled the Dyke and from which a stream (still visible) ran south-westwards. From the pond a small bronze bust of Commodus was recovered in the last century, and traces of masonry were found just north-west of it; these discoveries may suggest a local religious or administrative centre.

References

J.K. St Joseph, *J.R.S.* LXVII (1977), 160. C.W. Phillips (ed.), *The Fenland in Roman Times* (London, 1970), 212-13, map with Pl. XVII (oblique view in reverse direction before flattening by bulldozer). V.C.H. *Cambridgeshire* VII (1978), 49 with Pl. VA (panorama from north, before bulldozing). Excavations: J.G.D. Clark, *Antiq. Journ.* XXIX (1949), 145–63. Lincolnshire Car Dyke: B Simmons, *Britannia* X (1979), 183–96. Bust of Commodus: V.C.H. *Cambridgeshire* VII (frontispiece); J.M.C. Toynbee, *Art in Roman Britain* (London, 1962), Pl. V.

MARCH, Cambridgeshire (130–1)

The settlement lies 2.3 km north-east of March at a point where the east–west Roman road known as the Fen Causeway crosses an old artificial watercourse, the Flaggrass Waterway, which is seen as a wide dark band on 131, running from the modern lane towards the top of the photograph. Near the settlement this watercourse may have connected with another, the 'Rodham Farm Canal' which accompanies the Fen Causeway further east. The settlement is situated at the place where the Roman road leaves the gravel island on which March lies and resumes its course across the Fenland silts towards Norfolk.

132 Holbeach, Lincolnshire; Lamming's Bridge and Somerset House, agricultural and industrial settlements, looking N. TF 341160. AAQ 14: April 1960.

A large area of rectilinear enclosures can be seen extending between a north–south drove-way near the left margin of 130 and the west side of the watercourse; they also extend northwards into the next field, where the earthworks were levelled by ploughing in 1949. Most of the enclosures have yielded plentiful occupation debris, indicating that they contained houses; the sites of some of these buildings can be distinguished on 130. Unfortunately ploughing began in 1956 in the southern field as well.

The Flaggrass Waterway itself may have been already silted up or filled in during or before the lifetime of the settlement, for the spread of pottery from the latter continues over it without interruption. The Waterway is, however, accompanied (or perhaps replaced) by two side-ditches,

one of which defines the east side of the adjacent enclosures on the west bank, and the other the west side of an extensive area of rectangular fields stretching to north and east. In the background of both plates some boundary ditches from the settlement can be seen to cross the silted Waterway.

The relationship of the Roman road (Fen Causeway) to the settlement is not altogether clear. In 131 a wide light band, representing the gravel of the road, c. 10.5 m wide, enters the right-hand side of the picture half-way across the nearer modern field north of the lane; it then veers northward as if to cross the Flaggrass Waterway on a ford or causeway, west of which it gradually returns to the original alignment. But on the west bank the metalling of this road is cut by the

133 Rookery Farm, Spalding Common, Lincolnshire; agricultural site, looking NE (soil-marks). TF 214203. NH 70: March 1954.

ditches of more than one enclosure, and there are indications that before this occurred a more direct line for the road had been laid down a little nearer the camera. Over the watercourse itself the road-metalling may have sunk into the silt.

Finds from the settlement are mainly of a domestic character, spanning the whole Roman period; but there is also evidence that points to possible manufacture of pottery. An unusual quantity of querns (hand-mills) has led to the suggestion of trade in these objects, which would have had to be imported into this stoneless region.

References

C.W. Phillips (ed.), *The Fenland in Roman Times* (London, 1970), 221–2 with Map 13 and Pls. IVA (oblique view from NE before damage to N field); IVB (oblique view from SW (similar to our 130) after damage to N field); VA (our 131). T.W. Potter, *Britannia* XII (1981), 79–133.

HOLBEACH, Lincolnshire (132)

Ancient field systems are picked out by lynchets only on upland slopes. In flat ground such as the Fenlands of Lincolnshire and Cambridgeshire they are often revealed by the crop- or soil-marks

213

134 Grassington, North Yorkshire; Celtic field system, looking W. SE 003651. BLK 32: February 1973.

of their boundary ditches. In this view, however, two Fenland settlements are seen still in relief, not yet levelled by modern cultivation.

The sites are divided by the South Holland Main Drain, a modern drainage canal. A wandering drove-way now cut by the canal connects the two areas at the left of the plate; from it branch-roads run eastward, to link with fields and settlement enclosures; these are crossed by straight drainage ditches of more recent date. Limited excavation in the northern area yielded domestic remains from the settlement site west of the drove-way and industrial remains probably of salt-boiling, east of it. A great deal of pottery dating from the early second to the late third centuries has been found in the southern area. The irregularity of layout is typical of such Fenland sites; here and

there evidence of subdivision or of reorganisation can be seen.

There can be little doubt that earthworks of this general kind covered very extensive areas of the fertile silt Fenlands before the beginnings of modern agriculture that here followed the extensive drainage of the Fenland in the mid-seventeenth century. Since this photograph was taken, the earthworks in the more distant field have been levelled by tractor ploughing, and today only a few small areas of such earthworks remain undamaged anywhere in the region.

References

J.R.S. XXVI (1936), 248–9 (with plan of S area). C.W. Phillips (ed.), *The Fenland in Roman Times* (London, 1970), 309–10 (with Map 7).

214

ROOKERY FARM, SPALDING COMMON, Lincolnshire (133)

This photograph of the fertile silt fens south-west of Spalding was taken in winter, when the surface was drying after a period of wet weather – conditions that favour the development of very clear soilmarks. The photograph has recorded several phases of Fenland history. On the right are the side-ditches of a Roman road, a continuation of the so-called 'Baston Outgang', which follows a very straight course for 18 km north-eastwards from King Street towards Spalding across the fens, here only *c.* 2.6 m above sea-level. Straight engineered roads of this type are rare in the Roman Fenland.

From the main road, drove-ways lead to farmsteads and agricultural settlements. A rectangular farmstead enclosure measuring *c.* 75 by 58 m is seen on the north (left) of the road in the central foreground, with smaller enclosures both internal and external along its south boundary. The two sides of the principal enclosure are linked to the main road by narrow ditches outlining small fields or paddocks and, nearly opposite both of these ditches, other drove-ways branch off southwards. In the middle distance yet another drove-way runs north from the road in a series of straight lengths and is joined on its far side by ditches defining rectilinear fields. The rectangular farmstead enclosure has yielded surface finds of pottery of the second and possibly of the third century.

Besides the various straight lines of ditch already mentioned which represent a recognisable system of land use extending over a considerable area, the photograph has recorded a number of sinuous dark lines. One of these meanders across the foreground; part of its course is over the very same ground as is occupied by the rectangular enclosure already mentioned. It is joined by narrower winding tributary lines, one of which crosses the area of the enclosure. Another broad meandering mark is seen to left of centre and other elements of the system appear in the distance. These marks represent the natural streamcourses of the Fenland before the area was drained. There could hardly be a greater contrast between these sinuous marks and the straight lines of the Roman agricultural system. In this flat terrain where the ground-level may vary by only 0.5 m in several kilometres very careful attention to levelling is necessary if drainage channels, such as the long roadside ditches visible on the photographs, are to function effectively. It is however the proximity of the Roman road which has imposed a more than normally rectilinear character on the landscape here; quite close to the left-hand margin of the photograph a much more typically irregular Fenland settlement begins. The superficial resemblance of straight road and rectangular farmstead to similar features on a well-known photograph of centuriation in Apulia (southern Italy) is fortuitous. The straight road here is not part of a centuriated landscape (in which Roman surveyors divided up the land into carefully measured rectangles); nevertheless, the draining of the Fenland may be regarded as a remarkable achievement of Roman engineering, in that exact levelling was so crucial.

References

J.K. StJoseph, *J.R.S.* XLV (1955), Pl. XX (similar view). C.W. Phillips (ed.), *The Fenland in Roman Times* (London, 1970), 30, 288–9 with Map 4 and Pl. XII (b) (panorama from the W). Apulia: J. Bradford, *Antiquity* XXIII (1949), 68 with Pl. III.

GRASSINGTON, North Yorkshire (134)

Much of the high ground of the Pennines favoured a pastoral or mixed economy, as we shall see (135); but there is growing evidence of widespread cultivation in pre-Roman times of the lower, more fertile ground, as for instance on eleven sites where Hadrian's Wall and its associated structures have been found to overlie still earlier cultivated fields; and the spread of arable received powerful impetus under Roman control. One site particularly notable for the evidence it affords of agriculture lies near Grassington in the upper valley of the river Wharfe, some 21 km northwest of Ilkley. The photograph, taken when the ground was under a light covering of snow, shows the outlines of an extensive field system underlying modern field walls. The system covers more than 100 ha of the limestone benches that extend along Upper Wharfedale. So large a development must be considered Roman rather than Iron Age, a conclusion supported by the numerous sherds of pottery dating from the second to the fourth century which no doubt reached the fields when middens were spread – an operation all the more necessary because the thin soil covering the limestone can never have been very fertile. The extent of the system can probably be explained by the continuing requirement to supply the Roman army, a circumstance that may have brought prosperity to local farmers, and certainly led to an effort to encourage local production. There is no indication of veteran settlement here; the site and its scattered settlements appear to be entirely native in character.

The fields are marked by both lynchets and field-banks, and are, in the main, rectangular

135 Ewe Close, Cumbria (Westmorland); native settlement, looking SSW. NY 610135. AQL 101: January 1967.

rather than square in shape; their dimensions vary, but *c.* 115 by 23 m is a representative size. Running obliquely across the photograph, towards the left of the large central modern field, the line of a trackway is indicated by the presence on its lower (left) side of a series of small closes; these can be taken to indicate part of an associated settlement. Small circular house sites have been noted among the closes; but a large number of other scattered hut sites have also been recorded in the wood in the background, so that a nucleated village does not seem to be in question. A barrow is visible near the middle of the right-hand margin of the plate and, left centre, at a bend in a field wall, there is an oval banked enclosure measuring *c.* 45 by 23 m, with its entrance gap on the left near the wall. The earthwork is integral with three of the ancient field boundaries and has been thought to be a place of local assembly, corresponding to the moot of later times. However, other expla-

216

nations are possible, such as a cock-pit or bear-baiting pen, or even a pond if suitably lined with clay.

References

E. Curwen, *Antiquity* II (1928), 168–72 with plan. A. Raistrick and S.E. Chapman, *Antiquity* III (1929), 166–70 with map. *J.R.S.* XL (1950), Pl. VI, 1 (oblique view looking NE). J.K. StJoseph, *J.R.S.* XLIII (1953), 96. A. Raistrick, *Prehistoric Yorkshire* (Clapham, 1964), centre plate (oblique view looking SW).

EWE CLOSE, Cumbria (135)

It is well known that sites with low relief are best photographed in raking sunlight, preferably in winter when the vegetation is at its shortest; but the presence of frost or of a light covering of snow can often emphasise details of the plan in a remarkable fashion, as in this view of Ewe Close.

The site is that of a native stone-built settlement, 0.6 ha in extent, situated at a height of 260 m on limestone fells some 20 km south-east of Penrith. Like similar hillside settlements in the north and north-west of Britain which practised a mixed but mainly pastoral economy, Ewe Close presents few obvious indications of Romanization. However, it has been realised that the distribution of such communities, which became widespread for the first time in the Roman period, and especially the evidence of expanding population yielded by individual sites, are indications of the increased prosperity which stemmed from the *pax Romana*.

The settlement lies close to the Maiden Way, the main Roman road leading northward from Manchester to Carlisle, and is situated some 10 km north of its passage of the Lune Gorge (9); here the road has to cross the high ground north of Tebay on its way to the Eden valley at Brougham. Its well-preserved course can be seen skirting the west (right) side of the settlement. The road is crossed by two low earthen banks, part of a system of field boundaries. The suggestion conveyed by photographs that they are earlier than the settlement may be deceptive, and needs to be confirmed by digging. The village itself shows evidence of expansion and changes of plan which may be ascribed to the enlargement of a family group over several generations. The nucleus seems to have been the subrectangular enclosure nearest the road, containing a large circular house, 15 m in diameter, with its entrance in the north-east quadrant, and a second much smaller house, just beyond, in which was found a furnace. The enclosure has an entrance on the south side adjoining a group of nine small byres. The south-east corner of the enclosure wall has been taken down to allow an expansion in this direction, where a second enclosure (appearing more circular than in fact it is) has been added. It too contains houses, byres and yards. The large enclosure on the east (left) side of the photograph abuts the wall of this and so marks a third phase of expansion. In addition to a number of small yards and byres and a circular house, it also contains a rectangular building near its south-west corner together with traces of two others in the large yard in front of the round house. These may be taken to indicate increasing Roman influence.

The large number of byres and yards, and the small field system, strengthen the case for suggesting dependence upon pastoral farming. A stream flows only 300 m to the north. In fact the proportion of pastoral to arable fluctuates from farm to farm in the area; decisive factors were the altitude of the settlement and the fertility of the local land. At Crosby Ravensworth, only 1.5 km to the north-east but 60 m lower, there exists an extensive area of ancient fields.

Settlements of this sort, despite their primitive appearance, were by no means out of touch with the wider world, as the proximity of the main road indicates here; but they exhibit few signs of wealth or luxury, maintaining the traditional Iron Age economy of the region in which wealth was measured by the size of herds and flocks and of the family group, rather than in terms of material comfort.

References

W.G. Collingwood, *Trans. Cumb. and Westm. Antiq. and Arch. Soc.* (2nd series) VIII (1908), 355–68; IX (1909), 295–309 (excavation reports with plans). R.G. Collingwood, *ibid.* XXXIII (1933), 201–26 (general discussion). R.C.H.M., *Westmorland* (London, 1936), 83–4 (plan). R.G. Collingwood, *The Archaeology of Roman Britain* (London, 1930), 156 (plan). J.K. StJoseph, *J.R.S.* LIX (1969), Pl. VI 2 (oblique view looking SW). S. Applebaum in H.P.R. Finberg (ed.), *The Agrarian History of England and Wales* (Cambridge, 1972), 194, 202. R.J.A. Wilson, *Guide to the Roman Remains in Britain* (2nd ed., London, 1980), 264 (plan).

12

TEMPLES

The majority of sacred buildings in Roman Britain were of small size; only rarely did they exhibit the architectural character of the familiar classical form. A few classical Roman temples have been found in towns, the largest and best-known example being that of the deified Claudius at Colchester, where it formed part of the provincial centre for the Imperial Cult; but none of these is susceptible to aerial photography. In the third and fourth centuries a few temples were built on a basilican plan, such as those at Thistleton Dyer (139) and Lydney. But the most popular variety of religious building both in town and country was that known as Romano-Celtic, in which a small rectangular or circular shrine (*cella*) is surrounded by a concentric aisle or portico (91, 104, 136, 138).

This type of temple has a wide distribution across the northern provinces of the Roman empire, as far as Sarmizegethusae in Dacia (modern Romania); but it remains most plentiful in Britain, France and the Roman parts of Germany, and is thought to have originated in Gaul. Architecturally the type is merely an elaboration of an even simpler form, which consisted simply of a rectangular or circular shrine – a type of building which only exceptional circumstances can certainly distinguish from a domestic structure of the same plan. Recent studies have emphasised, however, that even in the Iron Age simple shrines of this sort existed more plentifully than was formerly imagined; and examples of Roman date are well attested both in Britain and on the Continent.

Celtic religion was often associated with groves or springs, mountains and rivers, which had a sacred character as the home or even the embodiment of a deity; these physical features also continued to form an element of Romano-British religious observance. Place-names derived from *nemeton*, the word used for sacred groves, occur in various parts of Britain (cf. Nymet, Nympsfield, Nympton). The former presence of groves is sometimes suggested by the plans of Roman temple enclosures, as at Gosbeck's Farm (136). The best-known centre in Roman Britain associated with a sacred spring is of course that at Bath, but it was not unique.

Temples were small because they were intended merely to house the statue of the god and the offerings made to him. In the sixth century Gildas (§ 4) records that weathered images were still to be seen in deserted shrines. A very fine limestone head of Mercury was found in 1979 at the temple at Uley, Glos., together with other parts of a more than life-size statue that illustrates the high artistic skill which could be commissioned for such work. Similar finds are rare because pagan shrines were frequently in the end destroyed by Christians, and because fragments of good stone were often taken for use in medieval buildings.

Religion met life at many points. Much can be learnt of the different deities, and of the relations of Romano-Britons to their gods, from a study of inscribed altars, votive finds and the curses (*defixiones*) inscribed on lead sheets in order to invoke divine assistance against thieves, enemies and even unresponsive loved ones. Celtic deities had many names, but the majority were probably local manifestations of a few divine beings possessing vaguely defined spheres of influence and powers. It was common for them to be assimilated to their nearest Roman counterpart, although sometimes with notable differences of function; and this process became more widespread as the new fashion of sculptural representation grew, for conceptions of art other than classical for such work had hitherto been largely lacking. The worship of gods of the classical pantheon and of others from the East was also introduced by such agencies as the army, merchants from the Continent and visiting officials. The result was a wide variety of available cults.

Although the shrines themselves were usually small, they often stood in large enclosures, whether the earthworks of prehistoric hill forts (3) or a specially walled *temenos*. These could accommodate crowds, for whose better control at seasons of festival a theatre was occasionally constructed, as at Gosbeck's Farm (137). Temples, in fact, played an important social role among the rural population and could attract periodic markets. Very often a settlement grew up in the vicinity, inhabited not only by the priests of the cult but also by purveyors of amulets, sellers of votive offerings and the professional scribes whose hand can

136 Gosbeck's Farm near Colchester, Essex; temple site, looking S. TL 9622. CR 52: June 1949.

sometimes be detected in the written *defixiones*. It remains true, however, that Britain lacks the many huge rural religious centres which are a characteristic of Roman Gaul, with their planned architecture and ancillary baths, theatres and inns. Only Gosbeck's and Lydney in Britain approach this scale of establishment.

In the countryside temples of Romano-British date were often built at sites already long hallowed. At Gosbeck's Farm (136) this is suggested by a pre-Roman ditched enclosure beneath the Roman *temenos*; elsewhere what are clearly Iron Age shrines have been found under or near a Roman successor, and sometimes the Roman temple is accompanied by a primitive-looking circular structure which preserves the memory and outline of the older shrine. In towns newly founded in Roman times continuity of cult-site is less likely to occur; temples were no doubt provided on new sites through the piety of the wealthy, as a civic duty or

in payment of a vow. At Verulamium there are indications that space was left vacant for a temple and its *temenos* although the building itself was not erected for forty years and its attendant theatre not for a further half century.

References

R.G. Collingwood and I.A. Richmond, *The Archaeology of Roman Britain* (2nd ed., London, 1969), Ch. 8. S.S. Frere, *Britannia, A History of Roman Britain* (3rd ed., London, 1978), Ch. 15. M.J.T. Lewis, *Temples in Roman Britain* (Cambridge, 1966). I.A. Richmond in P. Salway (ed.), *Roman Archaeology and Art, Essays and Studies by Sir Ian Richmond* (London, 1969), 166–80. W. Rodwell (ed.), *Temples, Churches and Religion in Roman Britain* (B.A.R. No. 77, Oxford, 1980). P. Salway, *Roman Britain* (Oxford, 1981), Ch. 21. D.R. Wilson, 'Romano-British Temple Architecture', *J. Brit. Arch. Assoc.* (3rd series) XXXVIII (1975), 3–27. For the Uley temple see A. Ellison in W. Rodwell, *op. cit.*, 305–28; M. Henig, *Antiquity* LV (1981), 43–4 with two plates.

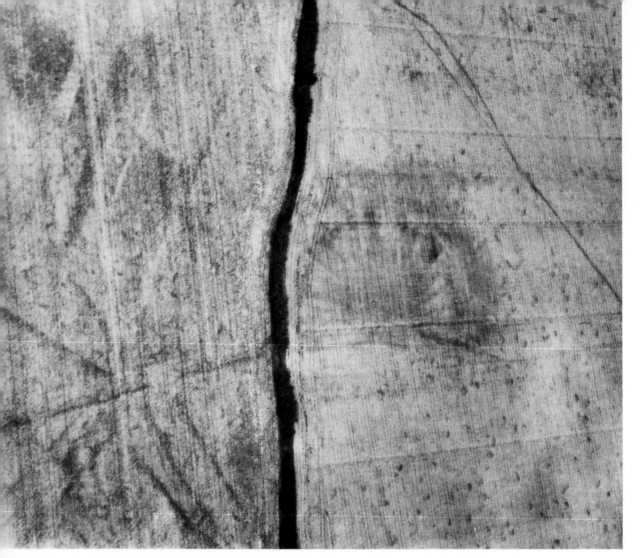

137 **Gosbeck's Farm; theatre,** steep oblique view, looking E. ZK 51: July 1959.

GOSBECK'S FARM, NEAR COLCHESTER, Essex (136–7)

These two photographs, taken during a drought, in years when the land was under corn, reveal a surprising amount of detail of buried features.

Gosbeck's Farm lies 3.75 km south-west of Colchester in an early nucleus of the dyke-defended site of Belgic Camulodunum ('the fortress of Camulos'). 136 shows a temple of Romano-Celtic plan (one square inside another) standing eccentrically within a double portico 100 m square, entered at the centre of the east side. The temple *temenos* stands at the west end of a much larger walled enclosure stretching 340 m to the east. The off-central location of the temple has been held to imply that a sacred grove or tree occupied the more important position within the *temenos*. It is known that trees and groves played a pre-eminent role in Celtic religion. The dark lines

of the crop-marks show that the walls have been robbed of their masonry.

Within the portico there is visible a broad dark mark of a square-shaped ditched enclosure with sharp angles, and an entrance causeway to the east. Excavation in 1936 showed the ditch to be *c*. 3.35 m deep and 10 m wide. This enclosure is in all probability pre-Roman, and marks the original sanctuary of the eponymous war-god Camulos. This god in Roman times was equated with Mars (e.g. *R.I.B.* 2166), and indeed diggers in 1842 recovered 'part of a platter stamped MARTI' on the temple-site. However, the find during ploughing north-east of the temple, *c*. 1945, of a fine bronze statuette of Mercury, 0.5 m tall, raises the possibility that Camulos had an alternative identification, or that more than one god was worshipped here.

137 shows an exceptional amount of structural detail of a rural theatre lying 200 m south of the

138 Weycock Hill, Berkshire; Romano-Celtic temple, looking ENE. SU 824777. OP 98: July 1954.

temple. In Gaul theatres often accompany temples at large rural religious sites, where the scale of accommodation shows that large periodic gatherings took place; examples may be cited at Sanxay and at Ribemont-sur-Ancre. Such theatres are often axially aligned with the temple to emphasise an architectural unity and, no doubt, an association of function. Gosbeck's Farm is, at present, the sole representative in Britain of such a large rural religious centre with a theatre, and here the two are not on the same axis. At Verulamium a closer architectural relationship can be observed between the two types of building, but in an urban environment. A theatre would have been a very convenient building in which to marshal large congregations at festivals, where enactments of sacred drama as well as ritual dancing and declamations might be expected. The site emphasises the continued devotion of the Trinovantian population to its ancestral cults and rites, despite the Romanization brought about by the foundation of the neighbouring *colonia* (a point reinforced by the presence nearby of the early fort at Stanway (50)); but the site also illustrates how these cults and rites themselves could not avoid eventually taking on the outward trappings of Romanized art and architecture.

The theatre was partially explored by excavation in 1967. The *cavea* had a diameter of 85 m; it consisted of a turf ramp retained by masonry walls. The turf-work had probably carried wooden benches sufficient for about 4000 spectators. An axial entrance passage led to the orchestra and two wide splayed entrances in each half gave access to staircases leading to the upper ranges of seating. The photograph shows radial lines positioned round the turf ramp, but these features were not recognised in the excavation. They perhaps mark framework-walls of timber or of specially laid turves designed to bind the main mass. There was an orchestra 30 m in diameter, retained by a wooden wall, together with a wooden stage 21 m long and 10 m wide.

The theatre had been built in the second half of the second century and was demolished during the third; it was found to overlie remains of a timber-framed theatre erected in the first half or middle of the second century, and furnished with seating carried on a timber grid.

Around the theatre can be seen the dark marks of long lines of ditch that surround one of a number of large irregular agricultural enclosures, extending over many hectares and presumably belonging in the main to the pre-Roman Belgic period.

References

M.V. Taylor, *J.R.S.* XL (1950), 107 with Pl. VIII, 2 (temple: this view). J.K. StJoseph, *J.R.S.* XLIII (1953), 90; LVIII (1968), 196 (theatre). M.R. Hull, *Roman Colchester*

221

139 Thistleton Dyer, Leicestershire (Rutland); temple site, looking N. SK 910171. VJ 78: July 1957.

(1958), 260–71 with Pls. XXXIX (temple, oblique) and XL (Mercury). R. Dunnett, *Britannia* II (1971), 27–47 (theatre); P. Crummy, *Britannia* VIII (1977), 88–9, Figs. 13–14 (maps showing temple and theatre in context). Sanxay: *Gallia* III (1944), 43–120. Ribemont-sur-Ancre: R. Agache, *La Somme Pré-romaine et Romaine* (Amiens, 1978), 404–10.

WEYCOCK HILL, Berkshire (138)

Of the many rural sanctuaries in Roman Britain, the majority were of the Romano-Celtic type, where a square shrine was surrounded by a square ambulatory. Variations of the type sometimes occur, as here, where the building is octagonal. The overall measurement is 28.5 m and the shrine or *cella* is 10.98 m across; both walls were over 1 m thick, implying a substantial superstructure. In many examples it is certain that the central shrine rose like a tower above the level of the roof of the ambulatory, but where both walls had foundations of similar width the superstructure possibly followed a different design. The Weycock temple has not been exactly dated, but was in use during the fourth century, a period of pagan revival in Britain.

These rural temples often stood within an enclosure (*temenos*), and although none is visible on this photograph, others are said to show that a rectangular enclosure existed. It seems certain that the *cella* was the home of the god, housing perhaps an altar and a statue, and that worship was usually an individual matter involving the offering of sacrifice or of gifts in payment of vows; but some sanctuaries had provision for the assembly of crowds probably at seasonal festivals, when there may also have been accompanying markets. There is some evidence that Celtic religion involved processions around the shrine, and this practice may be the reason for providing the outer portico.

References

V.C.H. *Berkshire* I (1906), 216. M.A. Cotton, *Berks. Arch. Journ.* LV (1956), 48–68; LIX (1961), 30 (*temenos*). M.J.T. Lewis, *Temples in Roman Britain* (Cambridge, 1966), *passim*.

THISTLETON DYER, Leicestershire (139)

The photograph shows an unusually elaborate rural shrine 11 km north-east of Oakham, in the territory of the Coritani; it was excavated in 1960–1 before destruction by quarrying. The temple is in the form of a *basilica* with nave and side aisles, and has a porch on the east front. The porch faces a long building, at right angles to the temple's axis, consisting of a corridor or portico and a range of rooms behind. Faint parch-marks suggest a walled enclosure surrounding the temple and attached to the ends of the building to form a *temenos*.

A full report of the excavation has not been published, but a summary account mentions five stone buildings, two of them associated with the temple. The discovery of Iron Age pottery and of no fewer than 13 native Coritanian silver coins suggests that a shrine existed here already before the end of the Iron Age. Beneath the floors of the temple was found a circular timber predecessor apparently of the first century A.D. This had later been replaced by another circular building now provided with masonry foundations; it was 12.5 m in diameter and had a red-and-white tessellated floor. Only after this building had survived long enough to suffer wear was it in turn replaced by the visible basilican temple at some date in the second half of the third century. The new temple was 18.8 m long by 13.7 m wide; its nave was divided in half by a transverse wall, the western half forming the sanctuary. In this an inscribed silver plaque was found, dedicated by a certain Mocuxsoma to the god Veteris, a somewhat obscure deity well-known in the region of Hadrian's Wall but otherwise unattested in the south. In the frontier district his devotees seem to have been confined to the lower classes of society, so that it appears unlikely that his cult could have been transferred to Thistleton by, for instance, a retired officer wealthy enough to build this temple. Indeed the name Mocuxsoma carries no suggestion that its owner belonged to the upper echelons of society. Moreover, there is the continuity of cult-site from pre-Roman times to consider. In truth, however, there are far too few dedications in southern Britain for certainty about the real distribution of native cults.

The classical basilican plan of the temple is very unusual among pagan shrines, although partly paralleled at Lydney, Gloucestershire; in its elevation the building must have resembled a church. Earlier finds from the field include fragments of a column base and Corinthian capital. No temples of normal Romano-Celtic plan (of one square within another) are yet known within the territory of the Coritani; their other shrines all seem to be simple circular or polygonal buildings, a fact which emphasises the unusual character of this one.

The temple lay not far from a large villa and attendant agricultural buildings, but its elaborate character points to more than just a local shrine. It may have been the centre of a cult drawing wealth from periodic markets and fairs which attracted large crowds, as various other rural religious centres are known to have done both in Britain and in Gaul

During the fourth century the floors were raised *c.* 30 cm with debris mainly consisting of slates taken from the roof, and two new walls were inserted across the nave; outside, the porch was taken down. This reconstruction marked the end of use of the building as a temple, for the latest occupation of the structure is thought to have been domestic.

References

J.K. St Joseph, *J.R.S.* XLVIII (1958), 98 with Pl. XV, 2 (this view). Excavations by E. Greenfield summarised in *J.R.S.* LI (1961), 175; LII (1962), 171–2 with plan. M.J.T. Lewis, *Temples in Roman Britain* (Cambridge, 1965), 84, 93–5 with Fig. 95 (plan) and Pl. IV (this view). M. Todd, *The Coritani* (London, 1973), 103–4.

13

TOMBS

Both cremation and inhumation were common in Roman Britain, inhumation becoming the prevailing rite in the later part of the period. The vast majority of the population was buried in cemeteries containing few monuments which have survived. The cemeteries themselves were placed outside the settlement to which they belonged, or outside what was for the time being the boundary, and often lay alongside roads. Under favourable conditions aerial photography can record the rows of grave-pits comprising the burial-ground, but these display few features which distinguish them from cemeteries of other periods; none is illustrated here. Even the use of stone sarcophagi is not a feature distinguishable from the air.

The practice of erecting a grave-stele or tombstone, usually carrying a portrait of the deceased, figured in relief together with an inscription, was introduced from the Continent by members of the Roman army and was then adopted by some civilian groups possessing the necessary financial resources; no tombstones survive *in situ* and they therefore fall outside the concern of aerial photography. On the Continent, families of substantial wealth formed the practice of constructing more monumental forms of tomb which, like the well-known Igel monument outside Trier, could be decorated with extensive sculpture in the round and in relief, depicting scenes of everyday activities together with others bearing on the after-life.

Even in Gaul and Germany the majority of such tombs are known to us only because the stones were later removed for reuse in the foundations of third-century town walls which were built in the aftermath of destructive barbarian invasions, when ruthless cannibalisation of neighbouring monuments was justified by emergency. Britain's town walls were built in altogether different circumstances and few have yielded comparable *spolia*. Nor were such grand sculptured tombs so common a feature in Britain. The component parts of the tomb of the Neronian procurator Julius Classicianus were indeed found in the foundations of a fourth-century tower added to the wall of London; what must have been an equally imposing funerary monument is known

from Corbridge (142), and the foundations of a few others survive.

The Corbridge tomb stood within a walled enclosure. Other walled cemeteries are known in Kent, and these contain an assortment of smaller tombs; they may represent family burial-grounds. Some excavated cemeteries have yielded similar groupings of burials within enclosures outlined in less durable materials, but records of this sort of feature can hardly be expected of the aerial camera.

Some tombs, such as one still to be seen near the fort of High Rochester, Northumberland, take the form of circular stone drums which may have been carried up as conical mounds; others comprising small rectangular structures in masonry were probably mausolea. In south-east Britain there exists a group of large earthen tumuli lacking stone substructures and resembling prehistoric barrows save that they are much larger and of steeper profile. Examples at the Bartlow Hills (140) and at Limlow Hill (141) are illustrated. The group has a close relationship with others in Belgic Gaul, and it illustrates an interesting cultural connection which is not fully understood. Both groups may originate in a common tradition transmitted to Britain during the folk-movements and conquests of the first century B.C.; alternatively the British tumuli may be explained in terms of intellectual and religious contacts, or of actual immigrants such as merchants, during Roman times. To judge by their rich contents, the tumuli were built for members of the tribal aristocracies, and they can sometimes be related to a neighbouring villa. In general, however, the burial-places of villa-owners are still to be discovered.

Reference

R.G. Collingwood and I.A. Richmond, *The Archaeology of Roman Britain* (2nd ed., London, 1969), Ch. IX with bibliography.

BARTLOW HILLS, ASHDON, Essex (140)

Four large burial mounds in a row survive of what was once a group of eight; before 1832, when they were removed, three others formed a second row

140 Bartlow Hills, Ashdon, Essex; Roman burial mounds, looking NW. TL 586449. AZ 45: July 1948.

west of (beyond) the surviving four, and there is a record of an eighth destroyed before 1586.

Of the three barrows destroyed in 1832 one can be dated to the late first century and the other two to the second. The earliest contained a burial deposited in a wooden chest, as probably did one of the others; the third covered a tile-built burial-chamber. The surviving barrow north of the railway was excavated in 1815, and the others were tunnelled into at various dates between 1835 and 1840. The three south of the railway all yielded traces of burial in wooden chests associated with rich collections of metal and other subjects; unfortunately these finds were almost all destroyed by fire in 1847. The largest tumulus is c. 13.7 m in height and 44 m in diameter; that to its south has a height of 10.6 m and a diameter of c. 30 m.

The barrows lie close to the remains of what may have been a very large villa, and two other villas lie within 2 km, all clustered in the upper valley of the Granta, a tributary of the river Cam, within a radius of 8 km of the small Roman town at Great Chesterford.

The Bartlow Hills seem to represent a family cemetery in which at least three generations of wealthy Trinovantian landowners were interred after cremation. The practice of barrow burial, though common in Essex, particularly in the second century, was not however confined to Trinovantian territory. Barrows of Roman date occur fairly widely in south-east Britain both south of the Thames and in Catuvellaunian territory, and the practice spread northwards into Lincolnshire and into the military regions of South Wales and Hadrian's Wall. They are no doubt linked with the large number of burials under barrows in Belgic Gaul and Lower Germany. The practice indeed may have been brought from the Continent in the late Iron Age, for pre-Roman *tumuli* are known at Lexden and elsewhere; however this may be, there was certainly a great increase of burial under barrows in both regions in the Roman period, sufficient to show a close cultural connection between them in the late first and second centuries. The rite may perhaps have gathered strength and respectability from the

225

141 Limlow Hill, Litlington, Cambridgeshire; Roman burial-ground, looking N. TL 323416. BZA 12: July 1976.

related Roman method of burial in earthen tombs supported on masonry substructures and ringed by stone walls, of which the Mausoleum of Augustus is the prime example. Small tombs of this form are known as far north as High Rochester in Northumberland.

References

V.C.H. *Essex* III (1963), 39–44 with Pl. IV (this view), V (plan) and VI–VIII (finds). R. Dunnett, *The Trinovantes* (London, 1975), 101–2. Roman barrows: G.C. Dunning and R.F. Jessup, *Antiquity* X (1936), 37–53 with Pl. II; R.F. Jessup, *J. Brit. Arch. Assoc.* (3rd series) XXII (1958), 1–11. R.F. Jessup, *Collection Latomus* LVIII (1962) (*Hommages à Albert Grenier*), 853–67 with Pl. CLXXVII (this view).

LIMLOW HILL, LITLINGTON, Cambridgeshire (141)

Limlow Hill is a rounded knoll 60 m high which forms an outlier some 2 km north of the low chalk ridge near Royston. Its top was formerly crowned

by a barrow, destroyed in 1888. Aerial photographs taken in 1934 by G.W.G. Allen revealed that the barrow had stood within a rectangular enclosure, which in turn lay within a circular hill fort. Trenches cut in 1937, however, threw doubt upon the reality of the hill fort; the crop-marks were found to represent a very shallow disturbance which was taken at the time as a marking-out trench for a defensive circuit planned but not executed. They are more probably of geological origin; very similar marks appear as broad meandering dark lines near the left of the photograph. The rectangular enclosure was shown to have been defined by a flat-bottomed ditch *c.* 7 m wide and 1.9 m deep, probably cut at some date in the late second century. It measures 64 m north-east–south-west and is approximately square.

The photograph reveals the broad, light-toned outline of the enclosure, with entrances in its south-west and north-east sides; the south-west (left) side was later overlaid by one of the headlands of the medieval strip fields of the parish, and this bank although by now largely ploughed away still shows on the photograph. A second, slighter, enclosure adjoins the main one near its east corner. Both enclosures are crossed by a narrow line in the form of a semicircle of *c*. 100 m radius round the south side of the hill. This may represent a pre-Roman palisade trench surrounding the summit. Towards the left margin of the photograph an oval crop-mark presumably indicates a Bronze Age barrow, and two more are represented by their ring ditches, one visible near the top centre of the photograph, and the second to the east of the large square enclosure. Excavation has shown that the large burial mound within the main enclosure was surrounded by a small ditch with external mound of upcast; the barrow itself is recorded as being 12.8 m in diameter and as much as 5.5 m high, and seems to have been built of alternate layers of chalk and turf. Beneath the barrow was a rectangular pit, 1.2 m long and 0.6 m deep, filled with large flints. This pit probably indicates burial in a wooden chest like those in the Bartlow Hills (140), for the Roman date of the mound is established by its steep profile, characteristic of Roman tumuli, and by its evident association with the second-century enclosing ditch, the only obvious source of the large amount of material required for so high a mound.

The outline of the barrow and what may be the site of the pit can still be identified on the 1934 photographs, where the pit lies north of a line joining the two entrances. By 1976, the date of the present photograph, more erosion had taken place; but much of the circle of the barrow's ditch can still be made out as a broad pale band lying somewhat eccentrically to the enclosure. Numerous other marks are revealed; those forming a pattern of blobs and irregular radiating lines are probably of geological origin; others that appear as closely spaced elongated rectangles may well relate to burials, although each rectangle is too large to represent an individual grave. These marks are seen most clearly to south of the barrow and less certainly to the east. If this identification is correct, they seem to respect the area occupied by the barrow. Skeletons accompanied by first- and second-century coins were recorded in or near the barrow in 1836.

We may conclude that the hill-top was used as a burial-place for some generations; the contemporaneity of the enclosure and barrow is strongly suggested by the layered structure of the barrow, probably composed of spoil from the enclosure ditch, which would have provided ample material. Indeed, the question may be asked, what happened to the chalk from the enclosure ditch itself if it

was not used for the barrow? There is no trace of a surrounding bank, and the silt now filling the ditch consists not of lumps of chalk, but of loam and plough-soil.

Once the barrow had been built, less than half the area of the enclosure would have been available for later burials. At Litlington, 1.5 km away to the north-west, is a large courtyard villa, near which a mausoleum and a walled cemetery are recorded. Limlow Hill is a site of most unusual character. We may conjecture that one of the land-owning family chose the summit as the position for a large barrow visible from his home and over great distances around. The space between the barrow and the rectangular enclosing ditch was subsequently used for more humble burials.

References

A.J. Kempe, *Archaeologia* XXVI (1836), 374 (burials). T.McK. Hughes, *Proc. Cambridge Antiq. Soc.* VI (1891), 395–6 (destruction of barrow). Cyril Fox, *The Archaeology of the Cambridge Region* (Cambridge, 1923), 194. O.G.S. Crawford, *Proc. Prehist. Soc.* II (1936), 101 with Pl. XXV (oblique from NW by G.W. Allen). *Idem, The Strip Map of Litlington* (Ordnance Survey, 1937), 3 with Pl. III (more distant oblique from NW). J.G.D. Clark, *Proc. Cambridge Antiq. Soc.* XXXVIII (1939), 170–6 with Pl. I (oblique from NW by G.W. Allen). V.C.H. *Cambridgeshire* VII (1978), 90 with Pl. IIIB (similar view to our photograph).

CORBRIDGE, Northumberland (142)

The photograph shows a thick-walled rectangular building almost 10 m (33 ft) square standing centrally within a walled enclosure 41 m (135 ft) square. The crop-mark bears some resemblance to a temple of Romano-Celtic plan save that the proportions are unusual; but excavation in 1958 proved the building to be a mausoleum, round which other humbler burials had clustered in the course of time. The central structure had massive foundations *c*. 3 m thick, which had evidently once supported a high tower-like monument; within it was a grave-shaft 1.2 m deep, which had formerly contained a wooden box or coffin, but all organic traces of the inhumation (if there ever was one) had been destroyed by the acid soil. Remains of a sculptured block depicting a lion standing over a stag, found buried near the south-east corner of the enclosure wall, and part of another lion, similarly buried at the south-west corner, suggest that the angles had supported pedestals decorated with the symbols of devouring Death. Pottery associated with the monument showed that it had been erected in the second quarter of the second century and that it was eventually dismantled in the second half of the

227

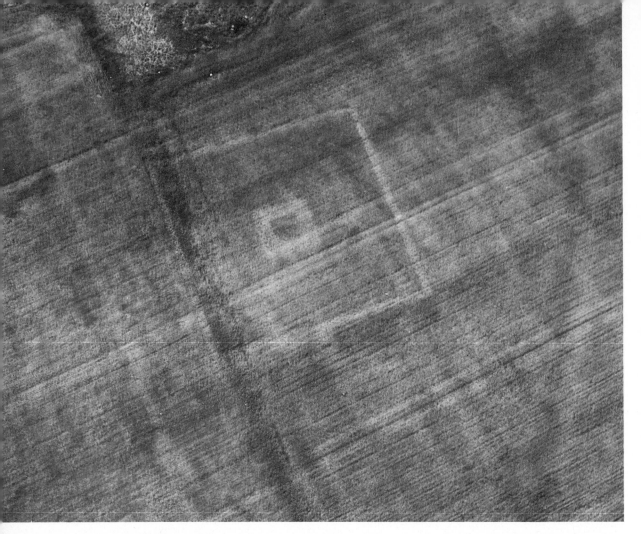

142 Corbridge, Northumberland; Roman mausoleum at Shorden Brae, looking SSW. NY 976649. DS 18: July 1949.

fourth. At least one of the burials outside the enclosure was of fourth-century date.

The mausoleum stood in a prominent position, above the scarp of Shorden Brae, and any tall monument in this position would have been visible over a wide area. The site lies 700 m west of the centre of the Roman site at Corbridge and close to the line of the Stanegate road. The date associates it with Corbridge rather than with the Agricolan base at Red House which lies only *c.* 340 m to its WNW. Until 163 Corbridge (see **30**) remained a fort, and it seems likely that the mausoleum was that of a Roman officer rather than of a civilian. The expected rite at this period would have been cremation, and traces of cremated bones should have survived if ever present. So there is a possibility that the building was a cenotaph, and perhaps the monument commemorated an officer who had been killed during the reconquest of Scotland.

References

J.K. St Joseph, *J.R.S.* XLI (1951), 55. J.P. Gillam and C.M. Daniels, *Arch. Aeliana* (4th series) XXXIX (1961), 37–62.

GLOSSARY

aedes Shrine in a military headquarters, centrally situated at the rear of the building to house the standards and the Emperor's image.

aestiva Summer quarters of a military force in the field.

agger A mound; term used either for the causeway of a Roman road or for the rampart of a camp.

ala A wing; term used for a unit of Roman cavalry either 500 or 1000 strong.

ascensus Sloping ramp, giving access to rampart-top.

auxilia The auxiliaries, non-citizen units in the Roman army, usually 500 or 1000 strong.

ballista Arrow- or stone-shooting catapult, the artillery of the Roman army.

berm Space between rampart and ditch.

burgus A watch-tower, signal-tower or other small fortification.

burh Saxon fortress, or fortified borough.

campus Parade-ground.

canabae Civilian settlement on military land near a fortress or fort.

carcares Chambers for beasts or gladiators in an amphitheatre.

cardo maximus Principal street, theoretically running north-south and at right angles to the *decumanus maximus*.

castellum aquae Water-cistern fed by an aqueduct and feeding distribution pipes.

castrum A fortified place.

cavea The part of a theatre containing spectators' seats.

century A formation of infantry literally consisting of 100 men, but in fact normally only 80.

civitas The territory of a tribe, a unit of local self-government; the word can also mean 'city' or Roman 'citizenship'.

clavicula The lunate curve inwards or outwards of a rampart at the gate of a camp.

clavicula, 'Stracathro type' In this type, described on p. 131, an external *clavicula* is supplemented by a straight length of rampart and ditch running obliquely outwards from the opposite side of the gate.

cohors equitata A part-mounted unit, in which the infantry is supplemented by 120 or 240 horsemen.

cohors peditata See cohort.

cohort A unit of Roman infantry, legionary or auxiliary, consisting of 6 or 10 centuries.

contubernium Quarters occupied by a mess of normally 8 men; term used for one of the units in a barrack-block and consisting of a back room for sleeping-quarters and a front room for equipment.

colonia A self-governing city of Roman citizens, often consisting of retired legionaries with land-allotments.

curia Senate-house or council-chamber.

cursus publicus The posting-system of the Roman Empire, for which inns and change-points for horses and vehicles were maintained along principal roads by local authorities.

decumanus maximus Principal street, theoretically running east-west and at right angles to the *cardo maximus*.

defixiones Prayers or curses inscribed usually on lead, and deposited at a shrine.

flash-lock Contrivance for releasing rush of water to enable a boat to proceed up or down stream.

fossa Ditch.

fossa Punica Ditch with one vertical and one oblique side.

forum Central market square and administrative centre of a city.

glandes Acorn-shaped shot, often of lead, for a *ballista* or sling.

gyrus Circular horse-training ring.

hiberna Winter quarters of a military force.

horreum Granary.

henge-monument A ritual enclosure of the Neolithic or Early Bronze Age with a bank outside the ditch and with either one, or two opposing, entrances.

insula An island; term used for a block of buildings surrounded by streets.

intervallum The space between a rampart of a fort or camp and the building-lines or tent-lines within.

laconicum A room in a bath-suite for sweating in hot dry – as opposed to steam – heat.

latera Praetorii Areas each side of the Headquarters building in a fortress or of the general's tent in a camp; term for the central range in a camp or fort.

legion Unit of some 5000 heavily-armed Roman citizen infantry consisting of 10 cohorts.

limes A frontier road or fortified frontier.

ludus Training or exercise area, such as a military amphitheatre.

lynchet A bank between fields (see p. 201).

macellum A provision market.

mansio An inn of the *cursus publicus*.

milliary A thousand strong.

mortarium Bowl-shaped and spouted vessel, usually with gritted interior surface, used for pounding or grinding herbs, etc.

municipium A self-governing chartered city of the second grade.

numerus A body of troops, a unit of lower grade than that of the *auxilia*.

oppidum A town; term sometimes applied to pre-Roman fortified centres.

opus signinum Roman hydraulic concrete partly composed of crushed brick.

pit-alignment A row of pits seemingly composing a land boundary of late prehistoric times.

porta decumana The rear gate of a Roman fort or camp.

porta praetoria The front gate of a Roman fort or camp, approached by the *via praetoria* leading from the Headquarters Building, or from the general's tent.

porta principalis dextra Gate at the right-hand end of the main transverse street (*via principalis*) of a fort or camp as viewed from the front of the Headquarters Building, or from the general's tent.

porta principalis sinistra Similar gate at the left-hand end of the transverse street.

praetentura The front division of a fort or camp, lying forward of the *via principalis*.

praetorium General's tent in a camp; residence of the commander in a fortress or fort; a principal posting station of the *cursus publicus*.

principia The Headquarters Building of a fortress or fort.

quingenary five hundred strong.

retentura The rear division of a fort or camp, lying behind the central range.

robbed Term used to describe a structure from which buiding-materials have been removed for reuse.

saltus Area of pasture; term sometimes used of a demesne in imperial ownership.

sarsen Residual sandstone boulder on chalk downland, left behind by the erosion of geological strata.

schola A building used for religious observance and relaxation by members of a corporation or guild.

slight (vb) To demolish a military structure, or deprive it of its defensive capacity.

temenos Sacred enclosure.

tessera Small cube of brick or stone used in mosaic or tessellated floors.

thermae Public baths.

titulum Outlying length of bank and ditch blocking direct approach to the gate of a camp or fort.

tribunal Raised platform for a commanding officer or magistrates.

turma Squadron of cavalry, usually of about 30 men, forming part of an *ala*.

turris A tower.

ultima ratio regis 'The King's final argument' – inscription on Spanish royal cannon.

vallum A rampart. The 'Vallum' of the Hadrianic frontier is miscalled, since its principal feature is a great ditch, but the term has been applied to it since the time of Bede.

vexillation A detachment of troops from a parent unit or units.

via decumana Street leading from behind the Headquarters Building to the rear gate of a camp or fort.

via praetoria Street leading from the front of the Headquarters Building, or general's tent, to the front gate of a camp or fort.

via principalis Main transverse street of a camp or fort, passing in front of the Headquarters Building or general's tent.

via quintana Transverse street running behind the Headquarters Building and *latera praetorii* in a camp or fort, parallel with the *via principalis*.

via sagularis Perimeter street in a fort, sometimes termed *intervallum* street.

vicus A small settlement, strictly one possessing some elements of local government; a term often applied to civilian settlements outside forts.

INDEX